Bill Nye and Boomerang

Or, The Tale of a Meek-Eyed Mule, and Some Other Literary Gems

Bill Nye

Alpha Editions

This edition published in 2021

ISBN : 9789354941252

Design and Setting By
Alpha Editions
www.alphaedis.com
Email - info@alphaedis.com

As per information held with us this book is in Public Domain.
This book is a reproduction of an important historical work. Alpha Editions uses the best technology to reproduce historical work in the same manner it was first published to preserve its original nature. Any marks or number seen are left intentionally to preserve its true form.

Contents

THE APOLOGY.	- 1 -
OSTROPHE TO AN ORPHAN MULE.	- 2 -
A MINERS' MEETING—MY MINE—A MIRAGE ON E PLAINS.	- 4 -
Camp on the New Jerusalem Mine, May 28, 1880.	- 4 -
THE TRUE STORY OF DAMON AND PYTHIAS.	- 7 -
CHAPTER I.	- 7 -
CHAPTER II.	- 9 -
CHAPTER III.	- 10 -
CHAPTER IV.	- 11 -
SAD MEMORIES OF THE DEAD YEAR.	- 12 -
HERE WE COME!	- 14 -
HERE WE COME! HERE WE COME!	- 14 -
13 BILL NYE'S 13	- 14 -
THE PRESS CORDIALLY INVITED.	- 17 -
PRESS COMMENTS.	- 18 -
A CARD.	- 18 -
LETTER FROM PARIS.	- 20 -
Paris, May 30th, 1878.	- 20 -

PREHISTORIC CROCKERY.	- 22 -
SUGGESTION'S FOR A SCHOOL OF JOURNALISM.	- 25 -
THE FRAGRANT MORMON.	- 28 -
RECOLLECTIONS OF THE OPERA.	- 29 -
A SUNNY LITTLE INCIDENT.	- 31 -
HE REWARDED HER.	- 33 -
THE MODERN PARLOR STOVE.	- 34 -
REMARKS TO ORIGINATORS.	- 35 -
QUEER	- 36 -
SIC SEMPER GLORIA HOUSEPLANT.	- 37 -
HOW TO TELL.	- 38 -
BIOGRAPHY OF COLOROW.	- 39 -
DIARY OF A SAUCY YOUNG THING.	- 40 -
KILLING OFF THE JAMES' BOYS.	- 41 -
A RELIC.	- 42 -
SOME REASONS WHY I CAN'T BE AN INDIAN AGENT.	- 43 -
THE PICNIC SNOOZER'S LAMENT.	- 45 -
BILLIOUS NYE AND BOOMERANG IN THE GOLD MINES.	- 46 -
TWO GREAT MEN.	- 48 -

DIRTY MURPHY.	- 49 -
A ROCKY MOUNTAIN SUNSET.	- 50 -
THE TEMPERATURE OF THE BUMBLE-BEE.	- 51 -
DRAWBACKS OF PUBLIC LIFE.	- 52 -
THE GLAD, FREE LIFE OF THE MINER.	- 54 -
SOME THOUGHTS OF CHILDHOOD.	- 56 -
THE NEW ADJUSTABLE CAMPAIGN SONG.	- 58 -
SITTING ON ON A VENERABLE JOKE.	- 60 -
A HAIRBREADTH ESCAPE.	- 62 -
MYSELF, DR. TALMAGE, AND OTHER DIVINES.	- 64 -
September 5, 1880.	- 64 -
FINE-CUT AS A MEANS OF GRACE.	- 67 -
THE WEATHER AND SOME OTHER THINGS.	- 68 -
THE PARABLE OF THE UNJUST STEWARD.	- 70 -
ODE TO SPRING.	- 72 -
THE PARABLE OF THE PRODIGAL SON.	- 73 -
THE INDIAN AND THE EVERLASTING GOSPEL.	- 76 -
THE MUSE.	- 79 -
CRITICISM ON THE WORKS OF THE SWEET SINGER OF MICHIGAN.	- 79 -
SHOEING A BRONCO.	- 85 -

PUMPKIN JIM; OR THE TALE OF A BUSTED JACKASS RABBIT.	- 88 -
CHAPTER I. PUMPKIN JIM.	- 88 -
CHAPTER II. GERALDINE CARBOLINE O'TOOLE.	- 90 -
CHAPTER III. STARTLING REVELATIONS.	- 91 -
CHAPTER IV. ALL'S WELL THAT ENDS WELL.	- 93 -
WILLIAM NYE AND THE HEATHEN CHINEE.	- 95 -
HONG LEE'S GRAND BENEFIT AT LEADVILLE.	- 98 -
YOU FOU.	- 100 -
THE LOP-EARED LOVERS OF THE LITTLE LARAMIE.	- 101 -
CHAPTER I. A TALE OF LOVE AND PARENTAL CUSSEDNESS.	- 101 -
CHAPTER II.	- 102 -
CHAPTER III.	- 103 -
CHAPTER IV.	- 105 -
SPEECH OF SPARTACTUS.	- 107 -
ADAPTED FROM THE ORIGINAL ESPECIALLY FOR THIS WORK.	- 107 -
CORRESPONDENCE.	- 110 -
Dalles of the St. Croix, September 8, 1880.	- 110 -
HE WENT OUT WEST FOR HIS HEALTH.	- 114 -

A QUIET LITTLE WEDDING WITHOUT ANY FRILLS	- 117 -
THOUGHTS ON SPRING	- 120 -
THE SAME OLD THING.	- 122 -
THE VETERAN WHO DIED WHILE GETTING HIS PENSION.	- 125 -
GINGERBREAD POEMS AND COLD PICKLED FACTS.	- 127 -
ORIGIN OF BEAUTIFUL SNOW,	- 129 -
UTE ELOQUENCE.	- 133 -
THE AGED INDIAN'S LAMENT.	- 135 -
[copyrighted: all rights reserved.]	- 135 -
HOW A MINING STAMPEDE BREAKS OUT.	- 137 -
THE GREAT ROCKY MOUNTAIN REUNION OF YALLER DOGS.	- 139 -
WHAT WOMAN'S SUFFRAGE HAS DONE FOR WYOMING.	- 141 -
SOME TESTIMONIALS, AND ONE THING AND ANOTHER.	- 141 -
ANSWERS.	- 141 -
PORTUGUESE WITHOUT A MASTER.	- 144 -
THE ROCKY MOUNTAIN HOG.	- 146 -
THE BUCKNESS WHEREWITH THE BUCK BEER BUCKETH.	- 148 -

BILLIOUS NYE AND THE AMATEUR STAGE.	- 149 -
A JOURNALISTIC CORRECTION.	- 151 -
OFFICE OF THE MEEK-EYED TARANTULA.	- 151 -
BANKRUPT SALE OF LITERARY GEMS.	- 151 -
OFFICE OF THE MORMON BAZOO.	- 151 -
THOUGHTS ON MARRIAGE.	- 152 -
A UTE PRESIDENTIAL CONVENTION.	- 154 -
THE CLUB-FOOTED LOVER OF PIUTE PASS.	- 159 -
A TALE OF LOVE AND COLD PIZEN.	- 159 -
CHAPTER THE FIRST.	- 159 -
CHAPTER THE TWICE.	- 160 -
CHAPTER THREE TIMES.	- 161 -
CHAPTER FOUR TIMES.	- 162 -
THE AUTOMATIC LIAR	- 163 -
SOME POSTOFFICE FIENDS.	- 165 -
AGRICULTURE AT AN ALTITUDE OF 7500 FEET.	- 168 -
THE GENTLE YOUTH FROM LEADVILLE.	- 169 -
A SNIDE JOURNALIST.	- 171 -
HE WAS BLIND.	- 174 -
THOUGHTS OF THE MELLOW PREVIOUSLY.	- 176 -
MY TOMBSTONE MINE.	- 178 -

Camp on Alder Gulch, June 18, 1880.	- 178 -
BANKRUPT SALE OF A CIRCUS.	- 181 -
GREELEY VERSUS VALLEY TAN.	- 183 -
THE ETERNAL FITNESS OF THINGS.	- 184 -
THEY UNANIMOUSLY AROSE AND HUNG HIM.	- 185 -
RHETORIC VS. WOODTICK.	- 187 -
Camp on the New Jerusalem Mine, June 15.	- 187 -
THE MODEL WIFE.	- 190 -
SOME OVERLAND TOURISTS.	- 193 -
CATCHING MOUNTAIN TROUT AT AN ELEVATION OF 8000 FEET.	- 196 -
TROUT FISHING.	- 197 -
HOME-MADE INDIAN RELICS.	- 199 -
THE PREVIOUS REPORTER.	- 202 -
THE PEACE COMMISSION.	- 203 -
EVIDENCE OF JOHNSON BEFORE THE COURT.	- 203 -
SOME ANSWERS TO CORRESPONDENTS.	- 206 -
ANSWER.	- 206 -
ANSWER.	- 208 -
THE CROW INDIAN AND HIS CAWS.	- 209 -
THE NUPTIALS OP DANGEROUS DAVIS.	- 211 -

THE HOLIDAY HOG.	- 213 -
SOME CENSUS CONUNDRUMS.	- 214 -
THE GENTLE POWER OF A WOMAN'S INFLUENCE.	- 216 -
THE NATIVE INBORN SHIFTLESSNESS OF THE PRAIRIE DOGS.	- 218 -
ANSWERS TO CORRESPONDENTS.	- 219 -
THE SECRET OF GARFIELD'S ELECTION.	- 222 -
PERILS OF THE BUTTERNUT PICKER.	- 224 -
A WORD OR TWO ABOUT THE SWALLOW.	- 227 -
LAUGHING SAM.	- 229 -
THE CALAMITY JANE CONSOLIDATED.	- 231 -
THE NOCTURNAL COW.	- 232 -
THE RELENTLESS GARDEN HOSE.	- 234 -
A WAIL.	- 235 -
THE GREAT, HORRID MAN RECEIVETH NEW YEAR CALLS.	- 236 -
JUST THE THING.	- 237 -
THANKS.	- 238 -
AN ANTI-MORMON TOWN.	- 239 -
A CHRISTMAS RIDE IN JULY.	- 240 -
EXAMINING THE BRAND ON A FROZEN STEER.	- 241 -

ONION PEELIN'S.

THE APOLOGY.

{In my Boudoir,

{Nov. 17, 1880.

Belford, Clarke & Co.:

Gentlemen:—In reply to your favor of the 22d ult., I herewith transmit the material necessary for a medium size volume of my chaste and unique writings.

The matter has been arranged rather hurriedly, and no doubt in classifying this rectangular mass of soul, I have selected some little epics and ethereal flights of fancy which are not as good as others that I have left out, but my only excuse is this: the literary world has been compelled to yield up first one well known historical or scientific work and then another, careful investigation having shown that they were unreliable. This left suffering humanity almost destitute of a reliable work to which it could turn in its hour of great need.

So I have been compelled to hurry more than I wanted to.

It affords me great pleasure, however, to know what a feeling of blessed rest and childlike confidence and assurance-and some more things of that nature-will follow the publication of this work.

Print the book in large coarse type, so that the old people can get a chance at it. It will reconcile them to death, perhaps.

Then sell it at a moderate price. It is really priceless in value, but put it within the reach of all, and then turn it loose without a word of warning. The Author.

Laramie City, Wyoming.

OSTROPHE TO AN ORPHAN MULE.

Oh! lonely, gentle, unobtrusive mule!
Thou standest idly 'gainst the azure sky,
And sweetly, sadly singeth like a hired man.

Who taught thee thus to warble
In the noontide heat and wrestle with
Thy ceep, corroding grief and joyless woe?
Who taught thy simple heart
Its pent-up, wildly-warring waste
Of wanton woe to carol forth upon
The silent air?

I chide thee not, because thy
Song is fraught with grief-embittered
Monotone and joyless minor chords
Of wild, imported melody, for thou
Art restless, woe begirt and
Compassed round about with gloom,

Thou timid, trusting, orphan mule!
Few joys indeed, are thine,
Thou thrice-bestricken, madly
Mournful, melancholy mule.
And he alone who strews
Thy pathway with his cold remains
Can give thee recompense
Of lemoncholy woe.

      He who hath sought to steer
Thy limber, yielding tail
Ferninst thy crupper-band
      Hath given thee joy, and he alone.
      'Tip true, he may have shot
Athwart the Zodiac, and, looking
O'er the outer walls upon
            The New Jerusalem,
      Have uttered vain regrets.

      Thou reckest not, O orphan mule,
      For it hath given thee joy, and
Bound about thy bursting heart,
      And held thy tottering reason
          To its throne.

      Sing on, O mule, and warble
In the twilight gray,
      Unchidden by the heartless throng.
      Sing of thy parents on thy father's side.
Yearn for the days now past and gone:
      For he who pens these halting,
      Limping lines to thee
      Doth bid thee yearn, and yearn, and yearn.

A MINERS' MEETING—MY MINE—A MIRAGE ON E PLAINS.

Camp on the New Jerusalem Mine, May 28, 1880.

I write this letter in great haste, as I have just returned from the new carbonate discoveries, and haven't any surplus time left.

While I was there a driving snow storm raged on the mountains, and slowly melting made the yellow ochre into tough plastic clay which adhered to my boots to such an extent that before I knew it my delicately arched feet were as large as a bale of hay with about the same symmetrical outlines.

A miners' meeting was held there Wednesday evening, and a district to be called Mill Creek District, was formed, being fifteen miles each way. The Nellis cabin or ranch is situated in the center of the district.

I presided over the meeting to give it an air of terror and gloom. It was very impressive. There was hardly a dry eye in the house as I was led to the chair by two old miners. I seated myself behind the flour barrel, and pounding on the head of the barrel with a pick handle, I called the august assemblage to order.

Snuffing the candle with my fingers in a graceful and pleasing style, and wiping the black off on my pants, I said: "Gentlemen of the Convention: In your selection of a chairman I detect at once your mental acumen and intelligent foresight. While you feel confident that, in the rose-colored future, prosperity is in store for you, you still remember that now you look to capital for the immediate development of your district.

"I am free to state that, although I have been but a few hours in your locality, I am highly gratified with your appearance, and I cheerfully assure you that the coffers which I command are at your disposal. In me you behold a capitalist who proposes to develop the country, regardless of expense.

"I also recognize your good sense in selecting an old miner and mineral expert to preside over your meeting. Although it may require something of a mental strain for your chairman to detect the difference between porphyry and perdition, yet in the actual practical workings of a mining camp he feels that he is equal to any emergency.

"After the band plays something soothing and the chaplain has drawn up a short petition to the throne of grace, I shall be glad to know the pleasure of the meeting."

Round after round of applause greeted this little gem of oratory. A small boy gathered up the bouquets and filed them with the secretary, when the meeting proceeded with its work. Most of the delegates came instructed, and therefore the business was soon transacted.

I located a claim called the Boomerang. I named it after my favorite mule. I call my mule Boomerang because he has such an eccentric orbit and no one can tell just when he will clash with some other heavenly body.

He has a sigh like the long drawn breath of a fog-horn. He likes to come to my tent in the morning about daylight and sigh in my ear before I am awake. He is a highly amusing little cuss, and it tickles him a good deal to pour about 13 1/2 gallons of his melody into my ear while I am dreaming, sweetly dreaming. He enjoys my look of pleasant surprise when I wake up.

He would cheerfully pour more than 13 1/2 gallons of sigh into my ear, but that is all my ear will hold. There is nothing small about Boomerang. He is generous to a fault and lavishes his low, sad, tremulous wail on every one who has time to listen to it.

Those who have never been wakened from a sweet, sweet dream by the low sad wail of a narrow-gauge mule, so close to the ear that the warm breath of the songster can be felt on the cheek, do not know what it is to be loved by a patient, faithful, dumb animal.

The first time he rendered this voluntary for my benefit, I rose in my wrath and some other clothes, and went out and shot him. I discharged every chamber of my revolver into his carcass, and went back to bed to wait till it got lighter. In a couple of hours I arose and went out to bury Boomerang. The remains were off about twenty yards eating bunch grass. In the gloom and uncertainty of night, I had shot six shots into an old windlass near a deserted shaft.

Boomerang and I get along first-rate together. When I am lonesome I shoot at him, and when he is lonesome he comes up and lays his head across my shoulder, and looks at me with great soulful eyes and sings to me.

On our way in from the mines we saw one of those beautiful sights so common in this high altitude and clear atmosphere. It was a mirage.

In the party were a lawyer, a United States official, a banker and myself. The other three members of the quartet, aside from myself are very modest men and do not wish to have their names mentioned. They were very particular about it and I have respected their wishes. Whatever Messrs. Blake, Snow or Ivinson ask me to do I will always do cheerfully.

But we were speaking about the mirage. Across to the northeast our attention was at first attracted by a rank of gray towers growing taller and taller till their heads were lifted into the sky above, while at their feet there soon appeared a glassy lake in which was reflected the outlines of the massive gray walls above. It was a beautiful sight. The picture was as still and lovely to look upon as a school ma'am. We all went into raptures. It looked like some beautiful scene in Palestine. At least Snow said so, and he has read a book about Palestine, and ought to know.

There was a silence in the air which seemed to indicate the deserted sepulchre of other days, and the grim ruins towering above the depths of clear waters on whose surface was mirrored the visage of the rocks and towers on their banks, all spoke of repose and decay and the silent, stately tread of relentless years.

By and by, from out the grey background of the picture, there stole the wild, tremulous, heart-broken wail of a mule.

It seemed to jar upon the surroundings and clash harshly against our sensitive natures. Some one of the party swore a little. Then another one came to the front, and took the job off his hands. We all joined, in a gentlemanly kind of way, in condemning the mule for his lack of tact, to say the least.

All at once the line of magnificent ruins shortened and became reduced in height. They changed their positions and moved off to the left, and our dream had melted into the matter of fact scene of twenty-two immigrant wagons drawn by rat-tail mules and driven by long-haired Mormons, with the dirt and bacon rinds of prehistoric times adhering to them everywhere.

What a vale of tears this is anyway!

We are only marching toward the tomb, after all. We should learn a valuable lesson from this and never tell a lie.

THE TRUE STORY OF DAMON AND PYTHIAS.

CHAPTER I.

The romantic story of Damon and Pythias, which has been celebrated in verse and song, for over two thousand years, is supposed to have originated during the reign of Dionysius I., or Dionysius the Elder as he was also called, who resigned about 350 years B.C. He must have been called "The Elder," more for a joke than anything else, as he was by inclination a Unitarian, although he was never a member of any church whatever, and was in fact the wickedest man in all Syracuse.

Dionysius arose to the throne from the ranks, and used to call himself a self-made man. He was tyrannical, severe and selfish, as all self-made men are. Self-made men are very prone to usurp the prerogative of the Almighty and overwork themselves. They are not satisfied with the position of division superintendent of creation, but they want to be most worthy high grand muck-a-muck of the entire ranch, or their lives are gloomy fizzles.

Dionysius was indeed so odious and so overbearing toward his subjects that he lived in constant fear of assassination at their hands. This fear robbed him of his rest and rendered life a dreary waste to the tyrannical king. He lived in constant dread that each previous moment would be followed by the succeeding one. He would eat a hearty supper and retire to rest, but the night would be cursed with horrid dreams of the Scythians and White River Utes peeling off his epidermis and throwing him into a boiling cauldron with red pepper and other counter-irritants, while they danced the Highland fling around this royal barbecue.

Even his own wife and children were forbidden to enter his presence for fear that they would put "barn arsenic" in the blanc-mange, or "Cosgrove arsenic" in the pancakes, or Paris green in the pie.

During his reign he had constructed an immense subteroranean cavernous arrangement called the Ear of Dionysius, because it resembled in shape and general telephonic power, the human ear. It was the largest ear on record. One day a workman expressed the desire to erect a similar ear of tin or galvanized iron on old Di. himself. Some one "blowed on him," and the next morning his head was thumping about in the waste paper basket at the General Office. When one of the king's subjects, who thought he was solid with the administration, would say: "Beyond the possibility of a doubt, your Most Serene Highness is the kind and loving guardian of his people, and the idol of his subjects," His Royal Tallness would say, "What ye givin' us? Do you wish to play the Most Sublime Overseer of the Universe and General Ticket Agent Plenipotentiary for a Chinaman?

"Ha!!! You cannot fill up the King of Syracuse with taffy." Then he would order the chief executioner to run the man through the royal sausage grinder, and throw him into the Mediterranean. In this way the sausage grinder was kept running night and day, and the chief engineer who run the machine made double time every month.

CHAPTER II.

I will now bring in Damon and Pythias.

Damon and Pythias were named after a popular secret organization because they were so solid on each other. They thought more of one another than anybody. They borrowed chewing tobacco, and were always sociable and pleasant. They slept together, and unitedly "stood off" the landlady from month to month in the most cheerful and harmonious manner. If Pythias snored in the night like the blast of a fog horn, Damon did not get mad and kick him in the stomach as some would. He gently but firmly took him by the nose and lifted him up and down to the merry rythm of "The Babies in Our Block."

They loved one another in season and out of season. Their affection was like the soft bloom on the nose of a Wyoming legislator. It never grew pale or wilted. It was always there. If Damon were at the bat, Pythias was on deck. If Damon went to a church fair and invited starvation, Pythias would go, too, and vote on the handsomest baby till the First National Bank of Syracuse would refuse to honor his checks.

But one day Damon got too much budge and told the venerable and colossal old royal bummer of Syracuse what he thought of him. Then Dionysius told the chief engineer of the sausage grinder to turn on steam and prepare for business. But Damon thought of Pythias, and how Pythias hadn't so much to live for as he had, and he made a compromise by offering to put Pythias in soak while the only genuine Damon went to see his girl, who lived at Albany. Three days were given him to get around and redeem Pythias, and if he failed his friend would go to protest.

CHAPTER III.

We will now suppose three days to have elapsed since the preceding chapter. A large party of enthusiastic citizens of Syracuse are gathered around the grand stand, and Pythias is on the platform cheerfully taking off his coat. Near by stands a man with a broadax. The Syracuse silver cornet band has just played "It's funny when you feel that way," and the chaplain has made a long prayer, Pythias sliding a trade dollar into his hand and whispering to him to give him his money's worth. The Declaration of Independence has been read, and the man on the left is running his thumb playfully over the edge of his meat ax. Pythias takes off his collar and tie, swearing softly to himself at his miserable luck.

CHAPTER IV.

It is now the proper time to throw in the solitary horseman. The horizontal bars of golden light from the setting sun gleam and glitter from the dome of the court house and bathe the green plains of Syracuse with mellow splendor.

The billowy piles of fleecy bronze in the eastern sky look soft and yielding, like a Sarah Bernhardt. The lowing herd winds slowly o'er the lea, and all nature seems oppressed with the solemn hush and stillness of the surrounding and engulfing horror.

The solitary horseman is seen coming along the Albany and Syracuse toll road. He jabs the Mexican spurs into the foamy flank of his noble cayuse plug, and the lash of the quirt as it moves through the air is singing a merry song. Damon has been delayed by road agents and washouts, and he is a little behind time. Besides, he fooled a little too long and dallied in Albany with his fair gazelle. But he is making up time now and he sails into the jail yard just in time to take his part. He and Pythias fall into each other's arms, borrow a chew of fine-cut from each other and weep to slow music. Dionysius comes before the curtain, bows and says the exercises will be postponed. He orders the band to play something soothing, gives Damon the appointment of Superintendent of Public Instruction and Pythias the Syracuse post-office, and everything is lovely. Orchestra plays something touchful. Curtain comes down. Keno. *In hoc usufruct Nux Vomica est.*

SAD MEMORIES OF THE DEAD YEAR.

It is with the deepest regret that I write in advance the obituary of the year 1879, and pay a last tribute to another landmark in our history before it be consigned to the boundless realms of the past. I do not write this as an item of local interest, because the year will fold its icy limbs and die at about the same time to the people of the East as to us. The limit of totality will strike us about the same. But I write of the last moments of 1879, as the subject seems to me.

The year now nearly gone has been fraught with almost innumerable blessings. None of us can look back over it without remembering many moments of pleasure. With what unalloyed bliss at this moment comes back to me the memory of that rich golden day of summer when the first watermelon billed the town and I mortgaged my little home and bought it. Then also I call to mind the day when the first strawberries began to be convalescent and were able to be out, and how forty or fifty of our leading business men formed a joint stock company and bought a whole box, Ah! life gives no richer recompense for its numberless ills than the proud moments when one buys the first box of unhappy dyspeptic berries of the season, and then compromises with one's creditors at ten cents on the dollar.

Then followed the ripe and radiant days of the Indian summer when the peaks of the distant mountains that bound the horizon, melt away into the soft warm sky, and the only sound that breaks the stillness is the merry roundelay of the John rabbit softly cooing to his mate. It is the choice season of the year when there is a solemn hush resting over the whole broad universe, a stillness like that which falls upon a peasant's dance when the "E" string of the leading violin dissolves partnership, and hits the bass violinist in the eye.

There are, indeed, many things for which we individually and as a people should be devoutly thankful. Think, for instance, how many Indians along our frontier have escaped violent deaths. Consider for a moment how a long and bloody war has been avoided by the more gentle sway of peace.

See how the olive branch waves, where a few months ago the tocsin of war echoed from the rugged hills of the West. The saber now hangs idly in its sheath and the alarums of war have petered out. See what a kind and considerate policy toward the wild untutored savage will do toward promoting the advance of universal civilization. By means of the Boston peace plan the opera and pin-pool and other adjuncts of wealth and refinement will be placed within the reach of the most illiterate and worthless sons of the forest.

It is true we are looked upon by other nations as the republic with a warm molasses poultice Indian policy; but right and softness and gentleness have overcome brute force and might. We of the West are too apt to be violent and radical in our treatment of the Indian. When he kills our family, all the family we have got, perhaps, too, and leaves us a lonely widower with the graves of our mangled household to remember him by, we are too prone to be bitter, and say mean, hateful things about him, and run him down and destroy his boom. We do not stop to consider that this is all the fun he has. We should learn to control ourselves, and look upon the Indian as a diamond in the rough. That's the way I do. I look upon Colorow as a regular Kohinoor, if he were only polished. I would be willing to polish him, too, if I had time and felt strong enough. I would hold his nose against an emery wheel, or something of that kind, very cheerfully, if my time were not all taken up.

But I have wandered away from what I was going to say relative to the old year and drifted into the Indian question, thus crowding out many sweet little things which I had mapped out to say of the snowy winding sheet which shrouds the dying year, and some more things of that kind, touching and beautiful in the extreme. I have allowed other matters to take the place of these little poetical passages and make a dull, prosy article of what I had intended to construct into a frail and beautiful fabric, with slender pinnacles, sublime arches and Queen Anne woodshed.

HERE WE COME!

HERE WE COME! HERE WE COME!

13 BILL NYE'S 13

Thirteenth Grand Semi-Annual FAREWELL CIRCUS AND HIPPODROME.

He eats nothing but fresh Ohio men.

Do not fail to see our Mammoth Street Parade, the Grand Oriental and Princely Pageant, over nine miles in length, and don't you forget it! It has been pronounced by the crowned heads of the world to be the most Scrumptuous Mighty and Magnificent Confederation of Wonders. Knights in full panoply—ladies without any panoply on. Endless ranks of gold bedizened cages, *recherche* chariots; boss camels, with or without humps; cages of mammoth reptilian angle-worms; lions stuffed with baled hay; petrified circus jokes; preserved seats; gazelle-like elephants, and a bang-up outfit generally.

It is well worth a journey of one hundred miles to see alone our mammoth band chariot, flecked with burnished gold, and costing $250 per fleck.

We will not be outflecked! Bear in mind the time and place!

GRANITE CANON, AUGUST 14TH. Afternoon and evening, with Grand Matinee for baldheaded men at 5 p.m. each day.

I challenge the world to produce the equal of this highly intellectual and amusing little cuss. He stands on four feet at one and the same time, in the mammoth pavilion, and at one price of admission, eating out of the hand with the utmost docility and reckless abandon. Boomerang is the only living performing trick stallion ever born in captivity.

MY MAMMOTH ELECTRIC LIGHT.

In connection with the untold and priceless splendor of the glittering pageant, I will introduce the Dynamo, Hydro-phosphatic, Perihelion Electric Light, in comparison with which the mid-day sun looks like a convalescent white bean. In brilliancy and refulgent splendor, it without doubt lays over and everlastingly knocks the socks off all other lights now in the known world.

This statement I am prepared to back up with the necessary kopecks.

The wonderful Tattooed Steer from Stinking Water. If not exactly as represented, your money will be refunded to you as you pass out the door.

This costly and truly picturesque Queen Anne Steer was secured at great cost to the management, and will positively appear every day in the regular programme, and within the mammoth pavilion. If he does not in every respect do as I advertise, and with one hand tied behind him, I will be responsible.

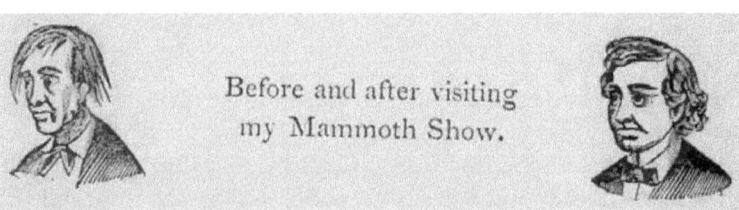

Before and after visiting my Mammoth Show.

The royal Mexican Plug, Billy English, and the truly remarkable mule with the genuine camel's hair tail, Winfield Scott Hancock.

These animals, with almost human intelligence, walk around the ring, stepping first on one foot and then on the other.

They have been procured at enormous expense and may be found only with my stupendous aggregation of trained animals.

They represent the perfect pyramid at each performance as represented in the above engraving.

The steer which performs upon the flying trapeze and horizontal bar.

The only steer that has ever successfully enacted the aeria-dive or eagle swoop.

The wonderful performing steer, Zazel, is the only one-horned, one-eared and bob-tailed steer ever born in captivity; This steer is found alone with Bill Nye's Great Cast-Iron Hippodrome and 27-Karat Utopian Giganticum.

THE PRESS CORDIALLY INVITED.

I extend to the members of the press everywhere a most hearty invitation. They will be furnished with luxuriant reclining chairs, porcelain cuspidores, and gold toothpicks to pick out the fragments of lemonade from their pearly teeth.

A special clown will be devoted to the members of the press.

A guide will have charge of visiting journalists to show them the curiosities, and see that they do not forget and carry anything away.

Members of the press will be allowed to sit on the top seats and let their feet hang down.

Do not fool with the animals.

PRESS COMMENTS.

The Owltown *Bunghole* says: "No living man has ever heretofore dared to perform all he advertised. Bill Nye certainly has secured the most wonderful and costly galaxy of arenic talent, and the most perfect and oriental conglomeration of grand, gloomy and peculiar zoological specimens from the four corners of the globe. The editor and his nineteen children, with his wife and hired girl, were passed in yesterday by the handsome and gentlemanly, modest and lady-like proprietor of Bill Nye's ownest own and simultaneous world-renowned hippodrome and menagerie."

A CARD.

A report has been set in circulation, probably by some unprincipled rival showmen, to the effect that I will not exhibit with my entire show at Granite Canon, but that the main show will be divided, the famous Trakene Stallion, Boomerang, going to Greeley; the Royal Mexican Plug Billy English, going to Whiskey Flat; the Mammoth Reptilian Angleworm going to Last Chance; the famous Trick Mule, Winfield Scott Hancock, going to Tie City, while the balance of the show would appear at Granite Canon.

I pronounce this and all similar reports the most flagrant, lying canards, as I shall not only appear at Granite Canon with my entire aggregation of my own and only jam-up-and-scrumptious show and North American Boss and Supreme Oriental and Collossal Menagerie, but at all points where I have advertised to appear. I make no show, but I can buy and sell every show on the road before breakfast, and don't you forget it.

I travel on my own special train, and regular passenger and express trains are held while I have the right of way with my elegant drawing-room and palace cars for the animals, and colossal silver chariots for the men.

I exhibit also under my acres and acres of canvas, and two-bits will admit you to all parts of the show.

Special trains will run to and from Granite Canon on the day of the show at regular rates.

Simultaneously yours,

Bill Nye.

LETTER FROM PARIS.

Paris, May 30th, 1878.

I am going to rest myself by writing a few pages in the language spoken in the United States, for I am tired of-the infernal lingo of this God-forsaken country, and feel like talking in my own mother tongue and on some other subject than the Exposition. I have very foolishly tried to talk a little of this tongue-destroying French, but my teeth are so loose now that I am going to let them tighten up again before I try it any more.

Day before yesterday it was very warm, and I asked two or three friends to step into a big drug-store on the Rue de La Sitting Bull, to get a glass of soda. (I don't remember the names of these streets, so in some cases I give them Wyoming names.) I think the man who kept the place probably came from Canada. Most all the people in Paris are Canadians. He came forward, and had a slight attack of delirium tremens, and said:

uZe vooly voo a la boomerang?"

I patted the soda fountain and said:

"No, not so bad as that, if you please. Just squeeze a little of your truck into a tumbler, and flavor it to suit the boys. As for myself, I will take about two fingers of bug-juice in mine to sweeten my breath."

But he didn't understand me. His parents had neglected his education, no doubt, and got him a job in a drug store. So I said:

"Look here, you frog-hunting, red-headed Communist, I will give you just five minutes to fix up my beverage, and if you will put a little tangle-foot into it I will pay you; otherwise I will pick up a pound weight and paralyze you. Now, you understand. Flavor it with spirituous frumenti, old rye, benzine—bay rum—anything! *Parley voo, e pluri-bus unam, sic semper go braugh!* Do you understand that?"

But he didn't understand it, so I had to kill him. I am having him stuffed. The taxidermist who is doing the job lives down on the Rue de la Crazy Woman's Fork. I think that is the name of the Rue that he lives on.

Paris is quite an old town. It is older and wickeder than Cheyenne, I think, but I may be prejudiced against the place. It is very warm here this summer, and there are a good many odors that I don't know the names of. It is a great national congress of rare imported smells. I have detected and catalogued 1,350 out of a possible 1,400.

I have not enjoyed the Exposition so much as I thought I was going to; partly because it has been so infernally hot, and partly because I have been a little homesick. I was very homesick on board ship; very homesick indeed. About all the amusement that we had crossing the wide waste of waters was to go and lean over the ship's railing by the hour, and telescope the duodenum into the æsophagus. I used to stand that way and look down into the dark green depths of old ocean, and wonder what mysterious secrets were hidden beneath the green cold waves and the wide rushing waste of swirling, foamy waters. I learned to love this weird picture at last, and used to go out on deck every morning and swap my breakfast to this priceless panorama for the privilege of watching it all day.

I can't say that I hanker very much for a life on the ocean wave. I am trying to arrange it so as to go home by land. I think I can make up for the additional expense in food. I bought more condemned sustenance, and turned it over to the Atlantic ocean for inspection, than I have eaten since I came here.

PREHISTORIC CROCKERY.

During my rambles through the Medicine Bow Range of the Rocky mountains recently, I was shown by an old frontiersman a mound which, although worn down somewhat and torn to pieces by the buffalo, the antelope and the coyote, still bore the appearance of having been at one time very large and high.

This, I was told, had, no doubt, been the burial place of some ancient tribe or race of men, the cemetery, perhaps, of a nation now unknown.

Here in the heart of a new world, where men who had known the region for fifteen or twenty years, are now called "old timers," where "new discoveries" had been made within my own recollection, we found the sepulchre of a nation that was old when the Pilgrims landed on the shores of Columbia.

I am something of an antiquarian with all my numerous charms, and I resolved to excavate at this spot and learn the hidden secrets of those people who lived when our earth was young.

I started to dig into the vast sarcophagus. The ground was very hard. The more I worked the more I felt that I was desecrating the burial place of a mighty race of men, now powerless to defend themselves against the vandal hands that sought to mar their eternal slumber.

I resolved to continue my researches according to the

Vicarious plan. I secured the services of a hardened, soulless hireling, who did not wot of the solemn surroundings, and who could dig faster than I could. He proceeded with the excavation business, while I sought a shady dell where I could weep alone.

It was a solemn thought, indeed. I murmured softly to myself—

> The knights are dust,
>
> Their swords are rust;
>
> Their souls are with
>
> The saints, we trust.

Just then a wood-tick ran up one of my alabaster limbs about nine feet, made a location and began to do some work on it under the United States mining laws.

I removed him by force and submitted him to the dry crushing process between a piece of micaceous slate and a fragment of deodorized, copper-stained manganese.

But we were speaking of the Aztecs, not the woodticks.

Nothing on earth is old save by comparison. The air we breathe and which we are pleased to call fresh air, is only so comparatively. It is the same old air. As a recent air it is not so fresh as "Silver Threads Among the Gold."

It has been in one form and another through the ever shifting ages all along the steady march of tireless time, but it is the same old union of various gaseous elements floating through space, only remodeled for the spring trade.

All we see or hear or feel, is old. Truth itself is old. Old and falling into disuse, too. Outside of what I am using in my business, perhaps, not over two or three bales are now on the market.

Here in the primeval solitude, undisturbed by the foot of man, I had found the crumbling remnants of those who once walked the earth in their might and vaunted their strength among the powers of their world.

No doubt they had experienced the first wild thrill of all powerful love, and thought that it was a new thing. They had known, with mingled pain and pleasure, when they struggled feebly against the omnipotent sway of consuming passion, that they were mashed, and they flattered themselves that they were the first in all the illimititable range of relentless years who had been fortunate enough to get hold of the genuine thing. All others had been base imitations.

Here, perhaps, on this very spot, the Aztec youth with a bright eyed maiden on his arm had pledged life-long fidelity to her shrine, and in the midnight silence had stolen away from her with a pang of vigorous regret, followed by the sobs of his soul's idol and the demoralizing, leaden rain of buckshot, with the compliments and best wishes of the old man.

While I was meditating upon these things a glad shout from the scene of operations attracted my attention. I rose and went to the scene of excavation, and found, to my unspeakable astonishment and pleasure, that the man had unearthed a large Queen Anne tear jug, with Etruscan work upon the exterior. It was simply one of the old-fashioned single-barrelled tear jugs, made for a one-eyed man to cry into. The vessel was about eighteen inches in height by five or six inches in diameter, and similar to the cut above.

The graceful yet perhaps severe pottery of the Aztecs convinces me that they were fully abreast of the present century in their knowledge of the arts and sciences.

Space will not admit of an extended description of this ancient tear cooler, but I am still continuing the antiquarian researches—vicariously, of course,—and will give this subject more attention during the summer.

SUGGESTION'S FOR A SCHOOL OF JOURNALISM.

A number of friends having personally asked me to express an opinion upon the matter of an established school of journalism, as spoken of by ex-May or Henry C. Robinson, of Hartford, Connecticut, and many more through the West who are strangers to me personally, having written me to give my views upon the subject, I have consented in so far that I will undertake a simple synopsis of what the course should embrace.

I most heartily indorse the movement, if it may be called such at this early stage. Knowing a little of the intricacies of this branch of the profession, I am going to state fully my belief as to its importance, and the necessity for a thorough training upon it. We meet almost everywhere newspaper men who are totally unfitted for the high office of public educators through the all-powerful press. The woods is full of them. We know that not one out of a thousand of those who are to-day classed as journalists is fit for that position.

I know that to be the case, because people tell me so.

I cannot call to mind to-day, in all my wide journalistic acquaintance, a solitary man who has not been pronounced an ass by one or more of my fellow-men. This is indeed terrible state of affairs.

In many instances these harsh criticisms are made by those who do not know, without submitting themselves to a tremendous mental strain, the difference between a "lower case" q and the old Calvinistic doctrine of unanimous damnation, but that makes no difference; the true journalist should strive to please the masses. He should make his whole life a study of human nature and an earnest effort to serve the great reading world collectively and individually.

This requires a man, of course, with similar characteristics and the same general information possessed by the Almighty but who would be willing to work at a much more moderate salary.

The reader will instantly see how difficult it is to obtain this class of men. Outside of the mental giant who writes these lines and two or three others, perhaps——

But never mind. I leave a grateful world to say that, while I map out a plan for the ambitious young journalist who might be entering upon the broad arena of newspaperdom, and preparing himself at a regularly established school for that purpose.

Let the first two years be devoted to meditation and prayer. This will prepare the young editor for the surprise and consequent profanity which in a few years he may experience when he finds in his boss editorial that God is spelled with a little g, and the peroration of the article has been taken out and carefully locked up between a death notice and the announcement of the birth of a cross-eyed infant.

The ensuing five years should be spent in becoming familiar with the surprising and mirth-provoking orthography of the English language.

Then would follow three years devoted to practice with dumb bells, sand bags and slung shots, in order to become an athlete. I have found in my own journalistic history more cause for regret over my neglect of this branch than any other. I am a pretty good runner, but aside from that I regret to say that as an athlete I am not a dazzling success.

The above course of intermediate training would fit the student to enter upon the regular curriculum.

Then set aside ten years for learning the typographical art perfectly, so that when visitors wish to look at the composing room, and ask the editor to explain the use of the "hell box," he will not have to blush and tell a gauzy lie about its being a composing stick. Let the young journalist study the mysteries of type setting, distributing, press work, gallies, italic, shooting sticks, type lice and other mechanical implements of the printer's department.

Five years should be spent in learning to properly read and correct proof, as well as how to mark it on the margin like a Chinese map of the Gunnison country.

At least fifteen years should then be devoted to the study of American politics and the whole civil service. This time could be extended five years with great profit to the careful student who wishes, of course, to know thoroughly the names and records of all public men, together with the relative political strength of each party.

He should then take a medical course and learn how to bind up contusions, apply arnica, court plaster or bandages, plug up bullet holes and prospect through the human system for buck shot. The reason of this course which should embrace five years of close study, is apparent to the thinking mind.

Ten years should then be devoted to the study of law. No thorough metropolitan editor wants to enter upon his profession without knowing the difference between a writ of *mandamus* and other styles of profanity. He should thoroughly understand the entire system of American jurisprudence, and be as familiar with the more recent decisions of the courts as New York people are with the semi-annual letter of Governor Seymour declining the Presidency.

The student will by this time begin to see what is required of him and will enter with greater zeal upon his adopted profession.

He will now enter upon a theological course of ten years. He can then write a telling editorial on the great question of What We Shall Do To Be Saved without mixing up Calvin and Tom Paine with Judas Iscariot and Ben Butler.

The closing ten years of the regular course might be profitably used in learning a practical knowledge of cutting cord wood, baking beans, making shirts, lecturing, turning double handsprings, preaching the gospel, learning how to make a good adhesive paste that will not sour in hot weather, learning the art of scissors grinding, punctuation, capitalization, prosody, plain sewing, music, dancing, sculping, etiquette, how to win the affections of the opposite sex, the ten commandments, every man his own teacher on the violin, croquet, rules of the prize ring, parlor magic, civil engineering, decorative art, calsomining, bicycling, base ball, hydraulics, botany, poker, calisthenics, high-low jack, international law, faro, rhetoric, fifteen-ball pool, drawing and painting, mule skinning, vocal music, horsemanship, plastering, bull whacking, etc., etc., etc.

At the age of 95 the student will have lost that wild, reckless and impulsive style so common among younger and less experienced journalists. He will emerge from the school with a light heart and a knowledge-box loaded up to the muzzle with the most useful information.

The hey day and springtime of life will, of course, be past, but the graduate will have nothing to worry him any more, except the horrible question which is ever rising up before the journalist, as to whether he shall put his money into government four per cents or purchase real estate in some growing town.

THE FRAGRANT MORMON.

On Tuesday morning I went down to the depot to see a large train of ten cars loaded with imported Mormons. I am not very familiar with the workings of the Church of Latter-day Saints, but I went down to see the 350 proselytes on their way to their adopted home. I went simply out of curiosity. Now my curiosity is satisfied. I haven't got to look at a Mormon train again, and it fills my heart with a nameless joy about the size of an elephant's lip, to think that I haven't got to do this any more. All through the bright years of promise yet to come I need not ever go out of my way to look at these chosen people.

When I was a boy I had two terrible obstacles to overcome, and I have dreaded them all my life until very recently. One was to eat a chunk of Limberger cheese, and the other was to look at a Mormon emigrant train.

After I visited the train I thought I might as well go and tackle the Limberger cheese, and be out of my misery. I did so, and the cheese actually tasted like a California pear, and smelled like the atter of roses. It seemed to take the taste of the Mormons out of my mouth.

I sometimes look at a carload of Montana cattle, or Western sheep, and they seem to be a good deal travel-worn and out of repair, but they are pure as the beautiful snow in comparison to what I saw Tuesday morning.

Along the Union Pacific track, on either side, the green grass and mountain flowers looked up into the glad sunlight, took one good smell and died. Cattle were driven off the range, and the corpses of overland tramps were strewn along the wake of this train, like the sands of the sea.

Deacon Bullard, Joe Arthur, Timber Line Jones and myself went over together. Deacon Bullard thought that the party was from Poland and went through the train inquiring for a man named Orlando Standemoff. I claimed that they were Scandinavians, and I followed him through the cars asking for a man named Twoquart Kettleson and Numerousotherson. Neither of us were successful.

One of these Mormons was overtaken near Point of Rocks, with an irresistable desire to change his socks (no poetry intended) and before the brakeman could lariat him and kill him, he had done so.

The Union Pacific will abandon this part of the road now and leave this point several miles away rather than spend two millions of dollars for disinfectants.

RECOLLECTIONS OF THE OPERA.

Most every one thinks that I don't know much about music and the opera, but this is not the case. I am very enthusiastic over this class of entertainment, and I will take the liberty to trespass upon the time and patience of my readers for a few moments while I speak briefly but graphically on this subject. A few evenings ago I had the pleasure of listening to the rendition of the "Bohemian Girl" by Emma Abbott and her troupe at the Grand Opera House. I was a little late, but the manager had saved me a pleasant seat where I could alternately look at the stage and out through the skylight into the clear autumn sky.

The plot of the play seems to be that "Arline," a nice little chunk of a girl, is stolen by a band of gypsies, owned and operated by "Devilshoof," who looks some like "Othello" and some like Sitting Bull. "Arline" grows up among the gypsies and falls in love with "Thaddeus." "Thaddeus" was played by Brignoli. Brignoli was named after a thoroughbred horse.

"Arline" falls asleep in the gypsy camp and dreams a large majolica dream, which she tells to "Thaddeus." She says that she dreamed that she dwelt in marble halls and kept a girl and had a pretty fly time generally, but after all she said it tickled her more to know that "Thaddeus" loved her still the same, and she kept saying this to him in G, and up on the upper register, and down on the second added line below, and crescendo and diminuendo and deuodessimo, forward and back and swing opposite lady to place, till I would have given 1,000 shares paid-up non-assessable stock in the Boomerang if I could have been "Thad."

Brignoli, however, did not enter into the spirit of the thing. He made me mad, and if it hadn't been for Em. I would have put on my hat and gone home. He looked like the man who first discovered and introduced Buck beer into the country. She would come and put her sunny head up against his cardigan jacket and put one white arm on each shoulder and sing like a bobolink, and tell him how all-fired glad she was that he was still solid. I couldn't help thinking how small a salary I would be willing to play "Thaddeus" for, but he stood there like a basswood man with Tobias movement, and stuck his arms out like a sore toe, and told her in F that he felt greatly honored by her attention, and hoped some day to be able to retaliate, or words to that effect.

I don't want any trouble with Brignoli, of course, but I am confident I can lick him with one hand tied behind me, and although I seek no quarrel with him, he knows my post office address, and I can mop the North American continent with his remains, and don't you forget it.

After awhile the "Gypsy Queen," who is jealous of "Arline," puts up a job on her to get her arrested, and she is brought up before her father, who is a Justice of the Peace for that precinct, and he gives her $25 and trimmings, or thirty days in the Bastile. By and by, however, he catches sight of her arm, and recognizes her by a large red Goddess of Liberty tattooed on it, and he remits the fine and charges up the costs to the county.

Her father wants her to marry a newspaper man and live in affluence, but "Arline" still hankers for "Thad.," and turns her back on the oriental magnificence of life with a journalist. But "Thaddeus" is poor. All he seems to have is what he can gather from the community after office hours, and the chickens begin to roost high and he is despondent apparently. Just as "Arline" is going to marry the newspaper man, according to the wishes of her pa, "Thaddeus" sails in with an appointment as Notary Public, bearing the Governor's big seal upon it, and "Arline" pitches into the old man and plays it pretty fine on him till he relents and she marries "Thaddeus," and they go to housekeeping over on the West Side, and he makes a bushel of money as Notary Public, and everybody sings, and the band plays, and she is his'n, and he is her'n.

There is a good deal of singing in this opera. Most everybody sings. I like good singing myself.

Emma Abbott certainly warbles first-rate, and her lovemaking takes me back to the halcyon days when I cared more for the forbidding future of my moustache, and less for meal-time than I do now. But Brignoli is no singer according to my aesthetic taste. He sings like a man who hasn't taken out his second papers yet, and his stomach is too large. It gets in the way and "Arline" has to go around it and lean up on his flank when she wants to put her head on his breast.

A SUNNY LITTLE INCIDENT.

Thursday evening, in company with a friend, I rode up into the city on the Rock Island train and was agreeably surprised by seeing a Rocky Mountain man, a few seats ahead, sitting with a lady who seemed to be very much in love with him, and he was trying the best he knew to out-gush her. Now the gentleman's wife was at home in Wyoming in blissful ignorance of all this business while he was ostensibly buying his fall and winter stock of goods in Chicago.

The most obtuse observer could see that the companion of this man was not his wife, for she was gentle toward him, and looked lovingly in his eyes. Every one in the car laid aside all other business and watched the performance.

Then I whispered to my friend and said, "That is not the wife of that man. I can tell by the way they look into the depths of each other's eyes and ignore the other passengers. I'll bet ten dollars he has seven children and a wife at home right now. Isn't it scandalous?"

"You can't always tell that way," said my friend. "I've seen people who had been married twenty years who were just as loving and spooney as that."

He was biting a little, so I kept at him till he put up the ten dollars and agreed to leave it with the man himself. It was taking an advantage of my friend, of course, but he had played a miserable joke on me only a few days before; so I covered the $10, and walking up to the man I slapped him on the shoulder and said, "Hullo, George. How do you think you feel?"

He looked around surprised and amazed, as I knew he would be, but he wouldn't let on that he knew me. So I slapped him on the shoulder again, and gurgled a low musical laugh that welled up from the merry depths of my joyous nature, and filled the car full of glad and child-like melody.

My friend came forward and said, "Mr. Van Horn, let me make you acquainted with Mr. Nye, of Wyoming, who lives in a wild country, where every one goes up to every one else and says, hello, George or Jim, no matter whether he is acquainted or not. You musn't pay any attention to it at all; he don't mean anything by it. It is his way."

It was Mr. Van Horn, who had lived in Illinois for thirty-five years and had been married ten years to the lady who sat with him. That evening my friend and I went to Hooley's to see Robson and Crane, in the "Comedy of Errors." The play is supposed to be funny. Several people laughed at the performance at various stages, but I did not, for just as I would get to feeling comfortable the man who sat next to me, and who claimed to be a friend of mine, would lean over, and say:

"Hullo, George; how do you think you feel?" Then he would burst forth into the coarsest and most vulgar laughter. How few people there are in the world who seem to thoroughly understand the eternal fitness of things, and how many there are who laugh gaily on in the presence of those who suffer in silence, and with superhuman strength stifle their corroding woe.

HE REWARDED HER.

A noble, generous-hearted man in Cheyenne lost a wallet on Saturday, at the Key City House, and an honest chambermaid found it in his room. The warm heart of the man swelled with gratitude, and seemed to reach out after all mankind, that he might in some way assist them with the $250 which was lost, and was found again. So he fell on the neck of the chambermaid, and while his tears took the starch out of her linen collar, he put his hand in his pocket and found her a counterfeit twenty-five cent scrip. "Take this," he said, between his sobs, "virtue is its own reward. Do not use it unwisely, but put it into Laramie County bonds, where thieves cannot corrupt, nor moths break through and gnaw the corners off."

THE MODERN PARLOR STOVE.

In view of the new and apparently complex improvements in heating stoves, and the difficulty of readily operating them successfully, a word or two as to their correct management may not be out of place at this time.

Some time since, having worn out my old stove and thrown it aside, I purchased a new one called the "Fearfully and Wonderfully Maid." It had been highly spoken of by a friend, so I set it up in the parlor, turned on steam, threw the throttle wide open, and waited to see how it would operate. At the first stroke of the piston I saw that something was wrong with the reversible turbine wheel, and I heard a kind of grating sound, no doubt caused by the rubbing of the north-east trunnion on the face plate of the ratchet-slide. Being utterly ignorant of the workings of the stove, I attempted to remedy this trouble without first reversing the boomerang, and in a few moments the gas accumulated so rapidly that the cross-head gave way, and the right ventricle of the buffer-beam was blown higher than Gilroy's kite, carrying with it the saddle-plate, bull-wheel and monkey-wrench. Of course it was very careless to overlook what the merest school-boy ought to know, for not only were all these parts of the stove a total wreck, but the crank-arbor, walking-beam and throat-latch were twisted out of shape, and so mixed up with the feed-cam, tumbling-rod, thumb-screw, dial-plate and colic indicator, that I was obliged to send for a practical engineer at an expense of $150, with board and travelling expenses, to come and fix it up.

Now, there is nothing more simple than the operation of one of these stoves, with the most ordinary common sense. At first, before starting your fire, see that the oblique diaphragm and eccentric shaft are in their true position; then step to the rear of the stove and reverse the guide plate, say three quarters of an inch, force the stretcher bar forward and loosen the gang-plank. After this start your fire, throw open the lemon-squeezer and right oblique hydraulic, see that the tape-worm pinion and Aurora Borealis are well oiled, bring the rotary pitman forward until it corresponds with the maintop mizzen, let go the smoke stack, horizontal duodenum, thorough brace and breech-pin, and as the stove begins to get under way you can slide forward the camera; see that the ramrod is in its place, unscrew the cerebellum, allow the water guage to run up to about 750 in the shade, keep your eye on the usufruct, and the stove cannot fail to give satisfaction. The Fearfully and Wonderully Maid may not be a cheap or durable stove, but for simplicity and beauty of execution, she seems to excel and lay over, and everlastingly get away with all other stoves, by a very large majority.

REMARKS TO ORIGINATORS.

It is the wild delight which comes with the glad moment of discovery, and the feeling that he is treading on unexplored ground, that thrills the genius, whether he be a writer, a speaker, an inventor of electric light, or the man who firsts gets the idea for a new style of suspender.

Think how Carl Schurz must have broken forth into a grand piano voluntary, when he knew for a dead moral certainty that he had struck a new lead in the Indian policy. It was the sweet feeling of newness, such as we feel when for the first time we put on a new, rough flannel undershirt, and it occupies our attention all the time and brings us to the scratch.

Think how the 2571 originators of "Beautiful Snow" must have felt when they woke up in the night and composed seventeen or eighteen stanzas of it with the mercury at 43 degrees below par.

Think how Franklin must have felt when he invented electricity and knew that he had at last found something that could be used in sending cipher dispatches over the country.

Think how Hayes must have danced the highland fling around the executive mansion when the first idea of civil service reform dashed like a sheet of lightning through his brain.

These are only a few isolated illustrations of the unalloyed joy of discovery. They go to show, however, that the true genius and the true originator—whether he be simply the first man to work the vein of an idea, or the inventor of a patent safety-pin—is the man who makes the world better. He is the boss. He is the man to whom we look for delightful surprises and pleasant items of the world's progress. Then do not be discouraged, ye who linger along the worn-out ruts where others have travelled. Brace up and press onward. Perhaps you may invent a new style of spelling, or something unique in the line of profanity. Do not lose hope. Hope on, hope ever. Give your attention to the matter of improving the average Indian editorial. Or if you cannot do even this, go into your laboratory and work nights till you invent a deadly poison that will knock the immortal soul out of the average bedbug, or produce a frightful mortality among cockroaches, or book agents, or some other annoying insect. Invent a directory, or a glittering falsehood, or a napkin-ring, or a dog-collar, or a cork screw. Do something, no matter how small, for the advancement of civilization.

QUEER

An exchange says that the people of that locality were considerably excited the other day over a three-cornered dog fight that occurred there. This is not surprising. Had it been simply a combat between oblong or rectangular dogs, or even a short but common-place fight between rhombohedral or octagonal dogs it would not have attracted any attention, but an engagement between triangular dogs is something that calls forth our wonder and surprise.

SIC SEMPER GLORIA HOUSEPLANT.

Evidently it is an ill wind that blows nobody good. Although this severe weather froze up the water barrel and doubles the coal bill, I am filled with a great large feeling of gratitude and pleasure this evening, for the last pale house plant, which for two or three weeks has been sighing for immortality, last night about midnight, got all the immortality it wanted, and this morning no doubt it is blooming in the new Jerusalem. I am glad it will bloom somewhere. It never got up steam enough to bloom here.

The head of the house thought he heard the rustle of wings in the still hours of night, and arising in all the voluptuous sweep of his night robe, and with the clear white beams of the winter moon lighting up the angles and gothic architecture of his picturesque proportions, he stepped to the bedside of the sickly little thing to ask if there was anything he could do, any last words that the little plant would like to have preserved, or anything of the kind, but it was too late. John Frost had been there, and touched the little thing with his icy finger, and all was still. The agricultural editor breathed a sigh of relief and went back to rest, neglecting to awaken the other members of the house, because he did not want a scene.

Any one desiring a medium sized flower-pot as good as new, can obtain one at this office very reasonably.

HOW TO TELL.

For the benefit of my readers, many of whom are not what might be called practical newspaper men and women, I will say that if your time is very precious, and life is too short for you to fool away your evenings reading local advertisements, and you are at times in grave doubt as to what is advertisement and what is news, just cast your eye to the bottom of the article, and if there is a foot-note which says "*ty4-fritu, 3dp&wly, hcolnrm, br-jn7, 35tfwly, &df-codtf,*" or something of that stripe, you may safely say that no matter how much confidence you may have had in the editor up to that date, the article with a foot-note of that kind is published from a purely mercenary motive, and the editor may or may not endorse the sentiments therein enunciated.

BIOGRAPHY OF COLOROW.

Brigadier-General Wm. H. Colorow was born on the frontier in July, 1824, of poor but honest parents. Early in 1843, he obtained the appointment to West Point through the influence of his Congressmen. While at West Point he was the leader of the Young Men's Christian Association, and now, if the army officers knew the grips, passwords and signals of the Association, and would use them, much good might be accomplished in bringing the General to terms, as he still respects the organization. But most of the army officers are a little rusty in the secret work of the Y. M. C. A.

Lieutenant Colorow, after graduating at the head of his class, came west to engage in the scalp trade, in which he has been very successful. "Colorow's Great Oriental Hair Raiser and Scalp Agitator" is known and respected all over the civilized world.

He has also held the position of Master of Transportation on the air line route from Colorado to Kingdom Come. His promotion has been rapid and his career has been filled with wonderful incidents.

General Colorow is not above the medium height. He wears his hair straight, and parted in the middle—a habit he contracted while at West Point. He sometimes parts the white man's hair in the middle also. He does it with his little hatchet. He is rather inclined to the brunette order of architecture, with Gothic nose, Eastlake jaws, and ears of the Queen Anne style. His hair is turning gray and his face is burned and specked with powder, caused by an explosion which came near terminating an eventful career.

Brigadier-General Colorow owns considerable stock in some of the best North Park mines. Occasionally, he goes out to the Park to see how these mines are panning out. Then the miners, out of respect for his feelings, leave the mines and come into town to see what is the latest news from the front. Some of the miners have neglected to come in at times when the General was visiting the mines. They are there yet. I have a mine out there but I am getting along first-rate without it, and I have been thinking that when the General celebrates his silver wedding, I will send up this mine to his residence, wrapped up in a clean napkin, with his monogram worked on it.

DIARY OF A SAUCY YOUNG THING.

It may be wrong to publish the contents of a diary, but the following notes in a new diary found yesterday, are too good to lose:

Jan. 1, 1877. To-day is New Year's day. Last night was Sunday night. I remember it distinctly. George and I watched the old year out and the new year in. George is awful kind-hearted. He has quit using tobacco on my account. He hasn't taken a chew this year.

Jan. 3. I didn't get time to write anything yesterday.

Jan. 4. This is Thursday. Day after to-morrow will be Saturday, and the next day will be Sunday.

Jan. 8. George was here last evening. I found some tobacco in his overcoat. Can he be deceiving me? O what false hearts men have! We had popcorn last evening. George and I ate a milk-pan full. He says popcorn seems to supply a want long felt. I don't know where he heard that.

Jan. 9. Another long week before the blessed rest and quiet of the Sabbath. I met George yesterday near the postoffice, and he didn't laugh as he once laughed. I wonder what makes him so sad. Maybe it's going without tobacco, or perhaps it's a boil. O what a world of woe!

Jan. 10. George is trying to raise a moustache. It looks like a Norwegian's eyebrow. It is genuine camel's hair. George's mother treats him unkindly, because he has pearl powder on his coat sleeves Monday morning. Four more days and the peace and quiet of the Sabbath will be here. I am a great admirer of Sunday.

Jan. 11. To-day is Thursday. O pshaw, I can't keep a diary.

KILLING OFF THE JAMES' BOYS.

Now that a terrible mortality has again broken out among the James' boys, it is but justice to a family who have received so many gratuitous obituary notices, to say that the James' boys are still alive and enjoying a reasonable amount of health and strength.

Although the papers are generally agreed upon the statement that they are more or less dead, yet in a few days the telegraph will announce their death again. They are dying on every hand. Hardly a summer zephyr stirs the waving grass that it does not bear upon its wings the dying groan of the James' boys. Every blast of winter howls the requiem of a James' boy. James' boys have died in Texas and in Minnesota, in New England and on the Pacific coast. They have been yielding up the ghost whenever they had a leisure moment. They would rob a bank or a printing office, or some other place where wealth is known to be stored, and then they would die. When business was very active one of the brothers would stay at home and attend to work while the other would go and lay down his life.

Whenever the yellow fever let up a little the Grim Destroyer would go for a James' boy, and send him to his long home.

The men who have personally and individually killed the James' boys from time to time, contemplate holding a grand mass meeting and forming a new national party. This will no doubt be the governing party next year.

Let us institute a reform. Let us ignore the death of every plug who claims to be a James' boy, unless he identifies himself. Let us examine the matter and see if the trade mark is on every wrapper or blown in the bottle, before we fill the air with woe and bust the broad canopy of heaven wide open with our lamentations over the untimely death of the James' boys. If we succeed in standing them off while they live we can afford to control our grief and silently battle with our emotions when they are still in death, until we know we are snorting and bellowing over the correct corpse.

A RELIC.

The Hutchinson family gave a concert last evening at the Methodist church, according to advertisement, and were greeted with a fair house. The entertainment did not awaken very loud applause, nor very much of it. The songs were not new. Many of them I had almost forgotten, but they were trotted out last evening and driven around the track in pretty fair time.

The fresh little quartette entitled, "Tommy, don't Go," was brought forward during the entertainment. I could see that this song has failed very much since I last met it. Its teeth are falling out, and it is getting very bald-headed. It will probably make two or three more grand farewell concerts and then it will be found dead in its bed some morning before breakfast.

"Silver Threads Among the Gold" was omitted from the programme.

The old melodeon that I remember was rickety and out of repair when I was a prattling infant, was on the stage last evening. It is about the size of a mouth organ, but the tone is not as clear. It is getting wheezy, and a short breath shows that it is beginning to feel the infirmities of age. The pumping arrangement makes more noise than the music, and something is the matter with the exhaust pipe. But when the old man opened the throttle and gave her sand, she would make a good deal of racket for such a little thing. After the concert was over, Mr. Hutchinson rolled up the melodeon in his pocket handkerchief and took it home.

Take the entertainment up one side and down the other, I was not much tickled with it. For those who like to drift back into the musty centuries gone by, and shake hands with the skeletons of forgotten ages, it is all right; but the time has come when a troupe cannot travel upon anything but true merit, and the public require that those who ask for money shall give some kind of an equivalent.

SOME REASONS WHY I CAN'T BE AN INDIAN AGENT.

I see by the Western press that my name has been suggested to the Secretary of the Interior as a suitable one for the appointment of Indian Agent at the Uncompahgre Agency to succeed Berry; and, while I must express my grateful acknowledgment for the apparent faith and childlike confidence reposed in me by the people of Colorado, I must gently but firmly decline the proffered distinction.

In the first place, my other duties will not admit of it. My time is very much occupied at present in my journalistic work, and should there be a falling off in my chaste and picturesque contributions to the press, the great surging world of literature would be surprised and grieved.

Again, I could not entirely lay aside this class of work anyway, even were I to accept the position, and as I cannot write without being wrapped in the most opaque gloom and perfect calm I would be annoyed, I know, by the war-whoops of the savage when he got to playing croquet in the front yard, and whenever he got to shooting at me through the window while I was composing a poem, I am perfectly positive that I would get restless and the divine afflatus would cease to give down.

The true poet loves seclusion and soothing rest. That is the secret of his even numbers and smooth cadences. Look at Dryden, and Walt Whitman, and Milton, and Burns, and the Sweet Singer of Michigan. What could any of them have done with the house full of children of the forest who were hankering for a fresh pail of gore for lunch?

Further than this, I have not that gentle magnetic power over the untutored savage that some have. I am agitated all the time by a nervous dread that if I go near him I may lose my self-command and kill him. I would lose my temper some day when I felt irritable, I'm afraid, and shoot into a drove of them and mangle them horribly if they refused to dig the potatoes, or got rebellious and wouldn't do the fall plowing.

Then I would have to hunt up a suitable military post 200 or 300 miles away and stay there till the popular feeling in the tribe had cooled down a little.

Then, again, the Utes would invite me to attend the regular social hops during the winter, and I wouldn't know what to do, for it would be bad policy to refuse, and yet I don't know the first figure of the war-dance. I dance like a club-footed camel, anyway, and when I got mixed up in the scalp-dance the floor-manager would get mad at me probably, and chop some large irregular notches in me with a broad-ax.

Then their costumes are so low-necked and so exceedingly dress, and everything is so all-fired decolette, whatever that is. I would probably insist on wearing a liver-pad on a chilblain, and they wouldn't dance with me all the evening, and I would be a wall-flower, and they would call me a perfect dud, and would laugh at the way my liver-pad was cut, and I would go home and cry myself to sleep over the whole miserable affair.

So that perhaps it would be just as well to plug along as I am and not get ambitious. The life of the ostensible humorist may not be so fraught with untrammeled nature and sylvan retreats, and wild, picturesque canons, and bosky dells, and things of that kind, but it is cheering and comforting to put your hand on the top of your head and feel that it is still on deck, and, although wealth may not come pouring in upon you in such an irresistible torrent as you may desire, you know that if you can get enough to eat from day to day, and dodge the Vigilance Committee and the celluloid pie, you are comparatively safe.

Besides all this, I am afraid I am not in proper spiritual shape to go among the Indians., Suppose that on some softened, mellow, autumnal day they were all clustered about me with the bacon grease and war paint on every childlike countenance, and while I stood there in the midst of all the autumn splendor with the woods clothed in all the gorgeous apparel of the deceased year, telling them of the beauties of industry, and peace, and the glad unfettered life of the buckwheat promoter, or while I read a passage of Scripture to them and was explaining it, and they were looking up into my face with their great fawnlike eyes, all at once one of them should playfully shoot my wife—all the wife I had, too—or my hired girl! The chances are about even that I would throw down the Bible and fly into an ungovernable rage and swear, and be just as harsh, and rude, and unreasonable as I could be. Then, after I had hammered the immortal soul out of the entire tribe, and my wrath had spent itself, I would probably bitterly regret it all.

O it's of no use. I can't accept the position. I've been in the habit of swearing at the spring poet and the "constant reader" too long, and I know just as well as any one how it unfits me for every walk of life that requires meekness and gentle Christian forbearance.

THE PICNIC SNOOZER'S LAMENT.

Gently lay aside the picnic,
    For its usefulness is o'er,
And the winter style of misery
    Stands and knocks upon your door.

Lariat the lonely oyster
Drifting on some foreign shore;
Zion needs him in her business—
    She can use him o'er and o'er.

Bring along the lonely oyster,
    With the winter style of gloom,
And the supper for the pastor,
    With its victims for the tomb.

Cast the pudding for the pastor,
With its double iron door;
It will gather in the pastor
For the bright and shining shore.

Put away the little picnic
    Till the coming of the spring;
Useless now the swaying hammock
And the idle picnic swing.

Put away the pickled spider
And the cold-pressed picnic fly,
And the decorated trousers
    With their wealth of custard pie.

BILLIOUS NYE AND BOOMERANG IN THE GOLD MINES.

Whenever the cares of life weigh too heavily upon me, and the *ennui* which comes to those who have more wealth than they know what to do with settles down upon me, and I get weary of civilization, I like to load up my narrow-gauge mule Boomerang and take a trip into the mountains. I call my mule Boomerang because I never know where he is going to strike. He is a perpetual surprise to me in this respect. A protracted acquaintance with him, however, has taught me to stand in front of him when I address him, for the recoil of Boomerang is very disastrous. Boomerang is very much below the medium height, with a sad, faraway look in his eye. He has an expression of woe and disappointment and gloom, because life has been to him a series of blasted hopes and shattered ambitions.

In his youth he yearned to be the trick-mule of a circus, and though he fitted himself for that profession, he finds himself in the decline of life with his bright anticipations nothing but a vast and robust ruin. About all the relaxation he has is to induce some trusting stranger to caress his favorite chilblain, and then he kicks the confiding stranger so high that he can count the lamp-posts on the streets of the New Jerusalem. When Boomerang and I visit a mining camp the supplies of giant powder and other combustibles are removed to some old shaft and placed under a strong guard. In one or two instances where this precaution was not taken the site of the camp is now a desolate, barren waste, occupied by the prairie-dog and the jack-rabbit. When Boomerang finds a nitro-glycerine can in the heart of a flourishing camp, and has room to throw himself, he can arrange a larger engagement for the coroner than any mule I ever saw.

There is a new camp in the valley of the Big Laramie River, near the dividing line between Wyoming and Colorado. A few weeks ago the murmur of the rapid river down the canon and the cheerful solo of the cayote alone were heard. Now several hundred anxious excited miners are prospecting for gold, and the tent-town grows apace. Up and down the sides of the river and over the side of the mountain every little way a notice greets the eye announcing that "the undersigned claim 1,500 feet in length by 300 feet in width upon" the lode known as the Pauper's Dream, or the Blue Tail Fly, or the Blind Tom, or the Captain Kidd, or the Pigeon-Toed Pete, with all the dips, spurs, angles, gold and silver bearing rock or earth therein contained.

I have a claim further on in the North Park of Colorado. I have always felt a little delicate about working it, because heretofore several gentlemen from the Ute reservation on White River have claimed it. They are the same parties who got into a little difficulty with Agent Meeker and killed him. Of course these parties are not *bona fide* citizens of the United States, and therefore cannot hold my claim under the mining law; but I have not as yet raised the point with them. Whenever they would go over into the park for rest and recreation, I would respect their feelings and withdraw. I didn't know but they might have some private business which they did not wish me to overhear, so I came away.

Once I came away in the night. It is cooler travelling in the night, and does not attract so much attention. Last summer Antelope and his band came over into the park and told the miners that he would give them "one sleep" to get out of there. I told him that I didn't care much for sleep anyhow, and I would struggle along somehow till I got home. I told him that my constitution would stand it first-rate without rest, and I felt as though my business in town might be suffering in my absence. So I went home. The mine is there yet, but I would sell it very reasonably—very reasonably indeed. I do not apprehend any trouble from the Indians, but I have lost my interest in mines to some extent, The Indians are not all treacherous and bloodthirsty as some would suppose. Only the live ones are that way. Wooden Indians are also to be relied upon.

In digging an irrigating ditch on the Laramie Plains, last summer, the skeleton of an Indian chief was plowed up. I went to look at him. He had, no doubt, been dead many years; but in the dry alkaline divide, at an elevation of nearly 8,000 feet above sea level, his skull had been preserved pretty well. I took it in my hand and looked it over and shook the sand out of it, and convinced myself that life was extinct. An Indian is not always dead when he has that appearance. I always feel a little timid till I see his scapula, and ribs, and shin bones mixed up so that Gabriel would rather arrange a 15 puzzle than to fix up an Indian out of the wreck. Then I have the most child-like faith and confidence in him. When some avenging fate overtakes a Ute and knocks him into pi, and thus makes a Piute out of him, and flattens him out like a postage stamp, and pulverizes him, and runs him over the amalgator, and assays him so that he lies in the retort like a seidlitz powder, then I feel that I can trust him. I do not care then how much the cold world may scoff at him. Prior to that I am very reserved and very reticent.

That is why I presented my mine to the Ute nation as a slight token of my respect and esteem. Then I went away. I did not hurry much, but I had every inducement and encouragement to reach home at the earliest possible moment, and the result was very gratifying. Very much so, indeed. I left my gun and ammunition, but it did not matter. It wasn't a very good gun anyhow. I do not need it. Any one going into the park this summer can have it. It is standing behind the door of the cabin between the piano and the whatnot.

TWO GREAT MEN.

Mr. Thompson, Secretary of the Navy, passed through here on his way to San Francisco on Wednesday evening, with his party.

In company with Delegate Downey, Judge Blair and United States Marshal Schnitger, I went into the Secretary's special car and talked with him while the train stopped here.

The other members of the party did most of the talking and I eloquently sat on the back of a chair and whistled a few bars from a little operatta that I am having cast at the rolling-mill. I am not very hilarious in the presence of great at men. I am not so much at home in their society as I am in my own quiet little boudoir, with one leg over the piano, and the other tangled up among the $2,500 lace curtains and Majolica dogs.

Bye and bye I thought that I had better show the Secretary that I knew more than the casual observer would suppose, and I said, "Mr. Thompson, how's your navy looking this summer? Have you sheared your iron-clad rams yet, and if so, what will the clip average do you think?" He laughed a merry, rippling laugh, and said if he were at home he would swear that he was in the presence of the mental giant, William G. Le Duc.

I was very much pleased with the Secretary. This will insure the brilliant success of his Western trip.

He paid the Laramie plains a high compliment; said they were greener, and the grass was far superior to that of any part of the country through which he had passed. He said he was as positive of Garfield's election as he was of reaching San Francisco, and chatted pleasantly upon the general topics of the day.

I could see that he was accustomed to the very best society, for he stood there in the blinding glare of my dazzling beauty, as self-possessed and cool as though he were at home talking with Ben Butler and Conkling and Carpenter and other rising young men.

There is a striking resemblance between the Secretary and myself. We are both tall and slender, with roguish eyes and white hair. His, however, is white from age, and is a kind of bluish white. Mine is white because it never had moral courage or strength of character enough to be any other color. It also has more of a lemon-colored tinge to it than the Secretary's has.

We resemble each other in several more respects. One is that we are both United States officials. He is a member of the Cabinet, and I am a United States Commissioner. We are both great men, but I have succeeded better in keeping it a profound secret than he has.

DIRTY MURPHY.

On Thursday a man known by the Castillian nom de plume of Dirty Murphy, was engaged in digging out a frozen water-pipe in front of the New York House, when the glowing inspiration came upon him that the frozen earth could be blasted much easier than it could be dug, so he drilled a hole down to the pipe and put in a shot preparatory to lifting a large portion of the universe out by the roots and laying bare the foundations of the earth.

John Humpfner, the ram-rod of the New York House, feared that the explosion might break the large French plate glass windows of his palatial hotel, and so put a wash tub over the blast. What the exact notion of Mr. Humpfner was relative to the result in this case, I am unable to say, but when the roar of the universal convulsion had died away, and the result was examined by Mr. Humpfner and the Count de Dirty Murphy, they looked surprised.

Instead of blowing out a large tract of land and laying bare the entire water and gas system of the city, the blast blew out like a sick fire-cracker with a loose fuse, and, taking the washtub with it, sailed away into the realms of space. It crashed through the milky way and passed on in its mad flight into the boundless stretch of the unknown. Those who saw the affair and had no interest in the wash-tub, enjoyed it very much, but to the incorporators and bondholders who held the controlling interest in the tub, the whole thing seemed a hollow mockery and a desolate, dreary waste. Don Miguel de Dirty Murphy swooned on the spot. The hose has been playing on him ever since, but he has not returned to consciousness. The later geological formations have been washed away, and it is thought that by working a night shift, prehistoric and volcanic encrustations will be removed so that the pores may be opened and life and animation return, but it is a long, tedious job, and the superintending geologist is beginning to despair.

A ROCKY MOUNTAIN SUNSET.

Speaking of the hours of closing day reminds me that we have recently witnessed some of the most brilliant and beautiful sunsets here that I have ever seen. In justice to Wyoming, I will say that she certainly deserves a word for the gorgeous splendor of her summer sunset skies.

The air is perfectly pure, and at that hour the sighing zephyr seems to have sighed about all it wants to and dies away to rest. The pulse of tired Nature is almost still, and the luxurious sense of rest is upon the face of the silent world. The god of day drops slowly down the crimson west, as though he reluctantly bade adieu to the grassy plains and rugged hills. Anon the golden bars of resplendent light are shot across the deep blue of heaven, the fleecy clouds are tipped and bordered with pale gold, while the heavy billows of bronze are floating in a mighty ocean of the softest azure. The blue grows deeper and the gold more dazzling. The scarlet becomes intensified and the softened east takes up the magnificent reflection. The hills and mountains are bathed in the beams of this occidental splendor, and the landscape adorns itself in honor of nature's most wonderful diurnal spectacle.

It is certainly the boss. These mountain sunsets in the pure, clear air of Wyoming and Colorado, as thrilling triumphs of natural loveliness, most unquestionably take the cake.

The Italian sunset is a good fair average sunset, but the admission is too high. It also lacks expression and *embonpoint*, whatever that may be.

May be it is not *embonpoint* which it lacks, but it is something of that nature.

These beautiful sights awake the poet's soul within me, and on one occasion I wrote a little ode or apostrophe to the sunset, which was as sweet a little thing as I ever saw in the English language, but the taxidermist spoiled it. He left it out in the hot sun while he was stuffing a sage hen, and the poor little thing seemed to wilt and retire from the public gaze.

THE TEMPERATURE OF THE BUMBLE-BEE.

A recent article on bees says, "If you have noticed bees very closely, you may have seen that they are not all alike in size."

I have noticed bees very closely indeed, during my life. In fact I have several times been thrown into immediate juxtaposition with them, and have had a great many opportunities to observe their ways, and I am free to say that I have not been so forcibly struck with the difference in their size as the noticeable difference in their temperature.

I remember at one time of sitting by a hive watching the habits of the bees, and thinking how industrious they were, and what a wide difference there is between the toilsome life of the little insect, and the enervating, aimless, idle and luxurious life of the newspaper man, when an impulsive little bee lit in my hair. He seemed to be feverish. Whereever he settled down he seemed to leave a hot place. I learned afterward that it was a new kind of bee called the anti-clinker base-burner bee.

O, yes, I have studied the ways of the bee very closely. He is supposed to improve each shining hour. That's the great objection I have to him. The bee has been thrown up to me a great deal during my life, and the comparison was not flattering. It has been intimated that I resembled the bee that sits on the piazza of the hive all summer and picks his teeth, while the rest are getting in honey and beeswax for the winter campaign.

DRAWBACKS OF PUBLIC LIFE.

I always like to tell anything that has the general effect of turning the laugh on me, because then I know there will be no hard feelings. It is very difficult to select any one who will stand publicity when that publicity is more amusing to the average reader than to the chief actor. Every little while I run out of men who enjoy being written about in my chaste and cheerful vein. Then I hate to come forward and take this position myself. It is not egotism, as some might suppose. It is unselfishness and a manly feeling of self-sacrifice.

Last year I consented to read the Declaration of Independence, as my share of the programme, partially out of gallantry toward the Goddess of Liberty, and partly to get a ride with the chaplain and orator of the day, through the principal streets behind the band. It was a very proud moment for me. I felt as though I was holding up one corner of the national fabric myself, and I naturally experienced a pardonable pride about it. I sat in the carriage with the compiled laws of Wyoming under my arm, and looked like Daniel Webster wrapped in a large bale of holy calm. At the grounds I found that most everybody was on the speakers' stand, and the audience was represented by a helpless and unhappy minority.

At a Fourth of July celebration it is wonderful how many great men there are, and how they swarm on the speakers' platform. Then there are generally about thirteen venerable gentlemen who do not pretend to be great, but they cannot hear very well, so they get on the speakers' stand to hear the same blood-curdling statements that they have heard for a thousand years. While I was reading the little burst of humor known as the Declaration, the staging gave way under the accumulated weight of the Fourth Infantry band and several hundred great men who had invited themselves to sit on the platform. The Chaplain fell on top of me, and the orator of the day on top of him. A pitcher of ice water tipped over on me, and the water ran down my back. A piece of scantling and an alto horn took me across the cerebellum, and as often as I tried to get up and throw off the Chaplain and orator of the day and Fourth Infantry band, the greased pig which had been shut up under the stand temporarily, would run between my legs and throw me down again. I never knew the reading of the Declaration of Independence to have such a telling effect. I went home without witnessing the closing exercises. I did not ride home in the carriage. I told the committee that some poor, decrepit old woman might ride home in my place. I needed exercise and an opportunity to commune with myself.

As I walked home by an unfrequented way, I thought of the growth and grandeur of the republic, and how I could get rid of the lard that had been wiped on my clothes by the oleagineous pig. This year, when the committee asked me to read the Declaration, I said pleasantly but firmly that I would probably be busy on that day soaking my head, and therefore would have to decline.

THE GLAD, FREE LIFE OF THE MINER.

In the spring the young man's fancy lightly turns to thoughts of love. He also looks forward to some means by which he can earn the bread and oleomargarine on which he can subsist. There are several ways of doing this. Some take to agriculture and spend the long days of golden summer among the clover blossoms of the meadow, raking hay and hornets into large winrows, while they sniff the refreshing odor of the mignonette and the morning glory, and the boiling soft soap and potato bugs that have been mashed into the sweet bye-and-bye. Others, by a straightforward course become truthful newspaper men and amass untold wealth as funny men. Others proclaim the glad news of salvation at so much a proclaim.

Perhaps, however, the most exciting way to become wealthy in a speedy manner and in a surprising style is that of the miner. He buys some bacon, and tobacco, and flour, and whiskey, and a pick and some chewing tobacco, and a shovel and some whiskey, and an axe and some smoking tobacco and matches, and whiskey and blankets, and giant powder, and goes to the mountains to get wealthy.

He works all day hard, walking up hill and down, across ravines and rocky gulches, weary but happy and confident till night comes down upon him and he goes home to camp, and around the fire he enters the free-for-all lying match, and tired as he is gets away with the prize for scrub-lying. I have met miners who would with a little chance hold a pretty even race against the great stalwart army of journalists. I do not say this intending to reflect upon the noble profession of mining, for I have been taught to respect the pleasing lie which is told in a harmless way, to cheer the great surging mass of humanity who get tired of the same old truths that have been handed down from generation to generation.

One man who ran against me for justice of the peace two years ago and who, therefore, got left, is now independent, having sold out a prospect in sight of town for a good figure, while I plug along and tell the truth and have nothing under the broad blue dome of heaven but $150 per month and my virtue. Of course virtue is its own reward, but how little of glad unfettered mirthfulness it yields. Sometimes I wish I had a little looser notions about what is right and what is wrong. But it is too late now. I have become so hardened in these upright ways that when I do wrong it pretty nearly kills me.

This summer, however, I will get me a little blue jackass and put a sawbuck on his back, and pack some select oysters and gum-drops, and an upright piano, and a hammock, and some sheet music, and a camera, and some ice and frosted cake, and a Brussels carpet, and a tent on his back, and I will hie me to the mines, join the big stampede, fall down a prospect hole 200 feet deep, and my faithful jackass will pull me out, and I shall nearly freeze to death nights, and starve to death days, and I will have lots of fun.

I like the glad, free mountain life. I have tried it. Once I went out to the mountains and slept on the lap of mother earth. That is, I advertised to sleep, but I couldn't quite catch on. I lay on my back till two o'clock, A. M., looking up into the clear blue ether, while the stars above were twinkling. After they had about twinkled themselves out, I concluded I would not try to woo the drowsy god any more. I got up and made a pint of coffee, and drank it so hot that the alimentary canal was rolled together like a scroll. It felt as though I had swallowed a large slice of melted perdition, but it didn't warm me up any. Then I went up the mountain five miles to see the sun rise. In about four hours it rose. So did the coffee that I drank at two o'clock. Somehow the sunrise didn't seem to cheer me. It looked murky and muddy; all nature seemed to be shrouded in gloom. There was more gloom turned loose there than I have ever seen. I wanted to go home. I needed some one to pity me and love me a great deal. I needed rest and entire change of scene. I went away from there because the associations were not pleasant; roughing it doesn't seem to do me the required amount of good. I am too frail. I need more of the comforts of civilization, and less wealth of wild, majestic scenery. I find that my nature needs very little awe-inspiring grandeur, and a good deal of woven wire mattress and nutritious, digestible food.

SOME THOUGHTS OF CHILDHOOD.

Childhood is the glad springtime of life. It is then that the seeds of future greatness or startling mediocrity are sown.

If a boy has marked out a glowing future as an intellectual giant, it is during these early years of his growth that he gets some pine knots to burn in the evening, whereby he can read Herbert Spencer and the Greek grammar, so that when he is in good society he can say things that nobody can understand. This gives him an air of mysterious greatness which soaks into those with whom he comes in contact, and makes them respectful and unhappy while in his presence.

Boys who intend to be railroad men should early begin to look about them for some desirable method of expunging two or three fingers and one thumb. Most boys can do this without difficulty. Trying to pick a card out of a job press when it is in operation is a good way. Most job presses feel gloomy and unhappy until they have eaten the fingers off two or three boys. Then they go on with their work cheerfully and even hilariously.

Boys who intend to lead an irreproachable life and be foremost in every good word and work, should take unusual precautions to secure perfect health and longevity. Good boys never know when they are safe. Statistics show that the ratio of good boys who die, compared to bad ones, is simply appalling.

There are only thirty-nine good boys left as we go to press, and they are not feeling very well either.

The bad ones are all alive and very active.

The boy who stole my coal shovel last spring and went out into the graveyard and dug into a grave to find Easter eggs, is the picture of health. He ought to live a long time yet, for he is in very poor shape to be ushered in before the bar of judgment.

When I was a child I was different from other boys in many respects. I was always looking about to see what good I could do. I am that way yet.

If my little brother wanted to go in swimming contrary to orders, I was not strong enough to prevent him, but I would go in with him and save him from a watery grave. I went in the water thousands of times that way, and as a result he is alive to-day.

But he is ungrateful. He hardly ever mentions it now, but he remembers the gordian knots that I tied in his shirts. He speaks of them frequently. This shows the ingratitude and natural depravity of the human heart.

Ah, what recompense have wealth and position for the unalloyed joys of childhood, and how gladly to-day as I sit in the midst of my oriental splendor and costly magnificence, and thoughtfully run my fingers through my infrequent bangs, would I give it all, wealth, position and fame, for one balmy, breezy day gathered from the mellow haze of the long ago when I stood full knee-deep in the luke-warm pool near my suburban home in the quiet dell, and allowed the yielding and soothing mud and meek-eyed pollywogs to squirt up between my dimpled toes.

THE NEW ADJUSTABLE CAMPAIGN SONG.

I beg leave at this time to present to the public a melodious gem of song which I am positive cannot fail to give satisfaction.

It will withstand the rigors of our mountain clime as well as the heat and moisture of a lower altitude.

It is purely unpartisan, although it may be easily changed to any shade of political opinion. It is cheap, portable and durable, and filled with little pathetic passages that will add greatly to the enthusiasm of presidential contests.

It is true that some harsh criticism has been called down upon this little chunk of crystallized melody, as I may be pardoned for calling it, and it has been suggested that it is too much fraught with a gentle, soothing sense of vacuity, and that there is nothing in it particularly one way or the other.

This I admit to be in a measure true. There is nothing in it as a poem, but it must be borne in mind that this is not a poem. It is a campaign song.

Campaign songs never have anything in them. They don't have to.

Editorials and speeches have to express human ideas and little suggestions of original horse sense, but the campaign song is generally distinguished by a wild, tumultuous torrent of attenuated space.

They are like the sons of great men—we do not expect any show of herculean intellectual acumen from them.

Directions.—Set up the song with the feed bar down and pitman reversed. Then turn the thumbscrew that holds the asterisks in place, take them out and lay them away in the upper case, and in proper compartment.

Next set up desirable candidate, unless you can get candidate to set them up himself, slug the standing galley, oil the cross-head, upset the tripod, loosen the crown sheet a little, so that the obvious duplex will work easily in the lallygag eccentric, and turn on steam.

Should the box in which the lower case candidates are stored get hot, sponge off and lubricate with castor oil, antifat and borax in equal parts.

Keep this song in a cool place.

(Air—*Rally Round the Flag, Boys.*)
Oh, we'll gather from the hillsides,
We'll gather from the glen,

Shouting the battle cry of....,
And we'll round up our voters,
Our brave and trusty men,
    Shouting the battle cry of....

    Chorus.

Oh, our candidate forever,
    Te doodle daddy a,
Down with old...,
Turn a foodie diddy a,
And we'll whoop de dooden do,
    Fal de adden adden a,
And don't you never forget it.
Oh, we'll meet the craven foe
On the fall election day,
Shouting the battle cry of...,
And we'll try to let him know
That we're going to have our way,
Shouting the battle cry of,

    Chorus.

Oh, our candidate forever, etc.

Oh, we're the people's friends,
    As all can plainly see,
Shouting the battle cry of...,
And we'll whoop de dooden doo,
    With our big majority,
    And don't you never forget it.

    Chorus.

Oh, our candidate forever, etc.

SITTING ON ON A VENERABLE JOKE.

Near St. Paul, on the Sioux City road, I met the ever-present man from Leadville again.

I had met him before on every division of every railroad that I had traveled over, but I nodded to him, and he began to tell me all about Leadville.

He saw that I looked sad, and he cheered me up with little prehistoric jokes that an antiquarian had given him years ago. Finally he said:

"Leadville is mighty cold; it has such an all fired altitude, The summer is very short and unreliable, and the winter long and severe.

"An old miner over in California gulch got off a pretty good joke about the climate there. A friend asked him about the seasons at Leadville, and he said that there they had nine months winter and three months late in the fall."

Then he looked around to see me fall to pieces with mirth, but I restrained myself and said:

"You will please excuse me for not laughing at that joke. I cannot do it. It is too sacred.

"Do you think I would laugh at the bones of the Pilgrim Fathers, where are they? or burst into wild hilarity over the grave of Noah and his family?

"No, sir; their age and antiquity protect them. That is the way with your Phoenician joke.

"Another reason why I cannot laugh at it is this: I am not a very easy and extemporaneous laughter, anyway. I am generally shrouded in gloom, especially when I am in hot pursuit of a wild and skittish joke for my own use. It takes a good, fair, average joke that hasn't been used much to make me laugh easy, and besides, I have used up the fund of laugh that I had laid aside for that particular joke. It has, in fact, overdrawn some now, and is behind.

"I do not wish to intrench on the fund that I have concluded to offer as a purse for young jokes that have never made it in three minutes.

"I want to encourage green jokes, too, that have never trotted in harness before, and, besides, I must insist on using my scanty fund of laugh on jokes of the nineteenth century. I have got to draw the line somewhere.

"If I were making a collection of antique jokes of the vintage of 1400 years B. C., or arranging and classifying little bon-mots of the time of Cleopatra or King Solomon, I would give you a handsome sum for this one of yours, but I am just trying to worry along and pay expenses, and trying to be polite to every one I meet, and laughing at lots of things that I don't want to laugh at, and I am going to quit it.

"That is why I have met your little witticism with cold and heartless gravity."

A HAIRBREADTH ESCAPE.

To-day I got shaved at a barber-shop, where I begged the operator to kill me and put me out of my misery.

I have been accustomed to gentle care and thoughtfulness at home, and my barber at Laramie handles me with the utmost tenderness. I was, therefore, poorly prepared to meet the man who this morning filled my soul with woe.

I know that I have not deserved this, for while others have berated the poor barber and swore about his bad breath and never-ending clatter and his general heartlessness, I have never said anything that was not filled with child-like trust and hearty good will toward him.

I have called the attention of the public to the fact that sometimes customers had bad breath and were restless and mean while being operated on, and then when they are all fixed up nicely, they put their hats on and light a cigar and hold up their finger to the weary barber and tell him that they will see him more subsequently.

Now, however, I feel differently.

This barber no doubt had never heard of me. He no doubt thought I was an ordinary plug who didn't know anything about luxury.

I shall mark a copy of this paper and send it to him.

Then while he is reading it I will steal up behind him with a pick handle and kill him. I want him to be reading this when I kill him, because it will assist the coroner in arriving at the immediate cause of his death.

The first whiff I took of this man's breath, I knew that he was rum's maniac.

He had the Jim James in an advanced stage. Now, I don't object to being shaved by a barber who is socially drunk, but when the mad glitter of the maniac is in his eye and I can see that he is debating the question of whether he will cut my head off and let it drop over the back of the chair or choke me to death with a lather brush, it makes me nervous and fidgetty.

This man made up his mind three times that he would kill me, and some one came in just in time to save me.

His chair was near a window, and there was a hole in the blind, so that when he was shaving the off side of my face he would turn my head over in such a position that I could look up into the middle of the sun. My attention had never before been called to the appearance of the sun as it looks to the naked eye, and I was a good deal surprised.

The more I looked into the very center of the great orb of day the more I was filled with wonder at the might and power that could create it. I began to pine for death immediately, so that I could be far away among the heavenly bodies, and in a land where no barber with the delirium triangles can ever enter.

This barber held my head down so that the sun could shine into my darkened understanding, until I felt that my brain had melted and was floating around and swashing about in my skull like warm butter.

His hand was very unsteady, too. I lost faith in him on the start when he cut off a mole under my chin and threw it into the spittoon. I did not care very particularly for the mole, and did not need it particularly, but at the same time I had not decided to take it off at that time. In fact I had worn it so long that I had become attached to it. It had also become attached to me.

That is why I could not restrain my tears when the barber cut it off and then stepped back to the other end of the room to see how I looked without it.

MYSELF, DR. TALMAGE, AND OTHER DIVINES.

September 5, 1880.

I am beginning to-day to keep a diary. It is not an agreeable task, but I feel that the wild, glad bursts of unfettered thought which surge through my ponderous mind ought to be embalmed in eligible characters, and passed down to posterity.

The thought may arise in the mind of the reader that this is taking a low and contemptible advantage of a posterity that never in word or deed ever harmed me; but I care not. Other able men have perpetrated their diaries upon me when I was not in a condition to help myself, and now that I can hand down and transmit to nations yet unborn, the same great heritage unimpaired, there is a sweet consciousness of a revenge that has been fully glutted.

To day I have been to church. I do not speak of it as remarkable at all, for wherever I am, whether at home or abroad, my first thought is, where will I find a sanctuary?

The minister was quite classical and he pumped the congregation so full of heathen mythology that he came very near forgetting that he had a word to say on behalf of Christianity as the advance agent of Zion.

I do not wish to say one word that would sound like irreverence toward the cause which this man undertook to represent; but I want to jot down a little thought or two relative to this exponent, so that I may be placed squarely upon the record.

I have often thought when I have watched this class of ministers, with one hand resting in a graceful and negligent posture on the altar rail, while the self-conscious Demosthenes reeled off a 4th of July prayer to the miserable, wretched and undone sinners before him, how God has said that He is a jealous God; and I have wondered if these prayers, arranged with great care to meet the criticism of the worshippers, and with an off-hand disregard to the feelings of the Almighty that is very cool and very refreshing indeed, whether they ever lay hold of the throne of grace or not, and whether they ever lift up mankind or make the world better.

Speaking of divines, reminds me of the very pleasant trip I had over the Union Pacific on my way east with Brother Talmage. I call him Brother Tannage because he called me brother occasionally. He no doubt thought that in different walks of life, perhaps, but working in the same direction, we were both laboring to make the world better.

Brother Talmage, General Crook, myself and two or three other eminent men together occupied the sleeper Boise City. Brother Talmage and I one day were seized with the same irresistable desire, at the same moment, to change our shirts. He was a little nearer the wash-room than I was, so he got there first, and we stood up together smiling at each other sweetly, with a clean shirt in our hands, and didn't know exactly how to express ourselves.

I was the first to speak. I told the Doctor that it was of no consequence particularly, and I would wait. He said no, I must not wait for him, and insisted so cordially on my coming in there that we went in together and tackled the mysteries of our toilet at the same time.

It was pretty tough on me, for I had been accustomed while peeling off a damp shirt to go through a few little vocal exercises and dance around on one leg and howl.

Going from the mountains of Wyoming down into the tropical heat of Nebraska made me perspire a good deal, and nothing but the firm and irresistible restraint thrown about me by an eminent divine kept me from swearing.

But the Doctor did not get mad. When he shoved his bald head into his shirt a large smile was on his face, and when it emerged at the top and he waved his arms above his head and struggled to climb up into the shirt, so that he could look out over the battlements, he was still smiling. He was not only smiling, but he was smiling a good deal. Those who have seen Dr. Talmage smile know now he throws his whole soul into it.

If I could jam my head up through a wilderness of shirt and starch and saw off my windpipe as I looked out over the billowy, buttonless mass, and still smile, as Dr. Talmage does, I would give all my broad possessions in a moment.

This offer will hold good up to the 15th.

We got quite sociable and cordial toward the close, and I got the Doctor to reach up as far as he could on my spinal column and bring down the refractory end of a suspender, then I retaliated by going down into his true inwardness after a collar button that had dropped into oblivion.

While he was smiling with that glad, free smile of his, which he takes along with him instead of baggage, he told me a pretty good thing on the editor of the *Herald* of Salt Lake. He told it to me in confidence, he said, because he knew he could rely on a newspaper man. Then he laughed and seemed to think it was a good joke.

It seems that when Dr. Talmage was in Salt Lake, the *Tribune* published what purported to be an interview between a reporter of that paper and the Brooklyn divine.

Shortly afterward, and while Dr. T. was in San Francisco, he received a letter from the editor of the *Herald* and a marked copy of the paper, giving the Doctor a very flattering notice. In his letter the editor said: "I enclose a clipping from the *Tribune* purporting to be an interview between yourself and a reporter of that paper; will you be kind enough to write me whether it is or is not genuine?"

The Doctor looked the clipping carefully over, and as it was nothing but a blood-curdling account of the merits of Day's Kidney pad, he had no hesitancy in pronouncing the alleged interview a fraud. Still he never wrote the editor of the *Herald*, and he no doubt still wonders why it is that Dr. Talmage don't come forward and state the facts, so that the Gentile *Tribune* may be shown up.

The Doctor says that too much care cannot be used by the editor who wields the shears not to get his editorials mixed up with patent medicine advertisements.

FINE-CUT AS A MEANS OF GRACE.

The amateur tobacco chewer many times through lack of consideration allows himself to be forced into very awkward and unpleasant positions. As a fair sample of the perils to which the young and inexperienced masticator of the weed is subjected, the following may be given:

A few Sabbaths ago a young man who was attending divine worship up on Piety Avenue, concluded, as the sermon was about one-half done and didn't seem to get very exciting, that he would take a chew of tobacco. He wasn't a handsome chewer, and while he was sliding the weed out of his pocket and getting it behind his handkerchief and working it into his mouth, he looked as though he might be robbing a blind woman of her last copper. Then when he got it into his mouth and tried to look pious and anxious about the welfare of his never dying soul, the chew in his mouth felt as big as a Magnolia ham. Being new in the business, the salivary glands were so surprised that they began to secrete at a remarkable rate. The young man got alarmed. He wanted to spit. His eyes began to hang out on his cheek, and still the salivary glands continued to give down. He thought about spitting in his handkerchief or his hat, but neither seemed to answer the purpose. He was getting wild. He thought of swallowing it, but he knew that his stomach wasn't large enough.

In his madness he resolved that he would let drive down the aisle when the pastor looked the other way. He waited till the divine threw his eyes toward heaven and then he shut his eyes and turned loose. An old gentleman about three pews down the aisle yawned at that moment and threw his open hand out into the aisle in such a manner as to catch the contribution without any loss to speak of. He did not put his hand out for that purpose and did not seem to want it, but he got it all right.

He seemed to feel hurt about something. He looked like a man who has suddenly lost faith in humanity and become soured, as it were. Some who sat near him said he swore. Anyway, he lost the thread of the discourse. That part of the sermon he now says is a blank to him. It is several blanks. He called upon blank to everlastingly blank such a blankety blank blank, idiotic blank fool as the young man was.

Meantime the young man has quit the use of tobacco. He did not know at first whether to swear off or kill himself. The other day he said: "Only two weeks ago I stood up and said proudly I amateur. To-day, praise be to redeeming grace, I am not a chewer." (This joke for the first few days will have to be watered very carefully and wrapped in a California blanket, for it is not strong at all. However, if it can be worked through the cold weather it is no slouch of a joke.)

THE WEATHER AND SOME OTHER THINGS.

Sometimes I wish that Wyoming had more vegetation and less catarrh, more bloom and summer and fragrance and less Christmas and New Year's through the summer.

I like the clear, bracing air of 7,500 feet above the civilized world, but I get weary of putting on and taking off my buffalo overcoat for meals all through dog days. I yearn for a land where a man can take off his ulster and overshoes while he delivers a Fourth of July oration, without flying into the face of Providence and dying of pneumonia.

Perhaps I am unreasonable, but I can't help it. I have my own peculiar notions, and I am not to blame for them.

As I write these lines I look out across the wide sweep of brownish gray plains dotted here and there with ranches and defunct buffalo craniums, and I see shutting down over the sides of the abrupt mountains, and meeting the foothills, a white mist which melts into the gray sky. It is a snow storm in the mountains.

I saw this with wonder and admiration for the first two or three million times. When it became a matter of daily occurrence as a wonder or curiosity, it was below mediocrity. Last July a snow storm gathered one afternoon and fell among the foothills and whitened the whole line to within four or five miles of town, and it certainly was a peculiar freak of nature, but it convinced me that whatever enterprises I might launch into here I would not try to raise oranges and figs until the isothermal line should meet with a change of heart.

I have just been reading Colonel Downey's poem. It is very good what there is of it, but somehow we lay aside the *Congressional Record* wishing that there had been more of it.

Just as we get interested and carried away with it, having read the first five or six thousand words, it comes to an abrupt termination.

I have often wished that I could write poetry. It would do me a heap of good. I would like to write a little book of poems with a blue cover and beveled edges and an index to it. It would tickle me pretty near to death.

But I can't seem to do it. When I write a poem and devote a good deal of study and thought to it, and get it to suit me, the great seething mass of humanity, regardless of my feelings, get down on the grass and yell and hoot and kick up the green sward, and whoop at the idea of calling that poetry. It hurts me and grieves me, and has a tendency to sour my disposition, so that when a really deserving poet comes to the front I haven't the good nature and sweetness of disposition to enter dispassionately upon the subject and say a kind word where I ought to, but I will say of Colonel Downey's poem that it certainly has great depth and width and length, and as you go on, it seems to broaden out and extend farther on and cover more ground and take in more territory and branch out and widen and lay hold of great tracts of thought and open up new fields and fresh pastures and make homestead claims and enter large desert land tracts and prove up under the timber culture act and the bounty land act and throw open the Indian reservation to settlement.

The matter of decorating the Capitol with sacred subjects is one which would receive the hearty approval of all the people of the country, and I often wish that the Colonel had alluded to it in his poem.

I have some curiosity to know what his ideas are on that point.

I, for one, would be glad to see appropriate paintings of scriptural subjects decorating the walls of our national capitol, and have often been on the verge of offering to do it at my own expense.

A cheerful painting to adorn the walls back of the Speaker's desk, would be a study by some great artist, representing Sampson mashing the Philistines with the jawbone of an ass.

It would be historical and also symbolical; but principally symbolical.

Then another painting might be executed representing Balaam's ass delivering a speech on the Indian question. It would take first rate, and when visitors from abroad made a flying trip to Washington during the summer, and missed seeing Wade Hampton, and felt disappointed, they could go and see Balaam's ass, and go home with their curiosity gratified.

I have seen a very spirited painting somewhere; I think it was at the Louvre, or the Vatican, or Fort Collins, by either Michael Angelo, or Raphael, or Eli Perkins, which represented Joseph presenting a portion of his ulster overcoat to Potiphar's wife, and lighting out for the Cairo and Palestine 11 o'clock train, with a great deal of earnestness. This would be a good painting to hang on the walls of the Capitol, dedicated to Ben Hill and some other Congressional soiled doves.

Then there are some simpler subjects which might be worked up and hung in the Congressional nursery to please the children till the session closed for the day, and their miscellaneous dads came to carry them home.

I could think of lots of nice subjects for a painter to paint, or a sculptor to sculp, if I were to give my attention to it# But I haven't the time.

THE PARABLE OF THE UNJUST STEWARD.

Now there was a certain rich man in those days, who kept a large inn on the American plan.

And the hegira from other lands over against Kabzul and Eder, and Breckinridge and Kinah, and Georgetown and Dimmonah, and Kedesh and Roaring Forks, and Hador and Ithnan, and the Gunnison country and Ziph, and Telem and Silver Cliff, Beoloth and Hadattah, and even beyond Hazar—Gadah and Buena Vista, was exceedingly simultaneous.

And throughout the country roundabout was there never before an hegira that seemed to hegira with the same hegira with which this hegira did hegira.

And behold the inn was overrun day by day with pilgrims who journeyed thither with shekels and scrip and pieces of silver.

And the inn-keeper said unto himself, "Go to;" and he was very wroth, insomuch that he tore his beard and swore a large, dark-blue oath about the size of a man's hand.

For behold the inn-keeper gat not the shekels, and he wist not why it was.

Now, it was so that in the inn was one Keno-El-Pharo, the steward, and he stood behind the tablets wherein the pilgrims did write the names of themselves and their wives and their sons and their daughters.

And Keno-El-Pharo wore purple and fine linen, and fared sumptuously every day, and he drank the wines of one Mumm, and they were extra dry, and so even was Keno-El-Pharo from the rising of the sun until the going down thereof.

And behold one day the inn-keeper took a large tumble even unto himself, and also unto the racket of Keno-El-Pharo the son of Ahaz Ben Bunko.

And he said unto Keno, "Give an account of thy stewardship that thou mayest be no longer steward."

And Keno-El-Pharo cried with a loud voice and wept and fell down and rose up and went unto his place.

And he looked into the mirror, and patted the soap lock on his brow and he saw that he was fair to look: upon.

But he was exceedingly sorrowful and he said, What shall I do? for my lord taketh away the stewardship, and verily it was a good thing to have.

Alas! I know not what to do. I cannot get a position as mining expert, and to beg I am ashamed. I am resolved what I will do. And he smiled unto himself, and the breadth of the smile was even six cubits from one end thereof even unto the other.

So he called unto himself one of his lord's debtors, and he said, How much owest thou my lord?

And he said, Even for seven days food and lodging at $3.50 per day, together with my reckoning at the bar, amounting to thirty pieces of silver of the denomination known as the dollar even of our dads.

And the steward said unto him, Take thy bill quickly and write fifteen.

And it was so. And he said unto another, How much owest thou my lord?

And he answered him and said, fifty pieces of silver.

And the steward said unto him, take thy bill and write twenty-five.

And it was so.

And behold these two guests of the inn were solid with Keno El-Pharo from that hour.

And when Keno-El-Pharo received the Oriental grand bounce from the inn-keeper, the guests of the inn, to whom Keno had shown mercy, procured him a pass over the road, and they whiled away the hours with Keno-El-Pharo, and he did teach them some pleasant games; and when the even was come he went his way unto Kansas City, and they with whom he had abode wot not how it was, for they were penniless.

And Keno-El-Pharo abode long in the land over against St. Louis, and he was steward in one of the great inns for many years, and he wore good clothes day by day and waxed fat, and he rested his stomach on the counter, and he said to himself, ha! ha!

ODE TO SPRING.

Fantasia for the Bass Drum; Adapted from the German by William Von Nye.

In the days of laughing spring time,
    Comes the mild-eyed sorrel cow,
With bald-headed patches on her,
    Poor and lousy, I allow;
And she waddles through your garden
O'er the radish beds, I trow.

Then the red-nosed, wild-eyed orphan,
    With his cyclopædiee,
Hies him to the rural districts
With more or less alacrity.
And he showeth up its merits
To the bright eternitee.

How the bumble-bee doth bumble—
    Bumbling in the fragrant air,
Bumbling with his little bumbler,
    Till he climbs the golden stair.
Then the angels will provide him
With another bumbilaire.

THE PARABLE OF THE PRODIGAL SON.

Now, there was a certain man who had two sons.

And the younger of them said to his father, "Father, give me the portion of goods that falleth to me."

And he divided unto him his living, and the younger son purchased himself an oil cloth grip-sack and gat him out of that country.

And it came to pass that he journeyed even unto Buckskin and the land that lieth over against Leadville.

And when he was come nigh unto the gates of the city, he heard music and dancing.

And he gat him into that place, and when he arose and went his way, a hireling at the gates smote upon him with a slung-shot of great potency, and the younger son wist not how it was.

Now in the second watch of the night he arose and he was alone, and the pieces of gold and silver were gone.

And it was so.

And he arose and sat down and rent his clothes and threw ashes and dust upon himself.

And he went and joined himself unto a citizen of that country, and he sent him down into a prospect shaft for to dig.

And he had never before dug.

Wherefore, when he spat upon his hands and lay hold of the long-handled shovel wherewith they are wont to shovel, he struck his elbow upon the wall of the shaft wherein he stood, and he poured the earth and the broken rocks over against the back of his neck.

And he waxed exceeding wroth.

And he tried even yet again, and behold! the handle or the shovel became tangled between his legs, and he filled his ear nigh unto full of decomposed slate and the porphyry which is in that region round about.

And he wist not why it was so.

Now, after many days the shovelers with their shovels, and the pickers with their picks, and the blasters with their blasts, and the hoisters with their hoists, banded themselves together and each said to his fellow:

Go to! Let us strike. And they stroke.

And they that strake were as the sands of the sea for multitude, and they were terrible as an army with banners.

And they blew upon the ram's horn and the cornet, and sacbut, and the alto horn, and the flute and the bass drum.

Now, it came to pass that the younger son joined not with them which did strike, neither went he out to his work, nor on the highway, least at any time they that did strike should fall upon him and flatten him out, and send him even unto his home packed in ice, which is after the fashion of that people.

And he began to be in want.

And he went and joined himself unto a citizen of that country; and he sent him into the lunch room to feed tourists.

And he would fain have filled himself up with the adamantine cookies and the indestructible pie and vulcanized sandwiches which the tourists did eat.

And no man gave unto him.

And when he came to himself he said, How many hired servants hath my father on the farm with bread enough and to spare, and I perish with hunger.

And he resigned his position in the lunch business and arose and went unto his father.

But when he was yet a great way off he telegraphed to his father to kill the old cow and make merry, for behold! he had struck it rich, and the old man paid for the telegram.

Now the elder son was in the north field plowing with a pair of balky mules, and when he came and drew nigh to the house he heard music and dancing.

And he couldn't seem to wot why these things were thus.

And he took the hired girl by the ear and led her away, and asked her, Whence cometh this unseemly hilarity?

And she smote him with the palm of her hand and said: "This thy brother hath come, that was dead and is alive again," and they began to have a high old time.

And the elder son kicked even as the government mule kicketh, and he was hot under the collar, and he gathered up an armful of profanity and flung it in among the guests, and gat him up and girded his loins and lit out.

And he gat him to one learned in the law, and he replevied the entire ranch whereon they were, together with all and singular the hereditaments, right, title, franchise, estate, both in law and in equity, together with all dips, spurs, angles, crooks, variations, leads, veins of gold or silver ore, mill-sites, damsites, flumes, and each and every of them firmly by these presents.

And it was so.

THE INDIAN AND THE EVERLASTING GOSPEL.

William Henry Kersikes, D.D., Philadelphia, Pennsylvania. Dear Sir:—Your esteemed favor of the 25th instant, is at hand, asking me to throw some light upon a few Indian conundrums propounded by you.

I thank you most heartily for the unfaltering trust in me expressed by your letter. One of my most serious difficulties through life has been a growing tendency on the part of mankind, to refuse to trust me as I deserved. It has placed me in an extremely awkward position several times. But your letter is trust and reliance and childish faith personified.

You have done wisely in writing to me for my views on this important national question, and I give them to you cheerfully and even hilariously. If they were all the views I had it would be the same. I would squeeze along without any rather than refuse you.

First I agree with you in your ideas relative to the cause of failure on the part of the Peace Commission. It was not calculated to soothe the ruffled spirits of the hostiles and produce in their breasts a feeling of rest and friendship and repose, but it was more in the nature of an arrogant demand for those who had in an unguarded moment snuffed out the light of the White river agent and the employes. This was not right or even courteous on the part of the Commission.

You seem to understand the wants and needs of the Indian more fully than any man with whom I am acquainted. By your letter I see at a glance that you are the man to deal with them. You shall be agent at White river hereafter. I will use my influence for your appointment. If you think I have no influence with the administration you are exceedingly off.

The emoluments of the office are not large, but what you lack in money will be made up to you in attention. You will get tons and tons of Indian affection. For every dollar that you would receive from the government you would get eleven dollars and fifty cents' worth of childlike trust and clinging affection. You could also write religious articles for the Western press, and blow in a good many scads that way. By working that scheme judiciously I have amassed quite a little fortune myself. Your leisure time could be filled up by organizing Temples of Honor, Subordinate Granges, etc.; or you could get in an evening now and then playing a social game of draw poker with your charge. They are all, you will find, more interested in "draw" than they are in the Trinity. You can also hoe potatoes and do good. If time still hung heavy on your hands you could devote it to constructing a sheet-iron roof for your scalp. When the Utes came in from the warpath, foot sore and weary, you could go about from lodge to lodge and nurse them and read the Scriptures to them and drive away the blue-tail fly and other domestic insects, and lull the suffering savage to rest with "Coronation" and other soothing melodies. But I must pass on to your next question.

Second—There have been several methods proposed for civilizing the wandering tribes of the House of Stand-up-and-eat-a-raw-dog, but few of them, I fear, will meet with your approval. My own plan is called the Minnesota plan. It was an experiment used on the Sioux nation at one time in its history, and consisted in placing the Indians upon a large elevated platform, and so arranging a fragment of lariat that in case the platform gave way, the lariat would support the performer by the neck.

The Indian is generally stolid and indifferent to pain, but you give him a fall of seven and a half feet, allowing him to catch by his neck, and it is fun to see him try to kick a large piece out of the firmament.

The Indian when called on to make the opening speech at a country fair does not make any demonstrations, but place him on one of these sleight-of-hand scaffolds, and let the bottom drop out, and he makes some of the most powerful and expressive gestures.

Third—I am not prepared to answer fully your third question, as I haven't the statistics where I can lay my hand on them. I think, however, that the denominations are about equally divided among the Indians. Colorow is a Presbyterian, Ouray is a member of the Dutch Reformed Church, while Jack is a close communion Baptist. Few of them are regular attendants upon divine worship. At some of the Ute churches, I am told, very frequently there are not enough present for a quorum, especially during the busy season when they are gathering the fall crops of scalps.

Fourth—As to the time which would be required to bring the entire outfit into the fold, I am a little unsettled as to the correct estimate. It might take some time. The roads might be blockaded, you know, or something of that kind; or some old buck might stampede and take up a good deal of time. At least, I would not advise you to hold your breath while listening for their glad hallelujahs to the throne. They might miss the connections in some way, and you would get very purple around the gills.

However, do not get discouraged. Keep up your lick. Write on and speak on for this oppressed people. They deserve it. They have brought it on themselves. Get some more dough-faced idiots to unite with you in writing up the Indian question. It will be a good thing. Write to the Indians themselves personally. Of course it will be a horrible death for them to die, but they have richly merited it. Do not write to me again, however. I am not strong anyway, and I need rest. If you could, therefore, direct your remarks to the Utes themselves, and keep it up during the cold weather while they are hungry and weak, you will probably use up nearly all of them. If you will do so, I will see that the people of the West club together and give you a nice gold-headed cane.

THE MUSE.

CRITICISM ON THE WORKS OF THE SWEET SINGER OF MICHIGAN.

Through the courtesy of a popular young lady of Chicago, who recognizes struggling genius at all times, I have been permitted to carefully read and enjoy the lays of the sweet singer of Michigan; and I ask the reader to come with me a few moments into the great field of literature, while we flit from flower to flower on the wings of the Muse.

There are few, indeed, of us who do not love the heaven-born music of true poesy. Hardened, indeed, must he be whose soul is dead to the glad song of the true poet, and we can but pity the gross, brutal nature which refuses to throb and burn with spiritual fire lighted with coals from the altar of the gods.

I speak only for myself when I say that seven or eight twangs of the lyre stir my impressible nature so that I rise above the cares and woes of this earthly life, and I paw the ground and yearn for the unyearnable, and howl.

Julia A. Moore, better known as the Sweet Singer of Michigan, was born some time previous to the opening of this chapter, of poor but honest parents, and although she couldn't have custard pie and frosted cake every day she, was middling chipper, as appears by a little poem in the collection, entitled, "The Author's Early Life," in which she says:

> My heart was gay and happy:
> This was ever in my mind,
> There is better days a coming,
> And I hope some day to find
> Myself capable of composing.
> It was my heart's delight
> To compose on a sentimental subject
> If it came in my mind just right

This would show that the Muse was getting in its work, as I might say, even while yet Julia was a little nut-brown maid trudging along to school with bare feet that looked like the back of a warty toad. In my visions I see her now standing in front of the teacher's desk, soaking the first three joints of her thumb in her rosebud mouth, and trying to work her off toe into a knothole in the floor, while outside, the turtle-dove and the masculine Michigan mule softly coo to their mates.

A portrait of the author appears on the cover of the little volume. It is a very striking face. There are lines of care about the mouth—that is, part way around the mouth. They did not reach all the way around because they didn't have time. Lines of care are willing to do anything that is reasonable, but they can't reach around the North Park without getting fatigued. These lines of care and pain look to the student of physiognomy as though the author had lost a good deal of sleep trying to compose obituary poems. The brow is slightly drawn, too, as though her corns might be hurting her. Julia wears her hair plain, like Alfred Tennyson and Sitting Bull. It hangs down her back in perfect abandon and wild profusion, shedding bear's oil ever the collar of her delaine dress, regardless of expense.

I can not illustrate or describe the early vision of dimpled loveliness, which Julia presented in her childhood, better than by giving a little gem from "My Infant Days:"

> When I was a little infant,
>
> And I lay in mother's arms,
>
> Then I felt the gentle pressure
>
> Of a loving mother's arms.
>
>
> "Go to sleep my little baby,
>
> Go to sleep," mamma would say;
>
> "O, will not my little baby
>
> Go to sleep for ma to-day?"

When I read this little thing the other day it broke me alf up. It took me back to my childhood days when I lay in my little trundle bed, and was wakeful, and had a raging thirst, insomuch that I used to want a drink of water every fifteen seconds. Mamma didn't ask if I would "go to sleep for ma, to-day." She used to turn the bed-clothes back over the footboard, so that she could have plenty of sea room, and then she would take an old sewing-machine belt, and it would sigh through the agitated air for a few moments pretty plenty, till the writer of these lines would conclude to sob himself to sleep, and anon through the night he would dream that he had backed up against the Hill Smeltingg works. That's the kind of "Go to sleep for ma to-day," that comes up vividly to my mind.

But I must give another stanza or two from Julia's collection—as showing how this gifted writer can with a word dispel the chilling temperature of December, and run the thermometer up to 100 degrees in the shade. I will quote from the death of "Little Henry:"

>It was on the eleventh of December,
>   On a cold and windy day,
>Just at the close of evening,
>   When the sunlight fades away,
>Little Henry he was dying,
>   In his little crib he lay,
>With the soft winds around him sighing,
>   From early morn till close of day.

One of Julia's poems opens out in such a cheerful, pleasant way, that I wish I could give it all, but space forbids. She tunes her lyre so that it will mash all right, and then says:

>Come all kind friends, both far and near,
>O, come, and see what you can hear.

Then she proceeds to slaughter some one. In looking over her poems one is struck with the terrible mortality which they show. Julia is worse than a Gatling gun. I have counted twenty-one killed and nine wounded, in the small volume which she has given to the public. In giving the circumstances which attended the death of one of her subjects, and the economical principles of the deceased, she says:

>And he was sick and very bad,

> Poor boy, he thought, no doubt,
> If he came home in a smoking car
> His money would hold out.
> He started to come back alone,
> > He came one-third the way.
> One evening, in the car alone,
> > His spirit fled away.

That's the way Julia kills off a young man just as we get interested in him. You just begin to like one of her heroes or heroines and Julia proceeds to lay said hero or heroine out colder than a wedge. A sad, sad thing, which goes to the tune of Belle Mahone, starts out as follows:

> "Once there lived a lady fair,
> With black eyes and curly hair;
> She has left this world of care,
> > Sweet Carrie Monroe,"

To which I have added in my poor weak way—

> She could not her sorrows bear,
> For she was a dumpling rare;
> She has clum the golden stair,
> > Sweet Carrie Monroe.

> 'Twas indeed a day of gloom
> When we gathered in her room,
> While she cantered up the flume,
> > Sweet Carrie Monroe.

I will give but one more example of Julia's exquisite word painting, and then after a word or two relative to her style generally I will close.

After speaking tearfully of her life as a child, she says:

> My childhood days have passed and gone,
>
> And it fills my heart with pain,
>
> To think that youth will never more
>
> Return to me again.
>
> And now, kind friends, what I have wrote
>
> I hope you will pass o'er,
>
> And not criticize, as some have done,
>
> Hitherto herebefore.

I know that it ill becomes me to assume the prerogative of criticizing a poet's style or even to suggest any improvements, but sometimes an outsider may be able to stand off as it were and see little defects in a masterpiece which the author can not see.

My idea would be to take these poems and remove the crown sheet, then put in new running gear, upset and bush the pitman, kalsomine the boiler plate, drill new holes in the eccentric, rim out the gas pipe, raise the posterior eccentric to a level with the gang plank, slide the ash pan forward of the monkey wrench, securing it by draw bars to the topgallant mizzen. Then, throwing open the condenser and allowing the cerebellum to rest firmly against the vicarious whippety-whop, fair time may be made on a gentle grade.

If I were to suggest anything further it would be that Julia have entire change of air and surroundings. Michigan is too healthy for an ambitious obituary poet. She naturally has too much time on her hands. Let her go into the yellow fever districts next summer, where she can work in two or three of her cheerful little funeral odes every morning before breakfast. That's the place for her. It may kill her, but if it should we will trust in Providence to raise up some inspired idiot to take her place. We will struggle along anyway with George Francis Train and Denis Kearney and Dr. Mary Walker, even if Julia joins the glad throng of poets who let their hair grow long and kick up their heels in the green fields of Eden.

One more suggestion which will, I know, be accepted as coming from one who never says anything but in the kindest spirit. I think that Julia takes advantage of her poetic license. A poetic license, as I understand it, simply allows the poet to jump the 15 over the 14 in order to bring in the proper rhyme, but it does not allow the writer to usurp the management of the entire system of worlds, and introduce dog-days and ice-cream between Christmas and New Year. It does not in any way allow the contractor of prize funeral puffs to sandwich a tropical evening with the scent of orange blossom and mignonette, in between two December days in Michigan, that would freeze the lightning rods off the houses, and when the owners of cast iron dogs have to bring them in, and stand them behind the parlor stove.

Julia can't fool me much on a Michigan winter. When the seductive breath from the north comes soughing across Lake Superior, redolent with the blossom rock of the copper mines, and dead cranberry vines, and slippery elm bark, the poet or poetess who could maliciously crawl into a buffalo overcoat, and write a dirge that worked in "sighing soft winds," just for the benefit of one whose spirit is in a land where house plants never freeze, should have no poetic license. I would be in favor of having such license revoked, or raising the price so high that none but good, reliable, square toed poets could practice. I would suggest $500 per year for poets driving one horse, and dealing in native poems on death, spring, beautiful snow, etc., etc.; $1,000 per year for two horse, platform spring poets, retailers of imported poems; and $1,500 per year for poets who do a general business in manufactured Havana poems, or native wrappers with Havana fillers.

We have too many poets in our glorious republic who ought to be peeling the epidermis off a bull train; and too many poetesses who would succeed better boiling soap-grease, or spiking a 6 x 8 patch on the quarter-deck of a faithful husband's overalls.

I do not refer entirely to Julia in the last few lines, for Julia is not deserving of such criticism. She was never intended to do the drudgery of housework. She is too frail. She couldn't cook, because her cake would be sad, and her soft, wavy hair, like the mane of a Cayuse plug, would get in the cod-fish balls, and cling to the butter.

No, Julia, you don't look like a woman whose career as a housewife would be a success. From the mournful look in your limpid eye, I would say that your lignum-vitæ bread, and celluloid custard pie, and indestructible waffles, and fireproof pancakes, and burglar-proof chicken pie, would give you away. Your mind would be far away in the poet's realm, and you would put shoe blacking in the blanc mange, and silver gloss starch in the tea, and cod liver oil in the sponge cake. So, Julia, you may continue right along as you are doing. It don't do much harm, and no doubt it does you a heap of good.

SHOEING A BRONCO.

Recently I have taken a little recreation when I felt despondent, by witnessing the difficult and dangerous feat of shoeing a bronco.

Whenever I get low spirited and feel that a critical public don't appreciate my wonderful genius as a spring poet, I go around to Brown & Poole's blacksmith shop on A street, and watch them shoe a vicious bronco. I always go back to the office cheered and soothed, and better prepared to fight the battle of life.

They have a new rig now for this purpose. It consists of two broad sinches, which together cover the thorax and abdomen of the bronco, to the ends of which—the sinches, I mean—are attached ropes, four in number, which each pass over a pulley above the animal, and then are wrapped about a windlass. The bronco is led to the proper position, like a young man who is going to have a photograph taken, the sinches slipped under his body and attached to the ropes.

Then the man at the wheel makes two or three turns in rapid succession.

The bronco is seen to hump himself, like the boss camel of the grand aggregation of living wonders. He grunts a good deal and switches his tail, while the ropes continue to work in the pulleys and the man at the capstan spits on his hands and rolls up on the wheel.

SHOEING A BRONCO.

After a while the bronco hangs from the ceiling like a discouraged dish rag, and after trying for two or three hundred times unsuccessfully to kick a hole in the starry firmament, he yields and hangs at half mast while the blacksmith shoes him.

Yesterday I felt as though I must see something cheerful, and so I went over to watch a bronco getting his shoes on for the round-up. I was fortunate. They led up a quiet, gentlemanly appearing plug with all the weary, despondent air of a disappointed bronco who has had aspirations for being a circus horse, and has "got left." When they put the sinches around him he sighed as though his heart would break, and his great, soulful eyes were wet with tears. One man said it was a shame to put a gentle pony into a sling like that in order to shoe him, and the general feeling seemed to be that a great wrong was being perpetrated.

Gradually the ropes tightened on him and his abdomen began to disappear. He rose till he looked like a dead dog that had been fished out of the river with a grappling iron. Then he gave a grunt that shook the walls of the firmament, and he reached out about five yards till his hind feet felt of a Greaser's eye, and with an athletic movement he jumped through the sling and lit on the blacksmith's forge with his head about three feet up the chimney. He proceeded then to do some extra ground and lofty tumbling and kicking. A large anvil was held up for him to kick till he tired himself out, and then the blacksmith put a fire and burglar proof safe over his head and shod him.

The bronco is full of spirit, and, although docile under ordinary circumstances, he will at times get enthusiastic and do things which he afterwards, in his sober moments, bitterly regrets.

Some broncos have formed the habit of bucking. They do not all buck. Only those that are alive do so. When they are dead they are more subdued and gentle.

A bronco often becomes so attached to his master that he will lay down his life if necessary. His master's life, I mean.

When a bronco comes up to me and lays his head over my shoulder, and asks me to scratch his chilblain for him, I always excuse myself on the ground that I have a family dependent on me, and furthermore, that I am a United States Commissioner, and to a certain extent the government hinges on me.

Think what a ghastly hole there would be in the official staff of the republic if I were launched into eternity now, when good men are so scarce.

Some days I worry a good deal over this question. Suppose that some unprincipled political enemy who wanted to be United States Commissioner or Notary Public in my place should assassinate me!!!

Lots of people never see this. They sec how smoothly the machinery of government moves along, and they do not dream of possible harm. They do not know how quick she might slip a cog, or the eccentric get jammed through the indicator, if, some evening when I am at the opera house, or the minstrel show, the assassin should steal up on me, and shoot a large, irregular aperture into my cerebellum.

This may not happen, of course; but I suggest it, so that the public will, as it were, throw its protecting arms about me, and not neglect me while I am alive.

PUMPKIN JIM; OR THE TALE OF A BUSTED JACKASS RABBIT.

CHAPTER I.
PUMPKIN JIM.

It was evening in the mountains. The golden god of day was gliding slowly adown the crimson west. Here and there the cerulean dome was flecked with snowy clouds.

The flecks were visible to the naked eye.

Meanwhile the golden god of day, hereinbefore referred to, continued to glide adown the crimson west, with about the same symmetrical glide. It had done so on several occasions previous to the opening of this story.

The katydid was singing sleepily in the long grass, and the grizzly bear was trilling between eleven trills on the still air.

It was a spot where the foot of man had never trod, and the undisturbed temple of nature with its hallowed hush and never ending repose. The lofty pines were swaying softly to and fro in the gentle breeze of evening, and the babbling brook went babbling along down its rocky bed in the bottom of the canon, with a merry bab.

All at once, like a flash of dazzling light, a noble youth came slowly down the mountain side, riding an ambling palfrey of the narrow-guage variety, with a paint-brush tail on him—(that is the palfrey, of course.) The palfrey was a delicate buckskin color, with high, intellectual ears and Roman nose.

In crossing the stream the palfrey stubbed his toe, and fell on his noble rider, breaking the man's leg in three places, and jamming one of his ribs through the liver and into the ground, thus pinning him to the earth, and preventing him from rising.

The buckskin palfrey, with almost human foresight, and wonderful intelligence, found a soft place in the grassy bottom, and lay down.

There, in the slanting rays of the declining sun, and stretched out upon the sedgy brink of the clear mountain stream, far from the reach of man and miles beyond the outer line of civilization, lay Pumpkin Jim, the Yipping, Yelling Yahoo of Dirty Woman's Ranch.

He lay there partially submerged in the stream and partially in the clear, bracing atmosphere. Wild-eyed and beautiful he lay there, looking up into the glad realms of space, with that murderous glitter in his eye that wins a woman's love, and the sympathy of kind hearted philanthropists.

Occasionally he would raise his broken limb and try to use it, but it generally wilted and drooped like the leg of a rag doll.

Then he would struggle to raise himself up and drag his body out upon the bank, but the broken rib would tear out large chunks of his liver, and make him feel wretched and unhappy.

"Curses upon thee, thou base and treacherous mule!" he murmured, brokenly. "By my beard, thou hast poorly repaid me for my unremitting kindness to thee. Ah, alack, alack, alack—"

He was just about to alack some more, when a mellow, girlish voice came floating down the gulch and fell in large fragments near where he lay.

He gathered up some of the chunks of melody to see what the song might be. It was that wonderful masterpiece of Mozart's, "When Johnny Comes Marching Home."

Then he swooned.

The gurgling brook still continued to gurg. We will let it gurg.

CHAPTER II.
GERALDINE CARBOLINE O'TOOLE.

The melodious voice referred to in the preceding chapter was owned and operated by Geraldine Carboline O'Toole, the heroine of this classic tale.

Anon she came down the valley like a thing of life.

The limber sunbonnet which she wore had drifted to leeward and revealed her Grecian profile and peeled nose.

All at once her fawn-like eyes fell upon the prostrate figure, pale and still, and its toes turned toward the center of the zodiac.

A wild, frightened look came into her starry eyes, and a ghastly pallor overspread her young face, throwing her intellectual freckles into strong relief.

She stole forward and looked at the pale face of Pumpkin Jim as it lay upturned with the rosebud mouth slightly ajar, like the mouth of the Mississippi river.

Then she stooped, and, dipping up some of the clear, cold water in his hat, poured it into the rosy mouth. Slowly it trickled down his throat, and the wild panic and surprise created in his stomach by the novel fluid brought him speedily to consciousness.

"Where am I, and whence cometh this burning sensation in my liver?" faintly murmured Pumpkin Jim. "Methought some new and peculiar beverage didst cool my parching throat."

"Hist!" said Geraldine; "you must not excite yourself. You must brace up. Everything depends upon your keeping quiet instead of tearing up the ground with your broken rib."

"And whence comest thou, O beauteous vision, with the Aurora Borealis hair?"

"Didst I not tell thee," said Geraldine, "that thou mustest not converse, but remain quiet? Let it suffice, however, that I strayed away from a Sabbath school picnic at Cheyenne, and have wandered on carelessly for several hundred miles, wotting not whence I wist."

By this time the day god which we left gliding slowly adown the crimson west, had glode down the crimson west according to advertisement, and the solemn hush of night was coming on, broken anon by the long drawn shriek of the mountain lion, or the pealing of the thunder, which also reverberated anon through the otherwise solemn hush of night.

Darkness came on apace. It would be folly to attempt to prevent it, so we will let it come on apace.

CHAPTER III.
STARTLING REVELATIONS.

We will now suppose twenty-four hours to have passed Since the scenes narrated in the last chapter.

The gloaming is beginning to gloam.

It began to look as though if something were not done for Pumpkin Jim pretty previously, he would pass with a gentle, gliding movement up the flume.

He was growing fainter hour by hour, and the extreme torpidity of his liver, gave rise to grave apprehensions on the part of his gentle guardian.

His leg also gave him extreme pain and cause for uneasiness, to say the least. It had swollen to about the size of a flour barrel, and was still swelling as we go to press.

He opened his eyes with a low moan, and looked up into the limber sun-bonnet.

"Beauteous one, with the ethereal brow!" he began, but Geraldine blushed and bade him let up.

"Gentle lady," he began again, "I am aware that the crisis is near. Unless I have help very soon, in some form or other, I shall have clomb the golden stair. Already the circulation is impaired, and the transverse duplex has ceased to vibrate. Dissolution is coming on. My pulse grows feebler hour by hour, and I feel that another morning sun will find only my earthly tenement here. My spirit will have wung its way to the realms of eternal day."

"O, do not talk that way," sobbed Geraldine, filling her apron full of large, irregular fragments of grief. "It cannot, must not be!"

"Do not be over confident," said Pumpkin Jim. "Few men would have lived as I have with a rib running through the centre of the liver, and into the ground for nine or ten inches without great difficulty. The secret of my power of endurance, I will, however, confide to you, as this may be positively my last appearance. My true name is not Pumpkin Jim; that is only a *nom de plume*. My sure enough name is Jesse James—that is the secret of my longevity. I have been killed a great deal. I have lost my life in almost every State in the Union. At first it used to make me gloomy and taciturn to be killed so much; but latterly I became very much pleased and flattered by this attention. It is sad to think, however, that after being killed by some of our most prominent men, I should at last yield up the ghost in a lonely canon, at the urgent solicitation of a narrow-guage mule. But enough; it is useless to repine. All that I am kicking about is, that after dying in so many different styles, and in such desirable conditions, surrounded by all the comforts of civilization, and getting a large amount of newspaper space, and having a patent medicine portrait of myself published in the papers, I should succumb to the death-dealing jackass, in the solitude of the mountains.

"I cannot die again, however, without telling you of my love. I might occupy your time by telling you of my long and glittering career of crime, but it would take too long. I have nothing to lay at your feet but my untarnished record as a highway robber, and my all consuming love.

"It would ease the pain of my dying hour if you were to say to me that you returned my love."

Our hero then fell back upon the mossy bank and gasped for breath, while to all appearances the last moments of Pumpkin Jim had come.

It was a trying time for a young thing like Geraldine to pass through. She stooped over him and fanned him with her sun bonnet and whispered a few low musical words in his ear.

That did the business.

CHAPTER IV.
ALL'S WELL THAT ENDS WELL.

The magic words that Geraldine emptied into Pumpkin James' ear roused him, and his eyes opened with their old diabolical light. A slight grating sound was heard. It was the broken bone of our hero's off-limb coming back into its place and reuniting.

Then his rib came back out of the ground and waltzed into him, his liver healed up, and he arose and sat in the moonlight.

His first words were, "Ah, Geraldine, you have brought me back to life. Now would you please look around and see if there is any cold pie in the house, my very ownest own?"

This seemed to indicate that he had not fully recovered his mental faculties, as the most accessible cold pie was 327 miles from where they then were, and in a direct line.

Geraldine, however, set herself at once about procuring food for her soul's idol. Taking some salt she went out along the wooded slope to find a jack-rabbit on whose tail she could throw the salt, thus securing him as an easy prey.

She soon scared up one with a broken leg.

Most all of my gentle, refined, and intellectual readers of the Rocky mountains have frightened from his lair, at some time or other, a jack-rabbit with a broken leg. Jackrabbits with shattered limbs are very common in the West.

Geraldine followed hopefully on. Up hill and down, over low parks covered with hunch-grass, across little mountain streams, through long stretches of greasewood and sagebrush, starting the owl from some blasted pine tree, or frightening the smiling coyote from his course, onward and ever onward she flew like a hunted fawn.

Her every motion was grace and poetry itself. The limber sun bonnet flopped to and fro with a merry Runic flop, but the crippled John rabbit did not tarry. For an invalid, he seemed to make very fair time.

Occasionally he would look around over his shoulder, and laugh a merry, taunting laugh. Then he would give his attention to getting over the ground.

Geraldine got mad, and resolved to overtake her game and mete out to him a horrible death.

Now and then she would wildly throw a lump of salt in the direction of the fleeing rabbit; but it always failed to connect.

It was, indeed, an exciting chase, and, in fact, is yet, for as we go to press, Geraldine is still madly pursuing the ostensibly disabled jack-rabbit with a handful of common table salt poised in the air, ready to throw upon the tail of her rapidly retreating adversary.

Jesse James, alias Pumpkin Jim, waited a reasonable length of time for the return of Geraldine; but as she cometh not he said, he arose, and bestriding his narrow guage mule, he rode away.

He readily laid down his life again wherever he went, and although he died a miserable death in almost every corner of the earth, he never more met Geraldine Carboline O'Toole, the Italian Countess, to whom he was betrothed.

It is thought that she chased the crippled jack-rabbit into the realms of space.

WILLIAM NYE AND THE HEATHEN CHINEE.

The subject of agriculture, which really lies nearest my heart of anything I can think of, naturally brings to the front the oriental buckwheater.

The Chinaman, as an agriculturalist, is generally successful in a small way, and I love to watch him work. Whenever I get bilious and need exercise, I go over to the southend of town and vicariously hoe radishes for an hour or two till the pores are open, and I feel that delightful languor and the chastened sense of hunger and honesty which comes to the man who is not afraid to toil.

There is a feeling now too prevalent among our American people that the Chinaman should be driven away, but I do not join in the popular cry because I enjoy him too much, and he soothes me and cheers me when all the earth seems filled with woe.

My favorite oriental onion-promoter is called Tue Long. This, however, was a piece of side-splitting mirth on the part of his parents, for, as a matter of fact, he is too short.

He is considerably bronzed by the action of the sun and his out-of-door pursuits, so that his complexion has that radiant olive tinge that we see on the canvas-covered ham.

I go over to Tue Long's farm, in Sherrod's alkali addition to Laramie, when I feel that office work does not give me the physical exercise that I need, and I lean over the fence and tell Tue Long my experience with club-footed parsnips and early-fried potatoes. At first he used to listen to me with his mouth open, so that you could throw a Mason & Hamlin organ into it, but now he don't seem to pay much attention to what I say to him.

This shows that the Chinaman cannot keep pace with the rapid strides now being made by American agriculture.

One day last week I had lost my appetite, and needed active bodily exertion, so I strolled over to the rat-eater's rural retreat, to watch Tue Long a few hours, and see if I couldn't get up an appetite.

The wind was blowing pretty fresh, as it sometimes does in this lovely clime, and Tue Long was trying to hold down some vulcanized rubber beets, and moss-agate asparagus. He wasn't succeeding very well, for just as he would get the beets driven into the ground securely, the zephyr would spring up from the south and blow the moss-agate asparagus all over the military reservation. Then while he would be giving his attention to the asparagus, the wailing winds would blow down his fence, and turn the tail of Tue Long's morning wrapper over his head, and leave his spinal column sticking up into the summer sky.

It seemed to be a bad day for agriculture, and Tue Long would alternately uncork some brocaded profanity, and then chase his hat, or do up his hair in a fresh Grecian coil I leaned over the fence, and laughing a low gurgling laugh, I said:

"Tue Long, you must learn to control your fiendish temper. Agriculture requires patience and serenity of disposition. You must always be cheerful and gentle. Always be pleasant and amiable in your home life. When the mountain wind uncoils your back-hair, and you cannot hold down the flap of your dressing sacque, you must not get mad and swear; but fill the air with merry laughter, just as Confucius used to do. Be a philosopher, and frown down these little annoyances."

Now, when I was propagating my Scotch-plaid summer squashes, the squash-bugs got in one morning before breakfast, and ate the vines. Soon after that I tried a new kind of fire-proof squash, with a hunting-case on it; but the squash-bugs took a spade and pried open the hunting-case, and ate the supreme stuffing out of every individual squash. I then tried the Bessemer-steel squash, with plaster of Paris works inside, but the irrigation was defective, and it never matured.

But, did I forget myself and swear like a Guinea hen, the way you do? Did I break forth into petulant remarks, and lower myself in the estimation of my neighbors?

Not to any remarkable degree.

I went to the stockholders of the Pioneer Canal Company and said, "Here, gentlemen, I am an inexperienced agriculturalist, and I do not succeed. Nothing grows under my watchful care but the speckled squash-bug, and the fresh water cut worm. You are old, horny-handed sons of toil, and practical tillers of the soil; what shall I do?"

Then the secretary called a meeting of the stockholders, and the matter was discussed. The general custodian of peculiar seeds and rare bulbs was ordered to select certain seeds from the bureau, and give them to me for trial. Among these were the seeds of the early dwarf salad oil vine, the Northern spy horse radish, the black and tan Lima bean, the non-explosive codfish ball, the soda water melon, the grammatical sugar beet, and the anti-cut worm asbestos string bean.

These have all grown well and thrived when my neighbors, who were too proud to ask advice, have failed. I shall this year raise, no doubt, enough of the non-explosive codfish ball alone to place me far beyond the reach of want. But Tue Long is a thousand years behind the great irresistible tide of progress, and will cling to his celluloid beets and cottonwood cucumbers for ages yet to come.

HONG LEE'S GRAND BENEFIT AT LEADVILLE.

It will be remembered about nine months ago Hong Lee resolved to establish a branch laundry and shirt-destroying establishment—at Leadville, with the main office and general headquarters at Laramie. All at once he came back, and seemed to be satisfied at the old stand. So I would ask him his opinion of the future of the carbonate camp.

Hong Lee had just tied his hair up in a Grecian coil and secured it in a mass of shining braids, as I came in, and was giving some orders as to the day's work. One employe was just completing his devotions to a cross-eyed god in one corner, and another was squirting water out of his mouth like an oriental street sprinkler over the spotless front of a white shirt.

Hong Lee asked me to sit down on the ironing table and make myself at home. I asked him how trade was, and a few other unimportant questions, and then asked him what he thought of Leadville. I cannot give the conversation in the exact language in which it was given, as I am not up in pigeon English. He said he went over to Leadville, thinking that at $4.25 per dozen he could work up a good business and wear a brocaded overshirt with slashed sleeves and Pekin trimmings. Trade was a little dull here and he had more Chinamen than he could use, so he had concluded to establish a branch outfit at Leadville and make some scads.

I asked him why he did not remain at the camp and go through the pro—
- gramme.

He said that the general feeling in Leadville was not friendly to the Chinaman. The people did not meet him with a brass band, and the mayor didn't tender him the freedom of the city. On the contrary, they seemed cold and distant toward him. By and by they clubbed together and came to call on him. They were very attentive then. Very much so. Some had shot-guns to fire salutes with, and others had large clotheslines in their hands. Hong Lee felt proud to be so much thought of, and was preparing an impromptu speech on orange paper with a marking brush, when the chairman came and told him that a few American citizens had come, hoping to be of use to him in learning the ways of the city.

Then they took him out to the public square where Hong Lee supposed that he was to make his speech, and they proceeded to kick him into the most shapeless mass. They kicked him into a globular form and then flattened him out after which they knocked him into a rhomboid. This change was followed by thumping him into an isosceles triangle. When he looked more like a bundle of old clothes than a Chinaman, they took him with a pair of tongs, and threw him over the battlements.

GOING OVER THE BATTLEMENTS.

Hono-Lee returned to consciousness, and murmured, "Where am I?" or words to that effect. A noble mule-skinner passing by, touched him up with the hot end of his mule whip, and showed him the route to Denver.

Hong Lee says now, be it ever so humble, there's no place like home.

YOU FOU.

She is rather below the medium height, and her gait is the easy gliding movement of a club-footed Guinea pig. She has a mouth like a whippoorwill, and when she laughed at some little *bon mot*, such as I am always getting off, her upper lip was thrown back over her head, till it caught on a large Celestial hair-pin, and her attendant had to go up there with a monkey-wrench and unfasten it. It was the most heavenly smile I ever saw. It had so much depth and soul to it. I felt flattered, of course, but I was more guarded in my remarks after that. The Chinese, as a nation, cannot grapple with our American style of joke. They are not strong enough.

You Fou was held here on a telegram from Denver, until Monday, when she was released on writ of *habeas corpus*. I went up to see how the writ would work on a China woman. At first it 'didn't seem to catch on, but after awhile it began to work on her all right; and eventually turned her loose. But I wouldn't be a habeas corpus for $2 per day and board.

After being released on the writ, there being no warrant at that time, counsel told Ah Say, who had You Fou in charge, that the best thing for him to do would be to light out with great vehemence for some foreign strand, as the Denver officer would be here Monday evening with the required documents to take You Fou back to Denver. She was therefore taken to the palatial residence of Hong Lee, on Second, near A street, where she was rigged up in man's attire; but Sheriff Boswell stepped in, and through the gauzy disguise he discovered You Fou.

He arrested her. She was bathed in tears. It was the first bath she ever had. He took her and held her, figuratively speaking, until another telegram announced that the requisition of the Governor was countermanded, and You Fou lit out for her destination.

I shall write a little novelette next summer with this tale as a foundation, and it will be a good thing. I am having the cuts made now at a shoemaker shop here in town.

THE LOP-EARED LOVERS OF THE LITTLE LARAMIE.

CHAPTER I.
A TALE OF LOVE AND PARENTAL CUSSEDNESS.

The scene opens with a landscape. In the foreground stands a house; but there are no honeysuckles or Johnny-jump-ups clambering over the door; there are no Columbines or bitter-sweets, or bachelors-buttons, clinging lovingly to the eaves, and filling the air with fragrance. The reason for this is, that it is too early in the spring for Columbines and Johnny-jump-ups, at the time when our story opens, and they wouldn't grow in that locality without irrigation, anyway. That is the reason that these little adjuncts do not appear in the landscape.

But the scene is nevertheless worthy of a painter. The house, especially, ought to be painted, and a light coat of the same article on the front gate would improve its appearance materially. In the door of the cottage stands a damsel, whose natural lovliness is enhanced 30 or 40 per cent, by a large oroide chain which encircles her swan-like throat; and, as she shades her eyes with her alabaster hand, the gleam of a gutta percha ring on her front finger tells the casual observer that *she is engaged*.

While she is shading her eyes from the blinding glare of the orb of day, the aforesaid orb of day keeps right on setting, according to advertisement, and at last disappears behind the snowy range, lighting up, as it does so, the fleecy clouds and turning them into gold, figuratively speaking, making the picture one of surpassing lovliness. But what does she care for a $13.00 sunset, or the low, sad wail of the sage-hen far up the canon, as it calls to its mate? What does she care for the purple landscape and the mournful sigh of the new milch cow which is borne to her over the greet divide? She don't care a cent.

CHAPTER II.

It is now the proper time to bring in the solitary horseman. He is seen riding a mouse-colored bronco on a smooth canter, and, from his uneasiness in the saddle, it is evident that he has been riding a long time, and that it doesn't agree with him. He has been attending the spring meeting of the Rocky Mountain Roundup.

He takes a benevolent chew of tobacco, looks at his cylinder-escapement watch, and plunges his huge Mexican spurs into the panting sides of his bronco steed. The ambitious steed rears forward and starts away into the gathering gloom at the rate of twenty-one miles in twenty-one days, while a bitter oath escapes from the clenched teeth and foam-flecked lips of the pigeon-toed rider.

But stay! Let us catch a rapid outline of the solitary horseman, for he is the affianced lover and soft-eyed gazelle of Luella Frowzletop, the queen of the Skimmilk Ranche. He is evidently a man of say twenty summers, with a sinister expression to the large, ambitious, imported, Italian mouth. A broad-brimmed white hat with a scarlet flannel band protects his Gothic features from the burning sun, and a pale-brown ducking suit envelopes his lithe form. A horsehair lariat hangs at his saddle bow, and the faint suspicion of a downy mustache on his chiselled upper lip is just beginning to ooze out into the air, as if ashamed of itself. It is one of those sickly mustaches, a kind of cross between blonde and brindle, which mean well enough, but never amount to anything. His eyes are fierce and restless, with short, expressive, white eyelashes, and his nose is short but wide out, gradually melting away into his bronzed and stalwart cheeks, like a dish of ice-cream before a Sabbath school picnic.

Such is the rough sketch of Pigeon-toed Pete, the swain who had stolen away the heart of Luella Frowzletop, the queen of the Skimmilk Ranche. He isn't handsome, but he is very good, and he loves the fair Luella with a great deal of diligence, although her parents are averse to the match, for we might as well inform the sagacious and handsome reader that her parents are Presbyterians, whereas the hero of this blood-curdling tale is a hard-shell Baptist. Thus are two hearts doomed to love in vain.

CHAPTER III.

During all this time that we have been going on with the preceding chapter, Luella has been standing in the door looking away to the eastward, a soiled gingham apron thrown over her head, and a dreamy, far-away look in her mournful sorrel eyes. Suddenly there breaks on her finely moulded and flexible ear the sound of a horse's hoof.

"Aha!" she murmurs. "Hist! it is him. Blast his picture! Why didn't he have some style about him, and get here on time?" And she impatiently mashes a huge mosquito that is fastened on her swarthy arm.

Any one could see, as she stood there, that she was mad. She didn't really have any cause for it, but she was an only child, and accustomed to being petted and humored, and lying in bed till half past ten. This had made her high spirited, and she occasionally turned loose with the first thing that came to hand.

"You're a fine-haired snoozer from Bitter Creek; ain't ye?" said the pale flower of Skimmilk Ranche, as the solitary horseman alighted from his panting steed, and threw his arms about her with great *sang froid*.

"In what respect?" said Pigeon-toed Pete, as he held her from him, and looked lovingly down into her deep, sorrel eyes...

"O fairest of thy sect," he continued, as he took out his quid of tobacco, preparatory to planting a long, wide, passionate kiss on her burning cheek, "you wot not what you feign would say. The way was long, my ambling steed has a ringbone on the off leg, and thou chidest me, thy erring swain, without a cause." He knew that she would pitch into him, so he had this little impromptu speech all committed to memory.

She pillowed her sunny head on his panting breast for an hour or so, and shed eleven or eight happy tears.

"O lode star of my existence, and soother of my every sorrow," said he, with charming *naivete*, "wilt thou fly with me to-night to some adjacent justice of the peace, and be my skipful gazelle, my little *ne plus ultra*, my own *magnum bomum* and *multum in parvo*, so to speak? Leave your Presbyterian parents to run the ranche, and fly with me. You shall never want for anything. You shall never put your dimpled hands in dish-water, or wring out your own clothes. I will get you a new rosewood washing machine, and when your slightest look indicates that you want forty or fifty dollars for pin money, I will make out a check for that amount."

He had just finished his little harangue, whatever that is, and was putting in a few choice gestures, when the old man came around from behind the rain-water barrel with a shotgun, and told the impassioned swain that he had better skip. He told the ardent admirer of Luella that he had better not linger to any great extent, and as he said it in his quiet but firm way, at the same time fondling the lock on his shotgun, the lover lingered not, but hied him away to his neighing steed, and, lightly springing into the saddle, was soon lost to the sight. We will leave him on the road for a short time.

CHAPTER IV.

We will now suppose a period of three years to have passed. Luella had been sent to visit her friends in southern Iowa, partly to assuage her grief, and partly to save expenses, for she was a hearty eater. Here she met a young man named Rufus G. Hopper, who fell in love with her, about the first hard work he did, and when, metaphorically speaking, he laid his 40-acre homestead, with its wealth of grasshopper eggs, at her feet, she capitulated, and became his'n, and he became her'n.

Thus these two erstwhile lovers of the long ago had become separated, and the fair Queen of the Skimmilk Ranche had taken a change of venue with her affections. Still all seemed to be well to the casual observer, although at times her eyes had that far-away look of those who are crossed in love, or whose livers are out of order. Was it the fleeing vision of the absent lover, or had she eaten something that didn't agree with her?

Ah! who shall say that at times there did not flash across her mind the fact that she had sacrificed herself on the altar of Mammon, and given her rich love in exchange for forty acres of Government land? But the time drew nigh for the celebration of the nuptials, and still no tidings of the absent lover. Nearer and nearer came the 4th of July, the day set apart for the wedding, and still in the dark mysterious bosom of the unknown, lurked the absent swain.

These stars indicate the number of days which we must now suppose to have passed, and the glad day of the Nation's rejoicing is at hand. The loud mouthed cannon, proclaims, for the one hundredth time, that in the little Revolutionary scrimmage of 1776, our forefathers got away with the persimmons. Flags wave, bands play, and crackers explode, and scare the teams from the country. Fair rustic maids are seen on every hand with their good clothes on, and farmers' sons walk up and down the street, asking the price of watermelons and soda water. Bye and bye the band comes down street playing "Old Zip Coon," with variations. The procession begins to form and point toward the grand stand, where the Declaration of Independence will be read to the admiring audience, and lemonade retailed at five cents a glass.

But who are the couple who sit on the front seat near the speaker's stand, listening with rapt attention to the new and blood-curdling romance, entitled the "Declaration of Independence?" It is Luella and her bran new husband. The casual observer can discover that, by the way he smokes a cheap cigar in her face, and allows the fragrant smoke from the five cent Havana to drift into her sorrel eyes. All at once the band strikes up the operatic strain of "Captain Jinks," and as the sad melody dies away in the distance, a young man steps proudly forth, at the conclusion of the president's introductory speech, and in a low, musical voice, begins to set forth the wrongs visited on the Pilgrim Fathers, and to dish up the bones of G. Washington and T. Jefferson, in various styles.

What is it about the classic mouth, with its charming *naivete*, and the amber tinge lurking about its roguish outlines, which awakes the old thrill in Luella's heart, and causes the vital current to recede from its accustomed channels, and leave her face like marble, save where here and there a large freckle stands out in bold relief? It is the mouth of Pigeon toed Pete. Those same Gothic features stand out before her, and she knows him in a moment. It is true he had colored his mustache, and he wore a stand-up collar; but it was the same form, the same low, musical, squeaky voice, and the same large, intellectual ears, which she remembered so well.

It appeared that he had been to the Gunnison country, and having manifested considerable originality and genius as a bull whacker, had secured steady employment and large wages, being a man with a ready command of choice and elegant profanity, and an irresistable way of appealing to the wants of a sluggish animal. Taking his spare change, he had invested it in hand made sour mash corn juice, which he retailed at from 25 to 50 cents per glass. Rain water being plenty, the margin was large, and his profits highly satisfactory. In this way he had managed to get together some cash, and was at once looked upon as a leading capitalist, and a man on whom rested the future prosperity of the country. He wore moss-agate sleeve buttons, and carried a stem-winding watch. He looked indeed like a thing of life, and as he closed with some stirring quotation from Martin F. Tupper amid the crash of applause, and the band struck up the oratorio of "Whoop'em up'Liza Jane," and the audience dispersed to witness a game of base-ball. Luella took her husband's arm, climbed into the lumber wagon, and rode home, with a great grief in her heart. Had she deferred her wedding for only a few short hours, the course of her whole life would have been entirely changed, and, instead of plodding her weary way through the long, tedious years as Mrs. Hopper, making rag-carpets during the winter, and smashing the voracious potato bug during the summer, she might have been interested in a carbonate 'Bonanza, worn checked stockings, and low-necked shoes.

There are two large, limpid tears standing in her sorrel eyes, as the curtain falls on this story, and her lips move involuntarily as she murmurs that little couplet from Milton:—

"I feel kind of sad and bilious, because

My heart keeps sighing, 'It couldn't was.'"

SPEECH OF SPARTACTUS.

ADAPTED FROM THE ORIGINAL ESPECIALLY FOR THIS WORK.

It had been a day of triumph in Capua. Lentulus returning with victorious eagles, had aroused the populace with the sports of the amphitheatre, to an extent hitherto unknown even in that luxurious city. A large number of people from the rural districts had been in town to watch the conflict in the arena, and to listen with awe and veneration to the infirm and decrepit ring jokes.

The shouts of revelry had died away. The last loiterer had retired from the free-lunch counter, and the lights in the palace of the victor were extinguished. The moon piercing the tissue of fleecy clouds, tipped the dark waters of the Tiber rith a wavy tremulous light. The dark-browed Roman soldier moved on his homeward way, the sidewalk occasionally flying up and hitting him in the back.

No sound was heard save the low sob of some retiring wave, as it told its story to the smooth pebbles of the beach, or the unrelenting boot-jack struck the high board fence in the back yard, just missing the Roman Tom cat in its mad flight, and then all was still as the breast when the spirit has departed. Anon the Roman snore would steal in upon the deathly silence, and then die away like the sough of a summer breeze. In the green room of the amphitheater a Jittle band of gladiators were assembled. The foam of conflict yet lingered on their lips, the scowl of battle yet hung upon their brows, and the large knobs on their classic profiles indicated that it had been a busy day with them.

There was an embarassing silence of about five minutes, When Spartacus, borrowing a chew of tobacco from Trioforatum Aurelius, stepped forth and thus addressed them: "Mr. Chairman, Ladies and Gentlemen: Ye call me chief, and ye do well to call him chief who for twelve long years has met in the arena every shape of man or beast that the broad empire of Rome could furnish, and yet has never lowered his arm. I do not say this to brag, however, but simply to show that I am the star thumper of the entire outfit.

"If there be one among you who can say that ever in public fight or private brawl my actions did belie my words, let him stand forth and say it, and I will spread him around over the arena till the Coroner will have to gather him up with a blotting paper. If there be three in all your company dare face me on the bloody sands, let them come, and I will construct upon their physiognomy such cupolas, and royal cornices, and Corinthian capitols, and entablatures, that their own mothers would pass them by in the broad light of high noon, unrecognized.

"And yet I was not always thus—a hired butcher—the savage chief of still more savage men.

"My ancestors came from old Sparta, the county seat of Marcus Aurelius county, and settled among the vine-clad hills and cotton groves of Syrsilla. My early life ran quiet as the clear brook by which I sported. Aside from the gentle patter of the maternal slipper on my overalls, everything moved along with me like the silent oleaginous flow of the ordinary goose grease. My boyhood was one long, happy summer day. We stole the Roman muskmelon, and put split sticks on the tail of the Roman dog, and life was one continuous hallelujah.

"When at noon I led the sheep beneath the shade and played the Sweet Bye-and-Bye on my shepherd's flute, there was another Spartan youth, the son of a neighbor, to join me in the pastime. We led our flocks to the same pasture, and together picked the large red ants out of our indestructible sandwiches.

"One evening, after the sheep had been driven into the corral and we were all seated beneath the persimmon tree that shaded our humble cottage, my grandsire, an old man, was telling of Marathon and Leuctra and George Francis Train and Dr. Mary Walker and other great men, and how a little band of Spartans, under Sitting Bull, had withstood the entire regular army. I did not then know what war was, but my cheek burned, I knew not why, and I thought what a glorious thing it would be to leave the reservation and go on the warpath. But my mother kissed my throbbing temples and bade me go soak my head and think no more of those old tales and savage wars. That very night the Romans landed on our coasts. They pillaged the whole country, burned the agency buildings, demolished the ranche, rode off the stock, tore down the smoke-house, and rode their war horses over the cucumber vines.

"To-day I killed a man in the arena, and when I broke his helmet-clasps and looked upon him, behold! he was my friend. The same sweet smile was on his face that I had known when in adventurous boyhood we bathed in the glassy lake by our Spartan home and he had tied my shirt into 1,752 dangerous and difficult knots.

"He knew me, smiled some more, said 'Ta, ta,' and ascended the golden stair. I begged of the Prætor that I might be allowed to bear away the body and have it packed in ice and shipped to his friends near Syrsilla, but he couldn't see it.

"Ay, upon my bended knees, amidst the dust and blood of the anna, I begged this poor boon, and the Prætor answered: 'Let the carrion rot. There are no noble men but Romans and Ohio men. Let the show go on. Bring in the bobtail lion from Abyssinia.' And the assembled maids and mations and the rabble shouted in derision and told me to 'brace up' and 'have some style about my clothes' and 'to give it to us easy,' with other Roman flings which I do not now call to mind.

"And so must you, fellow gladiators, and so must I, die like dogs.

"To-morrow we are billed to appear at the Coliseum at Rome, and reserved seats are being sold at the corner of Third and Corse streets for our moral and instructive performance while I am speaking to you.

"Ye stand here like giants as ye are, but to-morrow some Roman Adonis with a sealskin cap will pat your red brawn and bet his sesturces upon your blood.

"O Rome! Rome! Thou hast been indeed a tender nurse to me. Thou hast given to that gentle, timid shepherd lad who never knew a harsher tone than a flute note, muscles of iron, and a heart like the adamantine lemon pie of the railroad lunch-room. Thou hast taught him to drive his sword through plated mail and links of rugged brass, and warm it in the palpitating gizzard of his foe, and to gaze into the glaring eyeballs of the fierce Numidian lion even as the smooth-cheeked Roman Senator looks into the laughing eyes of the girls in the treasury department.

"And he shall pay thee back till thy rushing Tiber is red as frothing wine; and in its deepest ooze thy life-blood lies curdled. You doubtless hear the gentle murmur of my bazoo.

"Hark! Hear ye yon lion roaring in his den? 'Tis three days since he tasted flesh, but to-morrow he will have gladiator on toast, and don't you forget it; and he will fling your vertebrae about his cage like the tar pitcher of a champion nine.

"If ye are brutes, then stand here like fat oxen waiting for the butcher's knife. If ye are men, arise and follow me. Strike down the warden and the turnkey, overpower the police, and cut for the tall timber. We will break through the city gate, capture the war-horse of the drunken Roman, flee away to the lava beds, and there do bloody work, as did our sires at old Thermopylae, scalp the western-bound emigrant, and make the hen-roosts around Capua look sick.

"O, comrades! warriors! gladiators!!

"If we be men, let us die like men, beneath the blue sky, and by the still waters, and be buried according to Gunter, instead of having our shin bones polished off by Numidian lions, amid the groans and hisses of a snide Roman populace."

CORRESPONDENCE.

Dalles of the St. Croix, September 8, 1880.

Yesterday we steamed up this beautiful river from Stillwater, and as I write, our boat is moored at the head of navigation, with the mighty, perpendicular walls of the St. Croix, shutting in the grassy waters below, while a hundred yards above us the foaming torrent is dashing against the invincible fortress of smooth, moss-grown rocks, with here and there a somber pine or graceful spruce clinging to a jutting shelf midway between the clear, calm sky above and the roaring, angry flood beneath.

Most every one has heard of the wonderful Dalles of the St. Croix. They are not, however, the sole feature of the locality entitled to notice. I consider the entire picture between Stillwater and the Falls one of surpassing loveliness. At this season of the year, the high, gray walls on either side of the lake and river are clad in garments of green and gold, which mock the pen of the poet, and strike the beholder dumb, as he stands in the royal presence of autumn.

The deep green of the stately pine, stands side by side with the golden glory of the poplar, and here and there the brazen billows and royal coloring of maple and oak, the hectic flush upon the features of the dying year, are spread out between the silent sky and the sandy beach; while softly mirrored in the glassy waters, the whole broad picture colored by a mighty, master hand, and with the myriad dyes from Nature's inexhaustible laboratory lies repeated, the echo of a thrilling vision.

There are two rival steamers plying on the Upper St. Croix. I do not remember their names, because they charged me full fare both ways. I can see that my memory is failing a little every day, and I am getting more and more prone to forget those who do not recognize my innate and spontaneous greatness at a glance, and extend the usual courtesies.

When we came down we towed a wheat barge loaded with 21,000 bushels of wheat, and it was pretty difficult most of the way.

The opposition boat went up the night before, and had taken up the water with a blotting-paper, so that every little while I had to roll up my pants about nine feet, and go out into the channel, and luff up on the starboard watch of the barge with a jenny pole and bring her to, so that she could find moisture.

Then I had a good deal of fun going ashore after ferns when the boat was aground. While the crew went aft and close-reefed the smoke-stack and hauled abaft the top-gallant, or side-tracked the wheat barge, my wife would send me ashore to gather maiden-hair ferns, and soft, velvety mosses, and sad, yearnful wood-ticks. O how I love to crawl around through the underbrush, and tear my clothes, and wilt my collar, and gather samples of lichens, and ferns and baled hay and caterpillars to decorate my Western home.

At first I thought I would not mention the little domestic cloud that has shot athwart my sky, but I cannot smother it in my own breast any longer.

St. Croix Falls is on the Wisconsin side of the river and Taylor's Falls on the Minnesota side. They are connected by a toll-bridge which charges you one and a half cents each, way for passage. One can stand halfway across this bridge and see up and down the river, with the Devil's Arm Chair at his right and the Dalles at his left. After supper I took a couple of friends down to the bridge and without letting them know the treat that I had in store for them, I went up to the gate-keeper and paid for all three of us both ways. Then I told them to enjoy themselves. It was a novel treat perhaps to throw open a toll-bridge to the enjoyment of one's friends, but I did it with that utter disregard of expense which has characterized my mining developments in the Rocky Mountains.

Then I took the boys over across the river and gave them the freedom of St. Croix Falls.

Jutting out into the river south of Osceola, is a high, rocky promontory called Cedar Point. Lonely and proud like a sentinel of the forgotten past, there stands a tall cedar tree on this natural battlement, devoid of foliage for some distance up the trunk.

This tree was the old mark that stood upon the dividing line between the Chippewa and Sioux territory. Below it, in the water-worn rock, is a large semi-circle, made by the action of the river, and this it was stated had been the footprint of the horse upon which the Great Spirit had ridden across the stream when he drew the line between these two mighty nations, and set the tree upon it to show his children the boundary between their respective territories. This was the Indian Mason and Dixon's line.

What a wild, weird suggestion of the crude legislation and amateur statesmanship of these two nations rises up before me as I write, and how I yearn to go into the details and try to enter the free-for-all contest and match a bob-tail Caucasian lie against these moss-grown prevarications of the red-man.

At Stillwater, my first wild impulse was to visit the State Penitentiary.

When I go into a new place I register my name at the most expensive hotel, and after visiting the newspaper offices I hunt up the penitentiary, if there be one, and if not, I go to the cooler. I do not go there under duress, as the facetious reader might suggest, but I go there voluntarily to see how the criminal business of the place is looking.

We went to the warden's office, and talked with him a little while, showed him that we were not loaded with giant powder and cross-cut saws, and then we were placed in charge of an usher, and sent through the building to view the mighty manufacturing interests that are carried on inside, where the striped criminals silently and doggedly are moving about at their varied occupations.

After awhile I got gloomy and began to whistle one of my tearful refrains in G. The usher told me to please put up my whistle, and I did so, partly to gratify him and partly because he had a temporary advantage over me. Most every one who has heard me whistle seems glad that his lines have fallen in such pleasant places; but this man, as I afterward learned, did not know the first principle of music. He groped along through life without knowing the difference between a symphony in B, and the low, sad song of the twilight cat.

Pretty soon we came to three men whose faces attracted my attention.

They were the Younger brothers. Their faces were easy of identification from the resemblance to wood cuts published at the time of their capture. I stood silently looking at them for some time.

Their countenances are a study for the reader of human character. Sullen, grim and depraved, they impress the beholder with their utter scorn for the laws and usages of the land. I asked the usher if I guessed right; but he turned away and told me it was against the rules of the institution to point out any one to visitors, or identify the convicts in any way. Then I knew that I was right, because he was so reserved.

I gave one of the men my card and entered into a conversation with him. It wasn't much of a conversation, however, because the usher broke in on me, and shut me off, as it were.

The description that I have given of the Younger brothers in this letter is not over full, owing partly to the fact that the usher wouldn't let me be as sociable with them as I wanted to be; and partly because I afterward discovered, casually, that they were not the Younger brothers.

Speaking of convicts reminds me of my experience with a poor, ignorant man at Laramie—the creature of circumstances—who was sentenced to three years in the Territorial penitentiary, for stealing a pair of flea-bitten bronchos. He was convicted mainly on the testimony of a man, who was afterward sent up for the same offence, and it was the general belief that the first-named man was entirely innocent. He was trusted about the penitentiary at all times, and allowed to go outside the walls without guard, but never betrayed the trust reposed in him.

I went to him and talked with him. His spirits and health were broken, and he told me, with tears in his eyes, that he hoped only for a merciful death to end his sufferings. While acting as guard to a party of convicts outside one day, they fell upon him and nearly killed him with a huge stone, and then leaving him bleeding and insensible.

He could not tell of his sufferings without crying. I undertook to enlist sympathy for him, and when I told his tale of misfortune to the governor and authorities in that thrilling way of mine, I had no difficulty in securing his pardon.

He came to my office and sobbed out his gratitude till I told him it was of no consequence, and begged him not to mention it, although it was the proudest moment of my life. He went to work for a citizen of Laramie, with the old, industrious, patient air, and I pointed him out with pride to my friends as a man whom I had rescued and brought back to a useful life.

One morning, however, before the pale dawn had streaked the eastern sky he took his employer's team and what money there was in the house and struck out for the Gunnison country. He did not know anything about mining, but he had such implicit confidence in himself that he started out alone and without letters of introduction to leading men in that country. It was a good thing that he did have perfect confidence in himself, for no one else had much confidence in him after that.

During that day a good many of my friends came around to see me. I didn't know I had so many friends. They all seemed to be in first-rate spirits. They seemed glad to see me, and laughed a good deal. Sometimes I couldn't see what they were laughing at, for my horizon was shrouded in gloom. It don't take much to make some people laugh.

I have never felt perfectly at ease with Governor Thayer since that. I know that he regards me as a confederate with that man, and he thinks that I got part of the money realized from the sale of that team, but I didn't. If it were the last statement I should make on earth I would still say?

As Heaven is my witness, that I have never realized a single dollar from the sale of that team.

HE WENT OUT WEST FOR HIS HEALTH.

In my capacity of justice of the peace and general wholesale and retail dealer in fresh, new-laid equity and evenhanded justice, I often meet with those who have seen better days, and who, through the ever-changing fortunes of the west, have fallen lower and lower in the social scale, until they stand up and are assessed as "common drunks," or "vags," or "assault and batteries," with that natural and easy grace which comes only to those who have been before the public in that capacity, so numerously, that it has ceased to indicate itself by the usual embarrassment of the amateur.

WENT OUT WEST.

Perhaps no surging sentiments of pity have stirred my very soul during my official career, like those that throbbed wildly athwart my system a few days ago.

It was a case of the most bitter disappointment of a young life. A youth from Chicago, came to me, near the close of day. I was just about to lock up the judicial scales for the evening, and secure the doors of the archives, preparatory to going out and "shaking" the mayor for the lemonade, after which I intended to breathe in a little fresh atmosphere and go home to dinner.

It had been a hard day in the temple of justice that day, and the court was weary.

It had dealt out even-handed justice at regular rates, since early morning, at so much per deal, till fatigue was beginning to show itself in the lines upon the broad, white brow.

Therefore, when a halting step was heard on the stair, there was a low murmur on the part of the court, and a half-surprised moan that sounded like the tail end of an affidavit.

The young man who entered the hallowed presence of eternal justice, and the all-pervading and dazzling beauty of the court in its shirt-sleeves, was of about medium stature, with shoes cut decollette, and Roman-striped socks clocked with brocaded straw-colored silk.

He wore an ecru colored straw hat, with navy-blue brocaded band, and necktie of old gold, with polka dots of humberta and cardinal, interspersed with embroidered horseshoe and stirrup in coucherde soleil and ultramarine.

His hair was dark and oleaginous, and his shirt was cream colored ground, with narrow baby-blue stripes, cutaway collar, and cuffs that extended out into space.

He also had some other clothes on.

But over all, and pervading the entire man, was the look of hopelessness and corroding grief. With all his good clothes on, he was a hollow mockery, for his eyes were heavy with woe.

The nose also was heavy with woe.

This feature in fact was more appropriately draped in token of its sadness than any of the rest. Few noses are so expressive of a general and incurable gloom as this one was. It had evidently at one time been a glad, joyous, and buoyant nose, but now it was despondent and low spirited.

There was a look of goneness and utter desolation about it that would stir the better impulses of the most heartless.

The feature had evidently tried to centralize itself, but had failed. Here and there narrow strips of court-plaster had gone out after it and tried to win it back, but they had not succeeded.

I said, "Mister, there seems to be a panic among your nose. It's none of my business, of course, but couldn't you get a brass band and call it together? Then you could hold a meeting and decide whether it had better resume or not."

The gentleman from Chicago went through the motions of wiping the wide waste and howling desolation where his once joyous nose had been, and then, putting away the plum-colored silk handkerchief with the orange border, he said "'Squire, I have been grossly deceived. You see in me the victim of a base misrepresentation. In Chicago this season of the year is extremely unhealthy. The intense hot weather carries away the innocent and the good, and I feared that my turn would come soon.

"I heard of the salubrious clime of your mountain city, where the days are filled with gladness and the burning heat of the mighty city by the inland sea never comes.

"I came here two brief days ago, and you can see with the naked eye what the result has been.

"It is not gratifying. The climate may in the abstract be all right, but there are certain sudden and wonderful atmospheric changes that I cannot account for, and they are very disastrous.

"I was sitting in a Second Street saloon to-day, talking about matters and things, when the conversation turned on physical strength. One thing led to another, and finally I made a little humorous remark to a young man there, which remark I have made in Chicago many times without disastrous results, but the air clouded up all of a sudden, and in the darkness I could see Roman candles going off and pin-wheels and high-priced rockets and blue-lights, etc.

"Shortly after that I gathered up what fragments of my face I could find and went down to the doctor's office.

"He held an inquest on my nose, and I paid for it.

"I shall go back to Chicago to-morrow. I shall not be as handsome as I was, but I have gained a good deal of information about the broad and beautiful west which is priceless in value to me.

"All I wished to say was this; if you see fit to mention this matter to the public, tone it down as much as possible, and say that for a bilious, nervous temperament, perhaps the air here is too bracing."

I have considered his sensitive feelings, and have tried to give the above account in fair and impartial terms.

A QUIET LITTLE WEDDING WITHOUT ANY FRILLS

Another class of those who frequent the temple of justice includes those who are in search of matrimony at reduced rates.

I remember one unostentatious little wedding which took place at the general headquarters of municipal jurisprudence, over which I preside, and during the earlier history of my reign.

It was quite a success in a small way.

I had just moved into the office, and had been engaged that morning in putting up a stove. The stove had seemed reluctant, and as my assistant was sociably drunk, I had not succeeded very well.

The pipe didn't seem to be harmonious, and the effort to bring about a union between the discordant elements, had not, up to the time of which I speak, produced any very gratifying results.

I had reached down into the elbow of the pipe several times, to see how it felt down there, and after satisfying my morbid curiosity in that respect, I had yielded to a wild and uncontrollable desire to scratch my nose with the same hand.

This had given me an air of intense sadness, and opaque gloom.

I stood on the top of a step-ladder trying to make the end of a six-inch joint of pipe go into the end of a five-inch joint, when the groom entered. He wanted to know if he could see the general manager, and I told him he could if he had a piece of smoked glass, and a $5 promissory note executed by old man Spinner.

Then he told me how he was fixed. He desired a small package of connubial bliss, and without delay.

The necessary preliminaries were arranged; the groom made an extempore effort to spit in the mosaic cuspidore, but was only partially successful, put on his hat and went out in search of Juliet.

She was very unique in her style, and entirely free from any effort to appear to the best advantage.

She wore her hair plain, *a la* Sitting Bull. It had been banged, but not with any great degree of system or accuracy. Probably it had been done with the pinking-iron or a pair of ice-tongs by an amateur banger.

She looked some like Mrs. Bender, only younger and more queenly, perhaps.

She swept into the arena with the symmetrical movement and careless grace of a hired man—only her steps were longer and less methodical.

Both bride and groom had come through with a band of emigrants from Kansas, and, therefore, they were out of swallow-tail coats and orange blossoms.

There was no airy tulle and shimmering satin, or broadcloth and spike-tail coat in the procession; at least there was none visible to the court.

The groom was bronzed and bearded like a pard, whatever that is, and wore a pair of brown-duck overalls, caught back with copper rivets and held in place by a lonely suspender. He also wore a hickory shirt with stripes running vertically. His hair looked like burnished gold, only he hadn't burnished it much since he left Kansas.

The entire emigrant train dropped in one by one to witness the ceremony, and seemed impressed with the overshadowing and awe-inspiring nature of the surroundings.

One by one they filed in, and, making their little contribution to the mosaic cuspidore, they leaned themselves up against the wall and wrapped themselves in thought.

I bandaged my finger, which I had skinned some in putting the stove together, wiped off what soot and ashes I had about my person and thought I would not need, and boldly solidified these two young hearts.

The ceremony was not very impressive, but it did the required amount of damage. That was all that was necessary.

The applicants seemed to miss the wedding-march and some other little preparatory arrangements, which I had overlooked, but I apologized to them afterward, and told them that when times picked up a little, and I got established, and the new fee-bill went into operation, I would attend to these things.

The wedding presents were not numerous, but they were useful, and showed the good sense of the donors.

The bride's mother gave her one of the splint-bottom chairs that one always sees tied to the rear of every well regulated emigrant wagon, and her father gave her a cream-colored dog, with one eye knocked out.

With his overflowing wealth of flea-bitten dogs, he might have done much better by her than he did, but he said he would wait a few years and if she were poor enough to need more dogs, he would not be parsimonious.

The young couple went up on Coyote Creek and went to housekeeping, and years have gone by since without word from them.

In the turmoil and hurry of life, I had almost forgotten them until Cole's circus was in town the other day.

That brought them to light.

They had done well in the dog business, and had succeeded in promoting the growth of a new kind of meek and lowly dog, with sore places on him for homeless and orphan flies.

They also had several children with reddish hair and large, wilted ears.

The youngest one was quite young, and cried when the calliope burst into a wild rhapsody of Nancy Lee.

When I saw the family, the mother was eagerly watching the parade, and at the same time trying to broil the baby's nose in the sun. It was almost done, when I was called away by other business, so I cannot say positively whether the child was taken home rare or well-done.

THOUGHTS ON SPRING

Spring is the most joyful season of the year. The little brooklets are released from their icy fetters and go laughing and rippling along their winding way. The birds begin to sing in the budding branches, and the soft South wind calls forth the green grass.

The husbandman then goes forth to dig the horseradish for his frugal meal. He also jabs his finger into the rosebud mouth of the wild-eyed calf, and proceeds to wean him from the gentle cow. The cow-boy goes forth humming a jocund lay. So does the hen. Boys should not go near the hen while she is occupied with her tuneful lay. She might seize them by the off ear, and bear them away to her den, and feed them to her young. The hen rises early in the morning so as to catch the swift-footed angleworm as he flits from flower to flower. The angleworm cannot bite.

In the spring the young man's fancy turns to thoughts of love. Love is a good thing.

The picnic plant will soon lift its little head to the sunshine, and the picnic manager will go out and survey the country, to find where the most God-forsaken places are, and then he will get up an excursion to some of these picturesque mud-holes and sand-piles; and the man who swore last year that he would never go to another picnic, will pack up some mustard, and bay rum, and pickles, and glycerine, and a lap-robe, and some camphor, and a spyglass, and some court-plaster; and he will heave a sigh and go out to the glens and rural retreats, and fill his skin full of Tolu, Rock and Rye, and hatred toward all mankind and womankind; and he will skin his hands, and try to rub the downy fluff and bloom from a cactus by sitting down on it.

I have attended picnics regularly for nearly ten years now, and I am a man of a good deal of firmness, too, but I cannot hold a cactus down on the ground with my entire weight, any better than when I first began; and I feel that I am getting farther and farther from redeeming grace.

With the approach of spring the correspondence between myself and Mr. Le Duc begins to get more brisk also. He writes me under date of March 20, saying that he is preparing for a more vigorous campaign this summer than ever before. He thinks the clip from his Cotswold hydraulic rams will exceed that of any previous year. He will also experiment in a scientific manner to perfect the laying of fancy Easter porcelain and decorated China eggs by Cochin China fowls. If they cannot manage it he will try some experiments on the egg plant. Mr. Le Duc is a man who is not easily discouraged by small obstacles. He will watch the habits of the grasshopper and curculio and bed-bug, also with great assiduity. I have begged him to transfer the bed-bug to the Indian Department. He always regards my suggestions very favorably, because, as he says, I am "so practical."

We are going to devote a part of the summer to grafting the saddle-rock oyster on the vegetable oyster-plant, and will spare no pains to secure an inland oyster that will stand this dry air and high, rigorous climate.

THE SAME OLD THING.

Recently I have had the pleasure of acting as chief mourner at a mountain picnic. This subject has been pretty well represented in romance and song already; but I venture to give my experience as being a little out of the ordinary.

The joy which is experienced in the glad, free life of the picnicker is always before the picnic. On the evening before he makes the excursion, he is too full of sacred pleasure and lavender-colored tranquillity for anything.

He glides about the house, softly warbling to himself the fragment of some tender love song, while he packs the corkscrews and matches, and other vegetables for the morrow.

I was placed in command of a party of ladies who had everything arranged so that all I needed to do would be to get into the buggy and drive to the mountains, eat my lunch, and drive back again.

I like to go with a party of ladies, because they never make suggestions about the route, or how to drive.

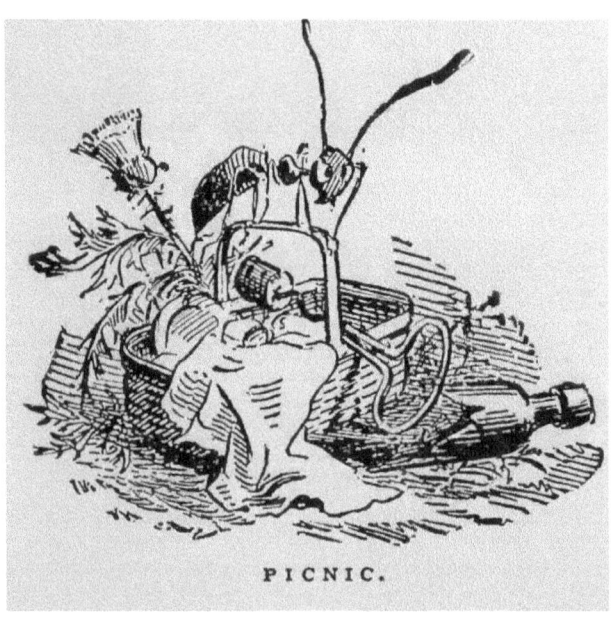

PICNIC.

They are just as full of gentle trust and child-like confidence and questions as they can be.

They get the lunch ready and get into the buggy, and keep thinking of things they have forgotten, till they get 400 miles from home, and they sing little pieces of old songs, and won't let the great, horrid man in charge of the excursion have any lunch when he gets hungry, because they are hunting for a romantic spot beneath the boughs of a magnificent elm, while every sane man in the Territory knows that there isn't an elm big or little, within 1,4321 1/2 miles.

We went up in the mountains, because we wanted to go where it would be cool. As a search for a cool resort, this picnic of ours was the most brilliant success. We kept going up at an angle of forty-five degrees from the time we left home until we had to get out and walk to keep warm. We got into one of the upper strata of clouds; and a cold mist mixed with fragments of ice-cream, and large chunks of hail and misery, about the size of a burglar-proof safe came gathering over us. Then we camped in the midst of the mountain storm, and the various ladies sat down on their feet, and put the lap-robes over them, and looked reproachfully at me. We hovered around under the buggy, and two or three little half-grown parasols, and watched the storm. It was a glorious spectacle to the thinking mind.

They began to abuse me because I did not make a circus of myself, and thus drive away the despair and misery of the occasion. They had brought me along, it seemed, because I was such an amusing little cuss. It made me a good deal sadder than I would have been otherwise. Here in the midst of a wild and bitter mountain storm, so thick that you couldn't see twenty yards away, with nothing to eat but some marble cake soaked in vinegar, and a piece of cold tongue with a red ant on it, I was expected to make a hippodrome and negro minstrel show of myself. I burst into tears, and tried to sit on my feet as the ladies did. I couldn't do it, so simultaneously and so extemporaneously, as it were, as they could. I had to take them by sections and sit on them. My feet are not large, but at the same time I cannot hover over them both at the same time.

Dear reader, did you ever sit amidst the silence and solitude of the mountains and feel the hailstones rolling down your back, melting and soothing you, and filling your heart with great surging thoughts of the sweet bye-and-bye, and death, and the grave, and other mirth-provoking topics? We had now been about two hundred years without food, it seemed to me, and I mildly suggested that I would like something to eat rather than die of starvation in the midst of plenty; but the ladies wouldn't give me so much as a ham handwich to preserve my life. They told me to smoke if I felt that I must have nourishment, and coldly refused to let me sample the pickled spiders and cold-pressed flies.

So in the midst of all this prepared food I had to go out into the sagebrush and eat raw grasshoppers and grease-wood.

Bye and bye, when we concluded that we had seen about all the mountain storm we needed in our business, and didn't pine for any more hail-stones and dampness, we hitched up again and started home. Then we got lost. The ladies felt indignant, but I was delighted. I never was so lost in all my life. When I was asked where I thought I was, I could cheerfully reply that I didn't know, and that would stop the conversation for as much as two minutes.

The beauty of being lost is that you are all the time seeing new objects. There is a charm of novelty about being lost that one does not fully understand until he has been there, so to speak.

When I would say that I didn't know where the road led to that we were traveling, one of the party would suggest with mingled bitterness and regret, that we had better turn back. Then I would turn back. I turned back seventeen times at the request of various members of the party for whom I had, and still have, the most unbounded respect.

Finally we got so accustomed to the various objects along this line of travel, that we pined for a change. Then we drove ahead a little farther and found the road. It had been there all the time. It is there yet.

I never had so much fun in all my life. It don't take much to please me, however. I'm of a cheerful disposition, anyhow.

Some of the ladies brought home columbines that had been drowned; others brought home beautiful green mosses with red bugs in them; and others brought home lichens and ferns and neuralgia.

I didn't bring anything home. I was glad to get home myself, and know that I was all there.

I took the lunch basket and examined it. It looked sick and unhappy. At first I thought I would pick the red ants out of the lunch; then I thought it would save time to pick the lunch out of the red ants; but finally I thought I would compromise, by throwing the whole thing into the alley.

I am now preparing a work to be called the "Pick Nicker's Guide; or Starvation Made Easy and Even Desirable!" It will supply a want long felt, and will be within the reach of all.

THE VETERAN WHO DIED WHILE GETTING HIS PENSION.

Many years ago, when business in my office was not very rushing, and time hung heavy on my hands, before I had attempted journalism, and no dream of my present dazzling literary success had entered my mind, I rashly offered to assist applicants for pensions in attracting the attention of the general government, at so much per head.

One hot day in July while I sat in my office killing flies with an elastic band and wondering if my mines would ever be quoted in the market, a middle-aged man came in and, spitting calmly into the porcelain cuspidore, began to tell me about his service as a soldier, and how he was wounded, and wished to secure a pension.

He said that several attorneys had already tried to procure one for him, but had failed to do so, giving up in despair. I examined the wound, which consisted of a large hole in the skull, caused by a gun-shot wound. He was almost entirely prevented by this wound from obtaining a livelihood, because he was liable at any moment to fall insensible to the ground, as the result of exercise or work. I told him that I would snatch a few moments from my arduous duties and proceed to do as he requested me.

Then I began a very brisk correspondence with the Interior Department. I would write to the Commissioner of Pensions in my vivacious but firm manner and he would send me back a humorous little circular showing me that I had been too hasty and premature. I never got mad or forgot myself but began a little farther back in the history of the world, and gradually led up to the war of the rebellion.

In reply the Commissioner would write back to me that my chronological table was at fault and I would cheerfully correct the error and proceed.

At this time, however, my client became a little despondent, several years having elapsed since we began our task. So to my other labors I had to add that of cheering up the applicant.

Time dragged its slow length along. Months succeeded months and the years sped on.

The Interior Department never forgot me. Every little while I would get a printed circular boiling over with mirth and filled with the most delightful conundrums relative to the late unpleasantness. These conundrums I would have my client answer and swear to every time, although I could see that he was failing mentally and physically. He would come into my office almost every day, and silently raise his right hand and with uncovered head stand there in a reverent attitude for me to swear him to something. Sometimes I had nothing for him to swear to, and then I would make him take the oath of allegiance and send him away. I wanted to keep him loyal if I could, whether he got his pension or not.

The last work had been nearly completed, and the claim had been turned over to the Surgeon-General's office, when the applicant yielded to the crumbling effect of relentless time, and took to his bed.

It was a sad moment for me. I could not keep back the silent tears when I saw the old man lying there so still and so helpless, and remembered how rosy, and strong, and happy he looked years and years ago, when he first asked me to apply for his pension.

I wrote the Department that if the claims could be passed upon soon, I would keep my client up on stimulants a short time, but that he was failing fast. Then I went to the bedside of the old man, and watched him tenderly.

When he saw me come into his room, although he could not talk any more, he would feebly raise his right hand, and I would swear him to support the Constitution of the United States, and then he would be easier. It seemed to me like a ghastly joke for the old man to swear he would support the Constitution of the United States, when he couldn't begin to support his own constitution; but I never mentioned it to him.

At last the blow fell. The Surgeon-General wrote me that owing to the lack of clerical aid in that office, and a failure of Congress to make any appropriation for that purpose, he was behind hand, and could not possibly reach the claim referred to before the close of the following year.

Then the old man passed into the great untried realm of the hereafter. But he was prepared.

With the aid of the government, I had given him an idea of Eternity and its vastness, which could not fail to be of priceless benefit to him.

After the government had used this pension money as long as it needed it, and was, so to speak, once more on its feet, the money was sent, and the old man's great-grand-children got it, and purchased a lawn-mower, a Mexican hairless dog, and some other necessaries of life with it.

I am now out of the pension business. It is a good thing, for I find that I am too impatient to attend to it. I am too anxious for tangible results in the near future. My desire to accomplish anything speedily is too violent and too previous.

GINGERBREAD POEMS AND COLD PICKLED FACTS.

In an old number of *Harper's Magazine*, will be found a little poem upon the subject of Joseph, the chief of the Nez Perces. There is a kind of mellow and subdued heroic light cast over the final defeat of this great North American horse thief, which is in perfectly pleasing harmony with the New England idea of the noble unlettered relic of a defunct race. This soft-voiced poet, who probably knows about as much of the true occidental pig-stealer, as the latter does about the Electoral College, starts out this little brass-mounted epic in the following elegant style of prevarication:

>From the northern desolation,
>
>Comes the cry of exultation,
>
>It has ended—he has yielded, and the stubborn fight won.
>
>Let the nation in its glory,
>
>Bow with shame before the story
>
>Of the hero it has ruined, and the evil it has done.

It is too true that here in the wild West people haven't the advantages that are accorded to the East, and in our uncouth ignorance, and meager facilities for obtaining information, we are, no doubt, too prone to ascribe to the hostile inebriate of the plains a character which does not compare very favorably with the boss hero in the poem hereto attached, and marked "Exhibit A." But the people on the frontier should not set themselves up to judge what they know nothing of. Why should frontiersmen, without colleges, without observatories, without telescopes, or logarithms, or protoplasms, or spectroscopes, or heliotropes, how should they, I ask, who can lay no claim to anything but that they are poor, unsophisticated, grasshopper sufferers; with nothing to refer to but the naked facts—the ruins of their desolated homes, and the ghastly, mutilated corpses of their wives and children—try to compete with the venerable philosophers who live where the Patent Office reports are made, and within the shadow of the building in which the *Illustrated Police Gazette* and other such reliable authorities have their birth, and in which are illustrated with graphic skill, the Indian raids of the border, using the same old cut which is taken from the "Death of Captain Cook," to illustrate every Indian outbreak from Nebraska to Oregon.

Is it nothing forsooth for a nomadic race of buffalo slayers and maple sugar makers and cranberry pickers to rise from the dust and learn to love the wise institutions of a free government? To lay aside the old hickory bow of the original red man and take up the improved breech-loader? To take kindly to mixed drinks and Sabbath school picnics and temperance lectures and base-ball matches? To live contentedly about the agencies, playing poker for the whiskies during the cold and cruel winter? Then when the glad song of the robin awakes the echoes in spring, and the air is filled with a thousand nameless odors, among which may be detected the balmy breath of the government sock, to hie him away to the valleys with his fishing rod and flies (and other curious insects), or to spend the glorious days of midsummer at the camp-meeting or the horse-race? We can never know how his poor heart must burn to kick off his box-toed boots and throw aside his dress coat and suspenders, and gallop over the green hills and kick up his heels and whoop and yell, and tear out the tongues of a few white women and be sociable.

They are indeed the nation's wards, a little frisky and playful at times, to be sure, but we must overlook that. There can be no reason nor justice in forbidding these freeborn descendants of these mighty races the inalienable right to lock up their front doors at the agency and put the key in their pockets, and light out, if they wish to, across the country, spreading gory desolation along their trail, eating the farmers' hard earned store, pillaging his home, murdering his household, burning his crops, riding their war horses over his watermelon vines, eating his winter preserves, scalping the hired man and wearing away the farmer's red-flannel undershirt wrong side to, and wrong side up if they want to. And if any ignorant upstart of the frontier, who feels a little sore over the loss of his family, undertakes to defraud these wild, free sons of the forest of any or all of their rights, let the lop-eared, slab-sided, knock-kneed, crosseyed, spavined, lantern-jawed, sway-backed, mangy, flannelmouthed poet of the educated and refined East write poetry about him till he is glad to apologize.

ORIGIN OF BEAUTIFUL SNOW,

The following letter is from Captain Jack relative to the expedition under his charge, sent out for the purpose of bringing in the murdering group of Utes, against whom the government seems to maintain a feeling, it not of enmity, at least of coolness, and perhaps unfriendliness.

The Indian is not generally supposed to be a humorist, or inclined to be facetious; but the letter below would seem to indicate that there is, at the least, a kind of grim, rough, uncouth attempt on his part to make a paragrapher of himself.

I am not at liberty to give my reasons to the public for the publication of this letter; nor even the manner of securing it. Those to whom my word has been passed relative to a strict secrecy on my part in the above connection, shall not be betrayed. Friends who know me are aware that my word is as good as my bond, and even better than my promissory note.

On the Wing, February 1, 1880.

Dear Sir:—I have a little leisure in which to write of our journey, and will dictate this letter to an amanuensis. [Amanuensis is a Ute word; but you will understand it in this connection. It does not mean anything wrong.]

We find much snow through the mountains, which impedes our progress very materially. We crossed a canyon yesterday where there was a good deal. I should think there might be 1,500 feet in depth of it. It filled the canyon up full, and bulged up ten or fifteen feet above the sides. I composed a short poem about it. I knew that it was wrong to do so; but almost every one else has composed a poem on the beautiful snow, then why should I, although I have not taken out my naturalization papers, be denied the sweet solace of song? I said:

> O drifted whiteness covering
> The fair face of nature,
> Pure as the sigh of a blessed spirit
> On the eternal shores, you
> Glitter in the summer sun
> Considerable. My mortal
> Ken seems weak and
> Helpless in the midst of

Your dazzling splendor,
      And I would hide my
Diminished head like
Serf unclothed in presence
Of his mighty King.

      You lie engulphed
Within the cold embrace
Of rocky walls and giant
Cliffs. You spread out
Your white mantle and
Enwrap the whole broad
Universe, and a portion
Of York State.

      You seem content,
Resting in silent whiteness
On the frozen breast of
The cold, dead earth. You
Think apparently that
You are middling white;
But once I was in the
Same condition. I was
Pure as the beautiful snow,
But I fell. It was a
Right smart fall, too.
    It churned me up a
Good deal and nearly
Knocked the supreme

Duplex from its intellectual
Throne. It occurred in
Washington, D. C.
       But thou
  Snow, lying so spotless
On the frozen earth, as
I remarked before, thou
Hast indeed a soft,
  Soft thing. Thou comest
Down like the silent
Movements of a specter,
And thy fall upon the
Earth is like the tread
Of those who walk the
Shores of immortality.
  You lie around all
Winter drawing your
Annuities till spring,
  And then the soft
Breath from the south with
Touch seductive bids you
Go, and you light out
With more or less alacrity.

      Then rest, O snow,
  Where thou hast settled
Down, secure in conscious
Purity. Avoid so far as
Possible the capital of

A republic, and the

Blessing of yours truly

Will settle down upon

You like—like—a

Hired man.

There are, no doubt, some little irregularities about this poem, but I scratched it off one night in camp when my chilblains were hurting me and itching so that I had to write a poem or swear a good deal.

We have not seen anything as yet to shoot at.

That is, of course, I refer to what we came here for. I shot at what I thought to be Douglas the other day, but it turned out to be an old Indian who was out skirmishing around after cotton-tails for his dinner. I snuffed his light out, however. By this time he is chasing cotton-tails in a better, brighter sphere, where the wicked cease from troubling and life is one prolonged Fourth of July. Occasionally we see a squaw and shoot her just for practice. I am getting so I'm pretty good on a wheel and fire.

Douglas ought to be easy to indentify, however, at a great distance, for his features are peculiar. He has a large nose. It is like a premium summer squash, only larger. I don't think I ever saw such a wealth of nose as his. Napoleon used to say that a large nose is indicative of strong character. According to this rule, Douglas must have a character stronger than an eight-mule team.

We start out early to-morrow and hope to bag something, but cannot tell how we will make it. I will report as soon as I get to where there is a telegraph. I do not allow any reporters along with me. A great many of them wanted to go along with me for the excitement. I told them, however, that I could furnish the press with such reports as I saw fit to furnish, and I did not want to take a young man away from the haunts of civilization and waltz him around among the hills of Colorado, for it isn't so much of a success as an editorial picnic after all. I often wish that I could run down to dinner as I did at Washington and eat all I need. I also yearn for the hot Scotch and the spiced rum of the pale-face, and the Scotch plaid lemon pie, and the indestructible blanc-mange, and the buckwheat cakes like door-mats that I got at Washington.

But I must attend to the business of the Great Father, and prepare the remains which he requires for his grand Indian funeral. Till then, adieu. Jack.

UTE ELOQUENCE.

(SPEECH OF OLD MAN COLOROW AT AN OLD SETTLER'S REUNION IN NORTH PARK, COLORADO.)

The following short oration, delivered by Colorow in the North Park, I send in as a sort of companion-piece to the letter written by Jack, and given in this work. Few people actually know the true spirit of Greek and Roman oratory that still lingers about the remnants of this people, now nearly driven from the face of the earth. I have never seen this speech in print, and I give it so that the youth of the nineteenth century may commit it to memory, and declaim it on the regular public school speech day.

"Mr. Chairman, Ladies and Gentlemen:—Warriors, we are but a little band of American citizens, encircled by a horde of pale-faced usurpers.

"Where years agone, in primeval forests, the swift foot of the young Indian followed the deer through shimmering light beneath the broad boughs of the spreading tree, the white man, in his light summer suit, with his pale-faced squaw, is playing croquet; and we stand idly by and allow it.

"Where erst the hum of the arrow, as it sped to its mark, was heard upon the summer air; and the panting hunter in bosky dell, quenched his parched lips at the bubbling spring, the white man has erected a huge wigwam, and enclosed the spring, and people from the land of the rising sun come to gain their health, and the vigor of their youth. Men come to this place and limp around in the haunts of the red man with crutches, and cork legs, and liver pads.

"Things are not precisely as they formerly were. They have changed. There seems to be a new administration. We are not apparently in the ascendancy to any great extent.

"Above the hallowed graves of our ancestors the buck-wheater hoes the cross-eyed potato, and mashes the immortal soul out of the speckled sqursh-bug. The sacred dust of our forefathers is nourishing the roots of the Siberian crab apple tree, and the early Scandinavian turnip.

"Our sun is set. Our race is run. We had better select a small hole in the earth into which we may crawl and then draw it in after us, and tuck it carefully about us.

"These mountains are ours. These plains are ours. Ours through all time to come. We need them in our business. The wail of departed spirits is on the winds that blow over this wide free land. The tears of departed heroes of our people fall in the rain drops, for their land is given away. To-day I look upon the sad wreck of a great people, and I ask you to go with me, and with our united hearts' blood win back the fair domain. Let two or three able-bodied warriors follow me and hold my coat while I mash' the white-livered snipe off the lowlands beyond recognition.

"Let us steal in upon the frontier while the regular-army has gone to his dinner and get a few Caucasians for breakfast.

"Arise, ye Goths, and glut your ire." [Applause.]

THE AGED INDIAN'S LAMENT.

[copyrighted: all rights reserved.]

Warriors, I am an aged hemlock. The mountain-winds sigh among my withered limbs. A few more suns and I shall fall amid the solemn hush of the forest, and my place will be vacant. I shall tread the walks of the happy hunting grounds, and sing glad hallelujahs where the worm dieth not and the fire-water is not quenched.

"Once I was the pride of my tribe and the swift-foot of the prairie. I stood with my brethren like the towering oak, and my prowess was known throughout my nation. Now I bow to the wintry blast and hump myself with a vigorous and unanimous hump. My eagle-eye is dimmed. The fleetness of my limbs is gone. The vigor of my youth is past. I do not shout now to my warriors, for the cliffs and rocks refuse to answer back my cry, and it sinks away like the sad moan of the low-grade refractory mule.

"When my brethren go forth to shoot the swift-footed ranchman as he gambols on the hill-sides, I cower above the camp-fire and rub mutton-tallow on my favorite chilblain through the still watches of the night.

"Warriors, I yearn for immortality. The White Father has said that over yonder the life is one of uninterrupted editorial excursions. No inflammatory rheumatism can ever enter there.

"I want to be a copper-colored angel and out-fly the boss angel of the entire outfit. I want to see Pocahontas and other great men who have clomb the golden stair. I want something to eat, so as to surprise my stomach. I want a long period of rest and soul-destroying inactivity.

"Warriors, my sun is set. I have lost my grip. My features are sharpened by age, and one by one my white teeth have resigned till but two are left, and they do not seem to mash by an overwhelming majority. I cannot masticate buffalo tripe or even relish my tarantula on toast as I once could.

"My twilight is fading into evening, and the day is gone. I hear the crickets chirp in the dead grass and I know that the night is at hand. Far away upon the gentle winds I hear the soft cooing of the Colorado tom-cat, and the thump of the stove lid as it misses the cat and strikes with a hollow, mournful sound against the corral. A few more moons and you will meet, but you will miss me. There will be one vacant chair.

"The veal-cutlet and the watermelon of the pale-face hold out no inducements to me. The circus and the icecream festival will miss me, for I shall be far away in the ether-blue, where the wicked cease from troubling and the weary are at rest. I shall be revelling in more eternal rest than I know what to do with.

"Farewell, my warriors. Make my humble grave low in the valley where the wild columbine and the Rocky Mountain flea can clamber over my last resting place, and carve upon the slab above my head the name of Minneconjo-presipitatenuxqonicatahskunkahcoquipahhahamazanpah kahconkaska. The-cross-eyed-caterpillar-who-walks-on-his-hind-legs-and howls-like-the-pale-face-pappoose-who-adver-tises-to-hold-down-the blonde-bumble-bee."

HOW A MINING STAMPEDE BREAKS OUT.

Dear reader, shall I give you a few symptoms of the mining epidemic in Mountain towns? All right. I will anyhow!

Symptom 1.—A long-haired man is seen pounding up a piece of quartz about the size of a man's hand.

Symptom 2.—Two men meander up to him and ask him where he got it.

Symptom 3.—The long-haired man looks down into the mortar, and lies gently to the inquiring minds who linger near.

Symptom 4.—More men come around. The long-haired man gets a gold-pan and doubles himself up over the ditch and begins to pan.

Symptom 5.—Two hundred more men come out of saloons and other mercantile establishments and join the throng.

Symptom 6.—The long-haired man gets down to black sand, and shows several colors about the size of a blue-jay's ear.

Symptom 7 times.—Several solitary horsemen start out, with some pack-mules, and blank location notices, and valley tan. The plot deepens. The telegraph gets red-hot. Men who have been impecunious, for lo, these many years, come around to pay some old bills. Poor men buy spotted dogs and gold-headed canes. Stingy men get reckless, and buy the first box of strawberries without asking the price.

I have caught the epidemic myself.

I am getting reckless. Instead of turning my last summer lavender pants hind side before, and removing the ham sandwich lithograph on the front breadths, I have purchased a new pair.

I never experienced such a wild, glad feeling of perfect abandon.

I go to church and chip in for the heathen, perfectly regardless of expense. If Zion languishes, I come forward and throw in the small currency with a lavish hand.

Banks, offices, hotels, saloons and private residences show specimens of quartz carrying free gold and carbonates, hard, soft, and medium soft, with iron protoxide of nitrogen, rhombohedral glucose indications of valedictory and free milling oxide of anti-fat in abundance.

Nellis, who lives near the Mill Creek carbonate claims, came in to town the other day to get an injunction against the miners, so that he could injunct them from prospecting in his cellar, and staking his pie-plant bed.

When he goes out after dark to drive the cow out of his turnip patch, he falls over a stake every little while, with a notice tacked on it, which sets forth that the undersigned, viz., Johnny Comelately, Joe Newbegin, Shoo Fly Smith, and Union Forever Dandelion claim 1,500 feet in length, by 600 feet in width for mineral purposes on this claim, to be known as "The Gal with the skim-milk Eye," together with all dips, spurs, angles or variations, gold, silver, or other precious metals therein contained.

Mr. Nellis says he is glad to see a "boom," and at first he did all he could to make it pleasant for prospectors; but lately he thinks that their sociability has become too earnest and too simultaneous.

I told him that the only way I could see to avoid losing his grip, and having his string-beans dug up prematurely, was to stake the entire ranche as a placer claim, buy him a Gatling gun that would shoot the large size of buckshot, and then trust in the mysterious movements of an overruling Providence.

I do not know whether he took my advice or not; but I am looking anxiously along the Mill-Creek road every day, for a six mule team loaded with disorganized remains, and driven by a man who looks as though he had glutted his vengeance, and had two or three gluts left over on his hands.

THE GREAT ROCKY MOUNTAIN REUNION OF YALLER DOGS.

Secretary Spates, the silver-tongued orator and gilt-edged mouth organ of Wyoming, acting general superintendent and governor extraordinary of Wyoming, expressed a wish the other day for a dog. He had a light yellow cane, and wanted a dog to match. He said that he wanted something to love. If he could wake up in the stillness of the night and hear his faithful dog fighting fleas, and licking his chops, and coughing, he (the secretary) would feel as though he was loved, at least? by one. Some friends thought it would be a pleasant thing to surprise Mr. Spates with a dog. So they procured a duplicate key to his room and organized themselves into a dog vigilance committee. There were several yellow dogs around Cheyenne that were not in use, and their owners consented to part with them and try to control their grief while they worried along from day to day without them. These dogs were collected and placed in the secretary's room.

Throwing a heterogeneous mass of dogs together in that way, and all of them total strangers to each other, in the natural course of things creates something of a disturbance, and that was the result in this case. When the secretary arrived, the dogs were holding a session with closed doors. The presiding officer had lost control, and a surging crowd of yellow dogs had the floor. Only one dog was excepted. He was struggling with all his strength against the most colossal attack of colic that ever convulsed a pale, yellow dog. Just as he would get to feeling kind of comfortable, a spasm would catch him on the starboard quarter and his back would hump itself like a 1,000-legged worm, and with such force as to thump the floor with the stumpy tail of the demoralized dog and jar the bric-a-brac on the brackets and what-nots of the Secretary of Wyoming Territory.

Just then the secretary arrived. He was whistling a trill or two from the "Turkish Patrol," when he got within earshot of the convention. Several people met him and asked him what was going on up in his room. The secretary blushed and said he guessed there was nothing out of character, and wondered if someone was putting up a Conkling story on him, to kill a Spates boom.

When he got to the door and went in, thirty-seven dogs ran between his legs? and went out the door with a good deal of intensity. More of them would have run between the secretary's legs, but they couldn't all make it.

Mr. Spates was mad. He felt hurt and grieved. The dogs had jumped on the bed and torn the pillow shams into minute bandages, and wiped their feet on the coverlid. They had licked the blacking off his boots, and eaten his toilet soap. One of them had tried on the secretary's dressing gown; but it was not large enough, and he had taken it off in a good deal of a hurry.

Long after it was supposed that the last dog had gone out, yellow dogs, of different degrees of yellowishness, and moving in irregular orbits, would be thrown from the secretary's room with great force. Some of them were killed, while others were painfully injured. It is said that there are fewer yellow dogs in Cheyenne now than there used to be, and those that are there are more subdued, and reserved, and taciturn, and skinned on the back, than they used to be; while the secretary has a far-away look in his eye, like a man who has trusted humanity once too often, and been everlastingly and unanimously left.

WHAT WOMAN'S SUFFRAGE HAS DONE FOR WYOMING.

SOME TESTIMONIALS, AND ONE THING AND ANOTHER.

The managing editor of a Boston paper, is getting material together relative to the practical workings of Woman's Suffrage, and as Wyoming is at present working a scheme of that kind, he wants an answer to the following questions:

1. —Has it been of real benefit to the Territory?

2. —If so, what has it accomplished?

3. —How does it affect education, morals, courts, &c.?

4. —What proportion of the women vote?

ANSWERS.

1. —Yes, it has indeed been of real benefit to the Territory in many ways.

Until woman's suffrage came among us, life was a drag—a monotonous sameness, and simultaneous continuousness. Now it is not that way. Woman comes forward with her ballot, and puts new life into the flagging energies of the great political circles. She purifies the political atmosphere, and comes to the polls with her suffrage done up in a little wad, and rammed down into her glove, and redeems the country.

2. —It has accomplished more than the great outside world wots of. Philosophers and statesmen may think that they wot; but they don't. Not a wot.

To others outside of Wyoming, woman's suffrage is a mellow dream; but here it is a continuous, mellow, yielding reality. We know what we are talking about. We are acquainted with a lady who came here with the light of immortality shining in her eye, and the music of the spheres was singing in her ears. She was apparently on her last limbs, if we may be allowed that expression. But woman's suffrage came to her with healing on its wings, and the rose of health again bloomed on her cheek, and her appetite came back like the famine in Ireland. Now she wrestles with the cast-iron majolica ware of the kitchen during the day, and in the evening works a cross-eyed elephant on a burlaps tidy, and talks about the remonetization of the currency.

Without attempting to answer the last two questions in a short article like this, we will simply give a few certificates and testimonials of those who have tried it:

Prairie-Dog Ranche, Jan. 3, 1880.

"*Dear Sir.* I take great pleasure in bearing testimony to the efficacy of woman's suffrage. It is indeed a boon to thousands. I was troubled in the east beyond measure with an ingrowing nail on the most extensive toe. It caused me great pain and annoyance. I was compelled to do my work wearing an old gum overshoe of my husband's. Since using woman's suffrage only a few months, my toe is entirely well, and I now wear my husband's fine boots with perfect ease. As a remedy for ingrowing nails I can safely recommend the woman's suffrage.

"Sassafras Oleson."

Miner's Delight, Jan 23, 1880.

"*Deer Sur.* Two year ago mi waife fell down into a nold sellar and droav her varyloid through the Sarah bellum. I thot she was a Gonner. I woz then livin' in the sou west potion of Injeanny. I moved to where i now am leaving sevral onsettled accounts where i lived. But i wood do almost anything to recover mi waifs helth. She tried Woman's Suffrins and can now lick me with 1 hand tied behind hur. i o everything to the free yuse of the femail ballot. So good bi. at Present

"Union Forever McGilligin."

Rawhide, Feb. 2, 1880.

"*Dear Sir.* I came to Wyoming one year ago to-day. At that time I only weighed 153 pounds and felt all the time as though I might die. I was a walking skeleton. Coyotes followed me when I went away from the house.

"My husband told me to try Woman's Suffrage. I did so. I have now run up to my old weight of 213 pounds, and I feel that with the proper care and rest, and rich wholesome diet, I mav be spared to my husband and family till next spring.

"I am now joyful and happy. I go about my work all day singing Old Zip Coon and other plaintive melodies. After using Woman's Suffrage two days I sat up in a rocking chair and ate one and three-fourths mince pies. Then I worried down a sugar-cured ham and have been gaining ever since.

"Ah! it is a pleasant thing to come back to life and its joys again.

"Yours truly, Ethel Lillian Kersikes."

PORTUGUESE WITHOUT A MASTER.

I am spending my leisure moments these days studying the Portuguese language.

It is not very generally used, it is true, but I might meet a Portuguese some day who wanted to hold a conversation with me very much, and I would feel more at ease if I could speak the language with elegance and precision.

I am working at the task silently and earnestly without a master, and I am sometimes a little mystified by the startling and original exhibitions of imported syntax and etymology as shown in the English translations given in the book which I am studying. It is a kind of Portuguese primer, designed and constructed by Jose De Fonseca and Pedro Carolino, and although the Portuguese part of it seems to be all right, I am at times a little annoyed at the novel arrangement of the English translations.

The authors in their preface seem to convey the impression that other compilers and writers who have attempted this thing have not seemed to meet the demands of the times, but Messrs. Fonseca & Carolino intimate that they have supplied a want long felt, and they seem tickled almost to death over the fact that they have the bulge on their predecessors. In their apparently modest way they say:

"The works which we are conferring for this labor found use us for nothing, but those who were publishing to Portugal or out, they were most all composed for some foreign or some national, acquainted in the spirit of both languages. It was resulting from that carelessness to rest these works fill of imperfections, and anomalies of style, and idiotisms, for this language in spite of the infinite typographical faults which sometimes invert the sense of the periods."

Parties who have become cloyed with the spicy fragrance of "Fifteen" might find pleasing diversion in the foregoing sentence. It is quaint and unique in its style, and although I consider it perfectly original, I am led to believe that there are little poetic gems from Walt Whitman in it.

Further on the authors in poetic prose say:

"We expect them, who the little book (for the care what we wrote him and for her typographical perfection) that may be worth the acceptation of the studious persons and especially of the youth at which we dedicate him particularly."

Ah, how well those dark-eyed dwellers in perpetual summer know how to inspire even the dull and commonplace sentences of a preface with a living, breathing soul! How the threadbare language of apology and modest braggadocio used by the hesitating but puffed up author ever since the first work published by Moses, is made to submit to the tropical influence of sunny Portugal, and comes forth breathing the seductive odors of that glad clime where the poet's song of undying love to the dark-eyed maid is ever throbbing in passionate pulsations upon the perfumed air.

But I must give a Portuguese translation rendered back into English, of the well known anecdote told on the physician who didn't take his own medicine:

"A physician eighty years of age, had enjoyed of a health unalterable. Their friends did him of it compliments every days. 'Mister Doctor,' they said to him, 'you are admirable man. What you make then for to bear as well?' 'I will tell you it, gentlemen,' he was answered them, 'and I exhort you in same time at to follow my example. I live of the product of my ordering without take any remedy who I command to my sicks.'"

One fault with American wit, in my estimation, is its coarseness and lack of polish. I have mentioned it a great many times and wept over it in extreme sorrow. Here, however, we have it down fine. The Portuguese joke is no doubt the most mirth provoking, and at the same time the most refined and delicate joke now made. We send our manufactures to all foreign countries to successfully compete with theirs; but our joke can never hold up its head and ask for the award or bronze medal where these Portuguese rib-ticklers and button-hole busters and suspender wrenchers are allowed to compete for the free for-all prizes. The Portuguese joke with facings of same held in place with bias folds of something else, is really the most *recherche* joke now on the market. Americans may for years to come be able to furnish a good, fair, stoga joke that will do to stub around home with, but they cannot design a joke that will do to dress up in and wear on great occasions. The low-neck, Oxford-tie, Portuguese burst of humor, hand-sewed, with sole leather counter and steel shank, and with the name of the author blown in the bottle, is bound to command the highest market price for a century or more to come.

We may command the smoking car and Congress trade, but Portugal must furnish the easy riding, gentle, picnic and croquet joke. It may be also fed to invalids with a spoon. A friend of mine who had been sick for nine years took a Portuguese joke that I gave him right out of the can without diluting it, and by that means gradually led up to fricasseed oat-meal gruel stuffed with sawdust and other rich dishes. It saved his life, but his intellect is impaired so that he don't know a calcium light from the splendor of the New Jerusalem.

THE ROCKY MOUNTAIN HOG.

In speaking of the domestic and useful animals of Laramie, it would not be right to overlook the hog. I do not allude to him as useful at all, but he is very domestic. He is more so than the people seem to demand. I never saw hogs with such a strong domestic tendency as the Laramie hogs have. They have a deep and abiding love for home, all of them, and they don't care whose home it is either.

There is a tremendous pressure of hog to the square inch here. The town is filled with homeless, unhappy and starving hogs.

THE ROCKY MOUNTAIN HOG.

They run between your legs during the day, and stand in your front yard and squeal during the night. Most of them are orphans. When Thanksgiving comes it will bring no joy to them. It will be like any other day.

About all the fun they have is to root a gate off the hinges, and then run off with a table cloth in their mouths. We should not be too severe, however, on the hog. What means has he of knowing that there is a city ordinance against his running about town? Kind reader, do you think the innocent little hog would openly violate a law of the land if he knew of its existence? Certainly not. It is pardonable ignorance on the part of the hog, the same as it is with the Indian, which causes him to break over the statutes and ordinances of his country.

Our plan, therefore, is to *civilize the hog*. Build churches and school houses for him. Educate him and teach him the ways of industry. Put a spade and a plow at his disposal, and teach him to till the soil. The natural impulses of the hog are good, but he has been imposed upon by dishonest white men.

Long before man came with his modern appliances, the hog was here. He owned the land and used it to raise acorns and grub-worms on. But the white man has entered on the fair domain, and, regardless of his solemn treaties, has taken this land and asks that the hog, the original owner of the soil, shall be penned up in a little reservation ten feet by twelve, made of cheap pine slabs.

Every principle of right, and justice, and equity, and humanity cries out against this tyrannical action on the part of the white man. Men who would scorn to do a dishonorable act, ordinarily, snatch the broad lands that were formerly owned by the hog, away from him, and deliberately go to raising wheat on them. This is not right. We should remember that the hog has certain rights which we are bound to respect.

Did you ever stop to think, dear reader, that the hog of the present day is but a poor, degraded specimen of the true aboriginal hog, before civilization had encroached upon him? Then do not join the popular cry against him. Once he was pure as the beautiful snow.

THE BUCKNESS WHEREWITH THE BUCK BEER BUCKETH.

Buck beer is demoralizing in its tendency when it moveth itself aright. It layeth hold of the intellect and twisteth it out of shape.

My son, go not with them who go to seek buck beer, for at the last it stingeth like the brocaded hornet with the red-hot narrative, and kicketh like the choleric mule.

Who hath woe? Who hath babbling? Who hath redness of eyes? He that goeth to seek the schooner of buck beer.

Who hath sorrow? Who striveth when the middle watch of the night hath come, to wind up the clock with the 15 puzzle.

He that kicketh against the buck beer and getteth left.

Verily, the buckness of the buck beer bucketh with a mighty buck, insomuch that the buckee riseth at the noon hour with a head that compasseth the town round about, and the swellness thereof waxeth more and more, even from Dan to Beer—sheba. (Current joke in the Holy Land.)

Who clamoreth with a loud voice and saith, verily, am not I a bad man? Who is he that walketh unsteadily and singeth unto himself, "The bright angels are waiting for me?" Who wotteth not even a fractional wot, but setteth his chronometer with the wooden watch of the watchmaker, and by means of a tooth-brush?

Go to. Is it not he who bangeth his intellect ferninst the bock beer, even unto the eleventh hour?

BILLIOUS NYE AND THE AMATEUR STAGE.

A great portion of my time at present is taken up in preparations for my appearance in a few weeks on the amateur stage.

Excursion trains will run from Denver on this occasion, and no pains will be spared to make the grand spectacular hoo-doo one long to be remembered.

Whenever any society or association desires to make a few thousand dollars for the relief of knock-kneed Piutes, or to purchase liver-pads for impecunious Senegambians, it only has to advertise that I am to appear on the amateur stage in a heavy part.

I am not a brilliant success in the "Say-wilt-be-mine" part. Just as I get the heroine up close to me near the footlights, and begin to hug her a little as I would at home, and I temporarily forget that a thousand eyes are upon me, it comes over me that my wife is in the audience and does not seem to enjoy the play. This throws a large four-dollar gloom over the entire surroundings, and I seem to lose my grip, so to speak.

Many years ago when I was young and, as one might say, in the hey-day of vigorous manhood, and had an appetite like a P. K. Dederick Perpetual Hay Press, I consented to take a leading part, and although I could generally worry through a little light comedy, I had not then learned how rough and uncouth I appeared as the heavy lover. I therefore consented to hug a beautiful young thing before five hundred people, and in the full glare of the footlights, whom I would not have dared to wink at in her father's parlor at midnight, with the lamp turned clear down.

I have an easy, gliding stage gait that is something between a "pace" and a "rack." It is full of the very poetry of motion.

I "racked" up to the heroine at the proper time and told her how I loved her and how it was tearing me all to pieces, and so forth. Just as I was coming to the grand flourish, however, I forgot a word, and while I was thinking that up, the remainder of the speech slowly drifted away to where I couldn't get at it.

To add to the general hilarity of the occasion the stage manager, who was furnishing at that moment some pale blue lightning and distant thunder, and who happened to be drunk, threw in a heavy snow storm that should have gone into another piece.

I stood there waiting and trying to think of my part about thirty years, I should think. Any way, the snow got knee deep and the heroine excused herself and went away to warm her feet. She told me to call her up by telephone when I could think of my piece.

I thought the audience would be mad and mob me, but it didn't. There seemed to be general good feeling and harmony all the way through. I told them that I could not call to mind the exact words of my part, but if those present would like to hear a little poem that had gone the rounds of the press a good deal and which I composed myself, entitled "The Burial of Sir John Moore," I would render it in my own choice and happy style.

It is not a humorous poem, but the audience seemed to think it was, for all the way through from the time the procession started out with Sir John till he was planted, everybody was tickled nearly to death.

Now I do not take the part of the leading lover any more. The awkward young man who carries dead bodies off the stage is good enough for me.

A JOURNALISTIC CORRECTION.

OFFICE OF THE MEEK-EYED TARANTULA.

We have, it appears, said something, casually, in our kind-hearted way, that the sensitive *Slimtown Harmonica* has taken to heart, and feels badly over, so we will try, as far as possible, to place ourself in a correct position. We spoke of the *Harmonica* in connection with another subject which we took the liberty to write upon, and did so simply with the idea of using the *Harmonica* as a *simile*. We find, however, that we were wrong. The *Harmonica* is not a *simile*. On the contrary, it is a parabola. It is a base, inferior isosceles, and its editor is nothing but a cosmopolitan hypothenuse; and if he wants to take it up, we may be found at our office at any time between the hours of A. m. and p. m. We were wrong in speaking of the Harmonica as a comparison or a *simile* but we want it distinctly understood that we know what the *Harmonica* and its editor are, and we are not afraid to say so, either. They are pre-Adamite, vicarious isotherms, and we think that it is time the people of the west were apprized of that fact too..

BANKRUPT SALE OF LITERARY GEMS.

OFFICE OF THE MORMON BAZOO.

Little boys who are required by their teacher to write compositions at school can save a great deal of unnecessary worry and anxiety by calling on the editor of this paper, and glancing over the holiday stock of second-hand poems and essays. Debating clubs and juvenile lyceums supplied at a large reduction. The following are a few selections, with price:

"Old Age," a poem written in red ink, price ten cents. "The Dog," blank verse, written on foolscap with a hard pencil, five cents. "Who will love me all the while?" a tale, price three cents per pound. "Hold me in your clean white arms," song and dance, by the author of "Beautiful Snow," price very reasonable; it must be sold. "She ain't no longer mine, nor I ain't hern," or the sad story of two sundered hearts; spruce gum and licorice taken in exchange for this piece. "God: his attributes and peculiarities," will be sold at a cent and a half per pound, or traded for a tin dipper for the office. Give us a call before purchasing elsewhere.

The stock on hand must be disposed of, in order to give place to the new stock of odes and sonnets on Spring, and contributions on "the violet" and the "skipful lamb."

THOUGHTS ON MARRIAGE.

Marriage is, to a man, at once the happiest and saddest event of his life. He quits all the companions and associations of his youth, and becomes the chief attraction of a new home.

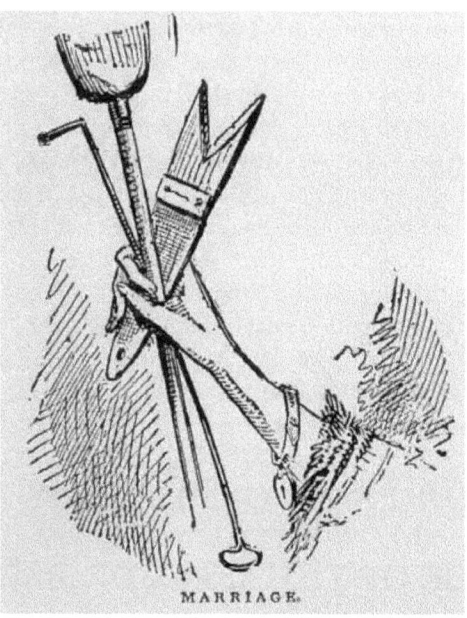

MARRIAGE.

Every former tie is loosened, the spring of every hope and action is to be changed, and yet he flees with joy to the untrodden paths before him. Then woe to the woman who can blight such joyful anticipations, and wreck the bright hopes of the trusting, faithful, fragrant, masculine blossom, and bang his head against the sink, and throw him under the cooking range, and kick him into a three-cornered mass, and then sit down on him. Little do women realize that all a man needs under the broad cerulean dome of heaven is love—and board and clothes. Love is his life. If some woman or other don't love him, and love him like a hired man, he pines away and eventually climbs the golden stair. Man is born with strong yearnings for the unyearnablc, and he does not care so much for wealth as he does for some one who will love him under all circumstances and in all conditions.

If women would spend their evenings at home with their husbands, they would see a marked change in the brightness of their homes. Too many sad-eyed men are wearing away their lives at home alone. Would that I had a pen of fire to write in letters of living light the ignominy and contumely and— some more things like that, the names of which have escaped my memory— that are to-day being visited upon my sex.

Remember that your husband has the most delicate sensibilities, and keenly feels your coldness and neglect. The former may be remedied by toasting the feet over a brisk fire before going to bed, but the latter can only be remedied by a total reform on your part. Think what you promised his parents when you sued for his hand. Think how his friends, and several girls to whom he had at different times been engaged, came to you with tears in their eyes and besought you not to be unkind to him. Do these things ever occur to you as you throw him over the card table and mop the floor with his remains? Do you ever feel the twinges of remorse after you have put an octagonal head on him for not wiping the dishes drier? Think what a luxurious home you took him from, and how his mother used to polish his boots and take care of him, and then consider what drudgery you subject him to now. Think what pain it must cause him when you growl and swear at him. Perhaps when you went away to your work you did not leave him wood and coal and water; does he ever murmur or repine at your neglect?

Ah, if wives knew the wealth of warm and true affection locked up in the bosoms of their husbands, and would draw it out, instead of allowing the hired girl to get all the benefit, what a change there would be in this earth of ours. But they never do until the companion of their joys and sorrows has winged his way to the ever-green shore and takes charge of the heavenly orchestra, and then for about two weeks you will see a violently red proboscis glimmering and sparkling under a costly black veil, after which the good qualities of the deceased will be preserved in alcohol, to be thrown up to No. 2 in the bright days to come.

Then, in conclusion, wives in Israel and other railroad towns, love your husbands while it is yet day. Give him your confidence. If your active corn manifests a wish to leave the reservation, go to your husband with it. Lean on him. He will be your solid muldoon. He will get an old wood rasp and make that corn look sick. He is only waiting for your confidence and your trust. Tell him your business affairs and he will help you out. He will, no doubt, offer to go without help in the house in order to economize, and he will think of numberless other little ways to save money. Do as we have told you and you will never regret it. Your lives will then be one great combination of rare and beautiful dissolving views. You will journey down the pathway of your earthly existence with the easy poetical glide of the fat man who steps on the treacherous orange peel. Your last days will be surrounded with a halo of love, and as your eyes get dim with age and one by one your teeth drop out, you can say with pride that you have never, never gone back on your solid pard.

A UTE PRESIDENTIAL CONVENTION.

The presidential conventions of last summer, and their attendant excitement, personal bitterness, and political sharpness, have called to my mind an occurrence in the history of a nation, of whose politics and whose statesmanship the civilized world knows but little.

Much has been said pro and con relative to the Indian character in general, and recently, of the Ute nation in particular, but those who knew the least have been most willing to shed information right and left, and to beam down upon the great reading world with the effulgence of the average cultivated lunatic.

I do not intend at this time to enlarge upon the question of western intolerance and eastern hero worship, as applied to the Indian nation, but simply to remark in my own gentle, soothing style, that those who know the Indian best, have the least respect and veneration for him.

At some other time I may say something relative to the Indian's home life, and attempt to show that while he appears in his public career to great advantage, both as a general and as a statesman, he is prone, like other great men, to little domestic irregularities. At this time, however, I intend simply to give some particulars of the great convention of 1875, which have never been brought to the eye of the reading public.

In the autumn of the above year at that delightful season when

> The maple turns to crimson,
> And the sassafras to gold.

When the soft and mellow light of the declining year sheds a subdued splendor of misty, dreamy languor over the snow-clad mountains and wooded canyons of Colorado, when the deep green of the mountain pine is darkly outlined against the pale gold of the poplar, and the cottonwood, and the willow, the chairman of the Republican central committee of the Ute nation, issued a call for a mammoth convention, to be held at Hot Sulphur Springs, for the purpose of nominating a candidate for head chief, to succeed Ula, whose term of office had expired by reason of his having violated the provisions of his first general order, in which he had pronounced himself as a champion of civil service reform.

The day for the grand convention had arrived, and Hot Sulphur Springs had become, all at once, a lively, bustling city. From every point of the compass came the wild shouts of the gathering delegates, with their credentials in one pocket, and their patriotism in pint bottles in the other.

The convention was called to order, and effected a permanent organization by electing Shavano as permanent chairman.

Shavano rose with stately gravity, bowed to the assembled convention, and walked to the platform, escorted by his trainer. He gracefully removed a quid of partially masticated government plug tobacco, and laying it carefully on the speaker's desk, said:

"Warriors of the Ute Nation, and Gentlemen of the Convention: We are gathered once more amid the solemn silence of the mountains, and under the dying leaves of the forest, to nominate a candidate to serve as executive of the Ute nation.

"Ula, the medicine man for this moon, who had hoped to be here, and who had his impromptu speech written for this occasion, will not be able to attend. I had hoped to see him here that he might act as secretary, but last evening he was shot by request.

"It seems that he had diagnosed the case of Prairie Dog, the son of Coyote, and had pronounced it to be membranous croup; but the coroner's inquest developed the fact that Prairie Dog had climbed the golden stair, the victim to a can of concentrated lye.

"A mighty nation, whose numbers are as the sands of the sea, can afford to let its medicine men fool around with its people and experiment with them till they meander up the flume, but the Ute nation is not large. It is a mere handful. We have only enough for a quorum, and we can not use any of them for scientific experiments. That is why Ula is on the evergreen shore instead of acting as our secretary to-day. At the request of the sorrowing friends of Prairie Dog, the medicine man's license was revoked, and Ula was fixed up for an extempore shot-pouch; so another person will have to act as your secretary.

"Warriors, I do not wish to trespass on your time. You have selected me as your chairman, and I thank you for the honor.

"We are now a small and powerless nation. Our war-cry is answered by the hilarious laughter of our foes. Once we were great. Our hunting grounds were without limit and our villages were as the leaves of the forest.

"To-day the white man plants his Swedish turnips above the graves of our ancestors. We are the orphan children of a great people and our sun is set.

"Once we were wealthy and powerful. Now we are poor and weak, and our wives cannot keep a hired girl.

"Why do the wails of our people echo among the canyons and desolated villages?

"Why are we left to mourn the loss of our wild horses and why are our own hillsides dotted with the locations and prospect holes of the pale face?

"Who is at fault that the graves of our fathers are staked as the 'Gilt Edge,' or the 'Bullion Lode,' or the 'Lucky Sal,' or the 'Calamity Jane,' or the 'Cross-Eyed Hannah with a Cork Limb?'

"I charge these woes of our people upon the puerile policy and fire-water reign of a democratic administration over the nation. [Deafening cheers.]

"Warriors and gentlemen of the convention: I have only one more word to say. I ask that the rotten fabric of the Ula, Bourbon, dyed-in-the-wool administration be overturned, that peace and prosperity may once more smile upon us.

"In conclusion I would ask the further pleasure of the convention." [Uproarious applause; the audience joining in "Old John Brown he had a little Injun."]

A committee on credentials was then selected, consisting of five members, of which Buffalo Tripe was chairman.

An adjournment to the following day at 10 A. m. was next taken by the convention.

The delegates were formally invited by the proprietor of the Jack Rabbit house to attend a little social walk-around and select scalp-dance on the following evening.

At the appointed hour the convention was called to order by the chair, and a report from the committee on credentials was called for.

Buffalo Tripe, on behalf of the committee, submitted the report that the delegates present were all entitled to seats, except that Dead Man's canyon had a double delegation.

The report of the committee on credentials was accepted, and the committee discharged. The chair then selected a new committee to examine the two delegations from Dead Man's canon, and instructed it to report adversely on the drunkest one.

This was regarded as a victory for the friends of Ouray, the favorite son from Stray Horse Gulch.

Nominations then being in order, the Silver-Tongued Cactus Plant from Middle Park arose majestically and said:

"Mr. Chairman and gentlemen of the convention: Our people have called us to do their work around the council fire and name for them a chief. [Loud cheers.] They look to us to-day for the assurance of their future prosperity.

"We stand in the moccasins of mighty men to-day with our tribes. Let us not betray their confidence. Let us be able to return to our squaws and pappooses with the smile of the Great Father upon us. [Applause.] It is a solemn moment for our whole nation, and the silence of a mighty forest amid the gathering storm is upon us. Mr. Chairman, I have the pleasure of nominating for our executive, Ouray, the man who never told a lie." [Thunders of applause and wild demonstrations throughout the entire wigwam.]

After the excitement had died away Hohne-pah-Snocke-monthegob, which in the Ute tongue means the man-with-the-patent-liver-pad, arose, and, laying aside a chew of tobacco about the size of an early rose potato, said:

"Mr. Chairman and delegates of the convention: I wish to put in nomination to-day Douglas, the amusing little cuss from Stinking Water. [Cheers.] I nominate him because he is a dark horse. As a candidate he is extremely brunette. His record is also on that order. I think he will run, as I may say, like a bay steer in the cucumber-patch. He is the swift-foot of the prairie, and the Mountain Zephyr of Cheyenne can not overtake him. He is also intellectual, and has written several little gems on spring. He is a philosopher, a scholar and a judge of whisky. He will harmonize the disaffected elements of our tribe, and secure the German vote. Douglas has a staving war record, and is lazy and shiftless enough to command the respect and esteem of the entire nation. The crisis seems to demand a standard-bearer who will meet the cunning of the pale face with the cunning of the red man, and I therefore make this nomination in order that I may go to my camp in the Gunnison country feeling that I have done my duty by calling the attention of my people to a man who is well calculated to lead us to success. Douglas has filled almost every position of trust or profit in our nation. He has held nearly every office within the gift of the people from watermelon stealer extraordinary up to most supreme bartender of the nation, and he has never betrayed a trust. I therefore do myself the great honor to place his name in nomination." [Cheers and bass drum solo.]

No more names were placed in nomination, and shortly afterward the convention had declared its preference for Ouray as its candidate.

He was called upon at his room by a committee and serenaded at the Jack-Rabbit House by a large band with torchlight procession.

On being called out, Ouray made a very short speech, as follows:

"Warriors and Fellow-Citizens of Indian Descent: I thank you for the honor you have conferred upon me to-day, and promise, if elected, to do all that I have agreed to do, besides what I may hereafter agree to do. I hope you will excuse me from making a long speech as I am very much worn out with my labors in securing this unexpected nomination. I also have an engagement to speak before the Young Men's Christian Association to-morrow, and also to address the Pocahontas Lodge of Good Templars the day following.

"I am very much overcome with surprise, this nomination having come entirely unsought, and compelled thus to receive a nomination forced upon me, together with the mental strain and constant worry necessary on my part to bring about this gratifying result, you will not be surprised that I thus abruptly close my remarks and bid you good-night."

This speech was greeted with round after round of applause, after which Douglas was called for by his friends. He did not meet with any great degree of success, for when he undertook to inhale a full breath and start his speech the friends of the regular nominee would present him with some antique eggs of the vintage of '49, and Douglas had to adjourn and rinse his mouth out with government whiskey. This occasioned delay and annoyance.

The delegates tripped the light fantastic till toward morning and then retired. In the afternoon they all arose with a light, maroon taste in their mouths, told the gentlemanly proprietor of the Jack-Rabbit House to charge their respective bills to the government, mounted their horses, and the most harmonious convention known to the world had become a matter of history.

THE CLUB-FOOTED LOVER OF PIUTE PASS.

A TALE OF LOVE AND COLD PIZEN.

CHAPTER THE FIRST.

Many years ago, when Wyoming was new and infested with the bear, the bunko-steerer, the buffalo and the bold, bad man, a little circumstance occurred there which is worthy of notice; and as it has never appeared in the newspapers, I give it as near as my memory will serve me in the narrative.

When Wyoming was a wilderness, and before the civilizing influence of the legislature and Pattee's lottery had toned down the rough outlines of the young commonwealth, there lived over on Horse Creek a ranchman whom we will call Henry Ward Beecher, as a kind of *nom de corral* as it were.

Henry Ward Beecher was a bachelor, and lived by himself. He did not know the loving influences and gentle yearnfulness of woman's society. His life was a howling wilderness, a wide waste of loneliness and wretchedness, because he was unmated.

Henry Ward Beecher did not know the pleasure of rising in the night and tangling his feet up in a corset lying on the floor, or of brushing his bald head in the morning with a hair brush so full of long, silky hairs that they would wind around his nose and tickle his bald head till he would wish he was dead. He was alone amid the solitude of the mountains, with no companion but a low grade, refractory mule and a flea-bitten, ecru-colored, mongrel dog, with one eye knocked out.

Henry thought, as year succeeded year, that he would make a change, and throw more joy into his humble life m some way or another, but he was making money, and kept busy all the time, so that he neglected it.

Finally one day in spring there came to the Ranche de Henry Ward Beecher a man from Ohio, named Obejoyful Jenkins. He had come west hoping to get a situation as president of a bank on the strength of being an Ohio man; but most all the banks seemed to have all the presidents they needed, so that Obejoyful concluded to compromise the matter, and herd sheep at twenty-five dollars per month and board. He struck Henry Ward Beecher and made a trade with him.

CHAPTER THE TWICE.

The two men soon became quite friendly, owing to their isolated condition, and told each other all their family secrets. Henry told Obejoyful how his grandfather was hung; and Obejoyful told Henry how he loved a girl in Ohio, named Oleander McTodd, and how he was going to send for her, and marry her as soon as he could raise the scads to bring her west.

Time flew on, and at last Obejoyful had saved up the collateral necessary to send for his soul's idol. He wrote to her, enclosing a post office money order for the amount necessary to pay emigrant fare to the railroad terminus, and also to buy *lignum vito* cookies, and fire-proof pie, at the lunch counters along the road.

About the day on which Oleander McTodd would naturally arrive at the ranche, Obejoyful was sent up on Stinking Water to round up a bunch of sheep that had escaped, and bring them back to the fold.

Then Henry Ward Beecher shaved' himself, put warm tallow on his boots, swept out the cabin for the first time in nineteen years, and waited for events to shape themselves.

CHAPTER THREE TIMES.

The orb of day rode slowly adown the crimson west. The snow-clad mountains stood leaning against the purple sky. They had done so on several occasions before. A woman, on an ambling palfrey of the cayuse denomination, rode down the mountain path to the cabin, and alighted. Henry Ward Beecher came to the door with some hesitation and no suspenders.

"Is't Obejoyful, me truant love, an inmate of this rural retreat, said a young, sweet voice, that sounded like the melody of a shingle mill.

"Nay, by my halidome he is't not. Gentle lady, on yester morn I did give him the grand bounce, and now he hath joined a hold-up outfit on the overland stage route. It pains me to tell to you this sad, sad news, for I wot ye art the damsel who erst was mashed on Obejoyful; but I cannot tell a lie; he is unworthy of you, and a cross-eyed, spavined snipe of the desert, and don't you forget it."

Then Oleander lifted up her voice to an elevation of about 14,000 feet above the level of the sea, and she wape with an exceeding great weep.

CHAPTER FOUR TIMES.

Henry Ward Beeeher let her weep till her surcharged orbs had ceased to give down, and then he brought out some valley tan that he had in the house for medicinal purposes and comforted her.

Then they got acquainted.

They sat in the gloaming, and Henry Ward Beecher turned the gas partly off, and held the hand of Oleander, and told her that Obejoyful had been a humorist on an Ohio paper, and otherwise destroyed the prospects of the absent lover in the eyes of Miss McTodd.

They looked into each other's eyes and knew that they were solid pards from that moment. Shortly afterward they rode away to the nearest justice of the peace, about 223 miles off, and were married.

Then they went home.

Obejoyful was there. He was also heeled; but H. W. B. got the drop on him. Then Obejoyful seemed filled with disgust, and he seemed oppressed and filled with nameless forebodings. He seemed to lose faith in mankind, also to some extent in womankind. He seemed to think that love wasn't exactly what it was represented to him by the agent. It didn't seem to be full weight, and there wasn't a prize in each and every package, as he had been led to suppose.

He then presented a bill to Henry Ward Beecher for $49.53, freight charges on Oleander McTodd; but H. W. B. swore with a great, blood-curdling, three-cornered oath that he would not pay it.

That night Obejoyful Jenkins procured some poison, and stole away to a quiet place, and wrote a note to tell his friends, when they found his body, why he had taken his own life. Then he commended his soul to Providence, poured out a glass of whisky, thought he would try it without the poison first. The draught revived him. He changed his mind and put the poison in Henry Ward Beecher's whisky, stole H. W. B.'s narrow-gauge mule Boomerang, and lit out for the North Park.

This is a true story. If the gentle reader has doubts about it I will produce the mule Boomerang, which is now in my possession and in a good state of preservation.

Hereafter, in order to save time and annoyance to my readers, true stories over my signature will be marked with a star, thus, *.

THE AUTOMATIC LIAR

Laramie City, August 23.—He came in gently but firmly, and felt in his pocket for something.

Finally he found what looked a little like an egg-beater and some like a new kind of speed indicator.

"I want to show you," he said kindly, "an office-dial to hang on your door, so that when you are away your clients will know where you are, and when you will return. For instance, by turning the thumb-screw, the dial will show:

"At court,

"At dinner,

"At supper,

"At bank,

"At post-office, etc., etc., etc., with the time you will return. There are sixty-four combinations which cover all cases of this kind necessary for the man of business, and it is no doubt the greatest achievement of mechanical ingenuity. Price, $ 1.50."

"No," said Mr. Biteoffmorethanhecouldchaw, "there are twenty-seven reasons why it would not be advisable for me to purchase your automatic bulletin. Firstly, I have but one client, and he can not read. He would only come and look at the indicator and kick it all to pieces and swear and go away. Secondly, your machine is incomplete, anyway. The inventor has signally failed to meet the popular want. It would only be an aggravation to the average attorney.

"I can think of a hundred things that ought to be added to a truthful indicator. Supposing that I have gone to the circus, or to a meeting of the vestry, or suppose I am drunk, or at a reunion of the Y. M. C. A., or out to eat a clove with a member of the bar, or at a camp meeting, or putting up the clothes-line at home? Or, going still further, suppose I am wringing out the clothes, or setting bread, or taking a bath, or wrestling with the delirium tremens, or toning down a rebellious corn, or putting Paris green on my squash bugs, or inspecting microscopically the homoeopathic fragment of ice that the kind-hearted ice man has prescribed for me?

"Or, going still further into detail, supposing that I am dead and cannot state with any degree of accuracy where I am or when I shall return, do you suppose that I would herald a glittering $1.50 lie to the world by saying that I was at the barber shop and would be back at 10:30?

"Do you think I would pay $1.50 for a machine to vicariously proclaim to the broad universe that I was at the bank, when I have no business with the bank?

"Do you suppose that I would advertise that I was at the post office when I was at the beer garden, or assert that I was at the court house, when, as a matter of fact, I was at that moment having a preparation of lemon-peel and other chemicals arranged for myself and another invalid in a cool retreat down town?

"No, sir! I spurn you and your cast-iron prevaricator, I promised my dying mother, who afterwards recovered, that I would never lie by machinery.

"If I cannot lie enough to keep up with the growing demand, I will resign like a man, and not call to my aid a cheap Jim Crow, hand-me-down-liar, costing $1.50 only.

"Always do right, and then you will never be put to shame.

"If you wish, you can leave the hall door ajar as you go out the main entrance."

Exeunt advance agent at upper left hand entrance, orchestra playing something soft and yielding.

SOME POSTOFFICE FIENDS.

The official count shows that only two and one-half per cent, of those who go to the postoffice transact their business and then go away. The other ninety-seven and one-half per cent, do various things to cheer up the postmaster and make him earn his money and wish that he had died when he was teething. They also make it exceedingly interesting for the other two and one-half per cent. When I go to the postoffice there is always one man who meets me at the door and pours out a large rippling laugh into my face, flavored with old beer and the fragrances of a royal Havana cabbage-leaf cigar that he is sucking. If he cannot be present himself he is vicariously on deck.

He asks me if my circus was a financial success, and how my custard pie plants are doing, and then fills the sultry air with another gurgling laugh preserved in alcohol.

I like to smell a hearty laugh laden with second-hand whisky. It revives me and intoxicates me. Still I am trying not to become a helpless slave to the appetite for strong drink in this form. There are other forms of intemperance that are more seductive than this one.

There is also a boy who never had any mail, and whose relatives never had any mail, and they couldn't read it if they did, and if some one read it to them they couldn't answer it. He is always there, too.

When he sees me he hails me with a glad smile of recognition, and comes up to me and stands on my toes and is just as sociable and artless and trusting and alive with childish glee and incurable cussedness as he can be. He stirs me up with his elbows, and crawls through between my legs until the mail is open, and then he wedges himself in front of my box so that I can't get the key into it.

Some day when the janitor sweeps out the postoffice he will find a short suspender and a lock of brindle hair and a handful of large freckles, and he will wonder what it means.

It will be what I am going to leave of that boy for the coroner to operate on.

Then there are two boys who come to the box delivery to settle the difficulties that arise during the day. They fight long and hard, but a permanent peace is never declared. It is only temporary, and the next day the old feud is ripe again, and they fight it all over once more.

There is also an amusing party who cheerfully stands up against the boxes and reads his letters, and laughs when he finds something facetious, or swears when the letter don't suit him. He also announces to the bystanders who each letter is from, and seems to think the great throbbing world is standing with bated breath quivering with anxiety to know whether his sister in Arkansas has successfully acquired triplets this year or only twins.

This, however, is an error, for the great, throbbing world, with characteristic selfishness, don't care a brass-mounted continental one way or the other. One day this man got a letter with a mourning envelope, and I heaved a sigh of relief, for, thought I, he will now go away and be alone with his great grief. But he did not. He stood up manfully and controlled his emotions through it all; and when he got through he broke into the old silvery laugh.

It seems that his brother in Oregon had run out of yellow envelopes, and had filled the one with the black border unusually full of convulsive mirth.

What a world of bitter disappointment this is anyhow!

Then there is the woman who playfully stands at the general delivery window, and gleefully sticks her fangs out into the subsequent week, and skittishly chides the clerk because he doesn't get her a letter, and he good naturedly tells her as he has done daily for seven years, that he will write her one to-morrow.

Then she reluctantly goes home to get rested so that she can come again and stand there the next day.

Then comes the literary cuss, who takes a weekly paper from Vermont with a patent inside to it. He reads it with the purest unselfishness to me, and points out the fresh, new-laid jokes that one always finds in the enterprising paper with the patent digestion.

He also explains the jokes to me, so that I need not grope along through life in hopeless ignorance of what is going on all about me.

There is a woman, too, who comes to the window and lavishly buys a three-cent stamp, and runs out her tongue, and hangs it over the stamp clerk's shoulder, and lays the stamp back against the glottis and moistens it, and has to run her skinny finger down her turkey gobbler neck to rescue it, and then she pastes it on the upper left-hand corner of the envelope, and asks the clerk to be sure and see that it goes. She then thoughtfully tells him who it is to go to, and gives a short biography of the sendee.

There can be no doubt that some women are more capable of doing certain kinds of business than men are. All classes of business requiring careful and minute explanations and concise and exhaustive directions can be better attended to by this class of women.

They enter joyfully upon the task of shedding collateral information in a way that would appall a man, and when they confide in you, you know that they are not keeping anything back. You almost wish sometimes that they would keep back a little of it and not rob themselvss.

Still, perhaps it is better that this class of women is not trusted with any great amount of business, for life is so brief, so evanescent, and so transitory.

It is but a step from the cradle to the grave anyway, and if a man stands on one leg an hour, and then on the other an hour, listening to extensive information every time he sells a stamp, he will die with his ambitions unfruitioned.

AGRICULTURE AT AN ALTITUDE OF 7500 FEET.

I herewith acknowledge the receipt of two bags of cane-seed from the Agricultural Department.

Mr. Le Duc is always thinking of me and evidently knew that I was yearning for some cane-seed. It will grow luxuriantly here on the spinal column of the American continent where winter lingers in the lap of spring till after the Fourth of July.

William says that this breed of sugar-cane "originated in Minnesota, and is claimed to have been the result of accidental hybridization."

I shall not allow anything of this kind myself if I can by the most tireless watchfulness avoid it. Accidental hybridization is what is demoralizing the sugar-cane of the whole country.

I shall plant this seed in drills two feet apart, mulching with rich top-dressing of retired gum boots and dead cats. I will then wait till the plant has germinated and appears above the surface, when I shall remove the boots and dead cats and rub the plants with a Turkish towel to promote a healthy circulation.

Then next fall while others who have sneered at me and called me a horny-handed buckwheater from the rural districts, are running up heavy bills for groceries, I will go out into my molasses orchard and pick a milk pan full of granulated sugar from my trees, or shell out enough maple sugar for breakfast at a slight cost and with the blessed consciousness that I did it all myself.

William is going to send me some more seeds that he thinks will do well in this tropical climate. If he could send me something that would be more hardy, like the early Swedish lemon-squeezer, or the mammoth custard-pie plant, or the Northern Spy cucumber tree, my reports to the department would be more cheerful than they are, but where plants have to wear their heavy California underclothes all through August they get discouraged and prefer to bloom in the sweet fields of Eden.

Last year I tried the hot-bed process, but it was not a signal success. This summer I shall use the hot-bed as an ice cream freezer. It wanted to act in that capacity last summer, but I had a freezer that did very well, so I foolishly used the hot-bed to assist the plants, although I know of several days in midsummer when my cabbage-plants had to get out of that hot-bed and run up and down the garden walk to keep their feet from freezing.

THE GENTLE YOUTH FROM LEADVILLE.

In addition to the other attractions about the depot, the old museum of curiosities from the Rocky Mountains has been re-opened. I like to go down and listen to the remarks of the overland passenger relative to these articles. There are two stuffed coyotes chained to the door, one on each side, and it amuses me to see a solicitous parent nearly yank his little son to pieces for going so near these ferocious animals. The coyotes look very life-like, and show their teeth a good deal, but it breaks a man all up when he finds that their digestive apparatus has been replaced with sawdust and plaster of Paris.

After a coyote gets to padding himself out with baled hay and cotton so as to look plump, he loses his elasticity of spirits, and we cease to respect him. Sometimes a tourist asks if these coyotes are prairie dogs.

A few days ago a man from Michigan, who has been here two weeks and wears a large buckskin patch where it will do the most good, and who is very bitter in his remarks about "tenderfeet," was standing at the depot, when a young man, evidently from a theological seminary, came along from the train whistling, "What a friend we have in Jesus." He walked up to the Michigan man, who began to look fierce, and timidly asked if he would tell him all about the coyote.

GENTLE YOUTH FROM LEADVILLE.

The Michigan man, who never had seen a live coyote in his life, volunteered to tell him some of the finest decorated lies, with Venetian blinds and other trimmings to them, while the young man stood there in open-mouthed wonder, with daylight visible between his legs as high as the fifth rib. I never saw such a picture of rapt attention in my life. As he became more interested, the Michigan man warmed up to his work and lied to this guileless youth till the perspiration rolled down his face. As the train started out, the delegate to the Young Men's Christian Association asked the Michigan man for his address. "I want the address of some good earnest liar," he said, "one who can lie by the day, or by the job, and endure the strain. I want a man to enter the field for the championship of America. Any communication you may wish to make will reach me at Leadville, Colorado. I have been in the Rocky Mountains ever since I was three years old, and have lived for weeks with no other diet but coyote on toast and raw Michigan man." He waved his hand at the M. man, and said: "If I don't see you again, hello!" and he was gone.

How many such little episodes we experience on our journey to the tomb!

A SNIDE JOURNALIST.

Recent occurrences here have seemed to absolutely demand that something be said relative to newspaper-men.

During my residence here I have been brought face to face with more fraud journalists than ever before, and I am forced to lift up my voice against it. I have met the ordinary-tramp who is pleased and happy if he be allowed to eat cold-grub and sleep beneath the twinkling stars, but the newspaper-tramp is meaner, more self assumed and has brighter prospects for perdition than all the rest. He stands out ahead of the rank and file of tramps as a kind of Major-General tramp, fearless and self reliant.

He feels the nobility of the profession of journalism, and indeed it is a calling of which its followers may well be proud, but the snide representative of the press is too proud. He puts on too many frills.

Perhaps I am too easily picked up in this manner, but I cannot help sympathizing with deserving newspaper men who lack many of the comforts of life. I have been there. I know what it is to battle with a cold world and wrestle with hunger. But now in the midst of prosperity, my heart goes out for these vagrants in such a way that just as I begin to get affluent, I find some subject for my charity, and I have to begin over again.

On Monday last a young man with a hopeful light in his eye, alighted from the eastern-bound train, and going into the Thornburg House, registered his name, at least we will play that it was his name, for no one else has since called in to claim it.

We will call him Brown as a matter of convenience. His front name, as I afterward learned, was Ward. I might say that, in putting this report together, another Ward has been heard from, but I leave that for the docile reader to do as he or she may see fit.

Mr. Brown then proceeded to get acquainted with the people of Laramie and be sociable. He was not so reticent as some prominent newspaper men are, but seemed to be the rollicking, jovial kind. He said that he was the travelling correspondent of the Salt Lake *Tribune* and also represented the Louisville *Courier-Journal*.

I wondered at the time what in the name of all that was handsome, the *Courier-Journal* wanted to pay a man and send him to the front for, with Laramie City as his objective point. Bye-and-bye he crossed my path and made himself known. Said he knew me by reputation, and then I began to get alarmed. I was afraid he was a detective. But he wasn't. I drew him out on the subject of Harry Watterson. He knew blank. Knew him well. Had slept with him. He and Hank had been drunk together several times.

Then I felt proud. He was an intimate friend of a great man, and sitting there talking with an unsophisticated youth like me just as naturally as life. It sounds like a book. I asked him up to my office, and made him sit in my best chair—the one with the four good legs—while I took the foundered one. I told him to make himself perfectly free with the luxuriant furniture of the office, and invited him to spit on the floor whenever it came handy. I told him that I knew great men didn't want to feel hampered while chewing tobacco, and that I wanted my guests to feel at ease.

He then took his knife, cut off a piece of tobacco, about the size of a paper weight, threw it back till it struck the gable-end of his mouth with a hollow thud, and proceeded to unroll the most gorgeous panorama of falsehoods that I ever listened to. Casually, while putting the fresco work on my floor, he took out a letter from Watterson, and showed it to me. Watterson writes about the same kind of a copper-plate hand that I do.

I wanted to take the letter and make a plaster cast of it, but Mr. Brown said Hank wouldn't like it. The letter went on in a free and easy way to joke Brown about looking too often on the maddening bowl, and then asked him to be a correspondent for the C. J.

The next day I came down town thinking about how easy it was for any one, by a straightforward, honest course, to rise in the world, and get acquainted with prominent men. Bye and bye I met the Sheriff. He asked me if I didn't want to go up to the jail and take a last look at my journalistic friend. I went up. Brown lay there in an easy position on an old blanket, in one of the cells.

The surroundings seemed to be in perfect harmony with the general appearance of Mr. Brown. He had taken off the large satin arrangement which served partly as a necktie, and partly to throw the public off its guard in relation to his shirt. The shirt was there, slightly disfigured, but still in the ring. It was the same shirt that he had started out in life with. He had outgrown it, and it looked feeble, but it was evidently determined to stay by Mr. Brown.

I looked at him and then broke into tears. Large $2.00 sobs convulsed my frame. I told him that he had basely imposed upon me, and led me to believe that he was a Republican, and now he had removed the mask as it were, and I could see that he was a Democrat. With these stone walls and iron grates, and that soiled shirt, I could no longer doubt.

I left him, resolving that hereafter I would not be betrayed by appearances. He will drift away into the mighty, surging mass of humanity, and we shall forget it. Perhaps, when the Governor of Maine holds a mass meeting and re-union at Augusta, he will be there. But he will drop out of my horizon like the memory of a red-headed girl, and I shall go on my way until some other newspaper man with a letter from Whitelaw Reid, or George Washington, or Noah, or some other prominent man, comes along, and then I shall, no doubt, open up to his view the same untold wealth of confidence and generous trust.

Those who are looking anxiously every mail for a copy of the Louisville *Courier-Journal* or the Salt Lake *Tribune*, containing a long letter about their town, will be disappointed. They will never come. Through the long visita of years and down through the mellow softened atmosphere of the Sweet Bye and Bye I hear the low, sad refrain, and it is refraining, "Never More." Instead of the merry prattle of Mr. Brown amid the loud echo of his expectorations as they fall with a startling crash upon the marble floor of my office, I only hear the rattle of the cast iron "come-alongs" and the tearful "Never More."

HE WAS BLIND.

While engaged the other day in writing a little ode to the liver pad, I heard a slight noise, and on looking toward the door I saw a boy with his hat in his hand standing on one leg and thoughtfully scratching it with the superior toe of the other foot.

I asked the freckled youth what I could do for him, and he said that there was a man at the foot of the stairs who wished to see me. I asked him then why in the name of a great republic and a free people he didn't see me. Then I told the boy that there was no admission fee; that it was the regular afternoon matinee, and it was a free show.

The frank and manly little fellow then came forward and told me that the man was blind.

It was not intended as a joke. It was a horrible reality, and pretty soon a man into whose sightless orbs the cheerful light of day had not entered for many years came up the stairs and into the office.

I said: "Ah, sir, I see that you are a poor, blind man. You cannot see the green grass and waving trees. While others see the pleasant fields and lovely landscape you wander on year after year in the hopeless gloom. Poor man. Do you not at times yearn for immortality and pine to be among the angels where the light of a glorious eternity will enter upon your sightless vision like a beautiful dream?"

This was a little sentiment that I had committed to memory, being an extract from the *Youth's Companion.*

He wiped away three or four scalding tears with his sleeve and said that he did. He was getting means, he said, to enable him to go to New York, where he was going to have his eyes taken out and refilled. He also intended to have the cornea filed down and a new crystal put in.

I asked him how much he thought it would cost. He said he thought it could be arranged so that $1,000 would pay the bill. At first I started to draw a check for that amount, and then I thought I would try him with a dollar first.

He took the dollar and walked sadly away.

It always makes me feel bad when I see a fellow creature who is doomed with uncertain steps and sightless eyes to tread his weary way through life, and I cannot be happy when I know that such misery is abroad in the land. I thought how much I had to be thankful for, how fortunate I had been to have all my senses and my bright and beautiful intellect, that I wouldn't take $400 for.

Then I wandered out to a saloon on A street to get a cigar. The blind man was there. He had just poured out about six fingers of Jamaica rum and was setting them up for the boys. I thought I would stand in with the arrangement, so I leaned up against the bar in very classic style and took two cigars at twenty-five cents apiece.

When he came to pay for the goods he shoved out the dollar I gave him, which I recognized, because it was a pewter dollar, and a very inferior pewter dollar at that.

The bartender kicked like a roan cow, and while the excitement was at its height I stole away to where I could be alone with my surging thoughts.

The blind man is still in town, but he is not succeeding very well. Unfortunately he has told several large openfaced lies and the feeling of pity for him has petered out, if I may be allowed that expression.

When he is sober he is going to have his eyes operated on at New York, and when he is drunk he is going to have them attended to in San Francisco. This gives the general appearance of insincerity to his remarks, and the merciless public yearns for him to pack his night shirt, like the Arabs and silently steal away.

THOUGHTS OF THE MELLOW PREVIOUSLY.

It is the evening of St. Valentine's Day, and I am thinking of the long ago. St. Valentine's Day is nothing now but a blessed memory. Another landmark has been left behind in our onward march toward the great hereafter. We come upon the earth, battle a little while with its joy? and its griefs, and then we pass away to give place to other actors on the mighty stage.

Only a few short years ago what an era St. Valentine's Day was to me.

THE REPORTER.

Now I still get valentines, but they are different and they affect me differently.

They are not of so high an order of merit artistically, and the poetry is more impudent and less on the turtle-dove order.

Some may be neglected on St. Valentine's Day, but I am not. I never go away by myself and get mad because I have been overlooked. I generally get valentines enough to paper a large hall.

I file them away carefully and sell them back to the dealer for next year. Then the following St. Valentine's Day I love to look at the familiar features of those I have received in the years agone.

One of these blessed valentines I have learned to love as I do my life. I received it first in 1870. It represents a newspaper reporter with a nose on him like the woman's suffrage movement. It is a large, enthusiastic nose of a bright bay color, with bias folds of the same, shirred with dregs of wine. How well I know that nose. The reporter is represented in tight green pants and orange coat. The vest is scarlet and the necktie is maroon, shot with old gold.

The picture represents the young journalist as a little bit disposed to be brainy. The intellect is large and abnormally prominent. It hangs out over the deep-set eyes like the minority juror on the average panel.

I can not help contrasting this dazzling five-cent valentine with the delicate little poem in pale blue and Torchon lace which I received in the days of yore from the redheaded girl with the wart on her thumb. With little of genuine pleasure have fame and fortune to offer us compared with that of sitting behind the same school desk with the Bismarck blonde of the school and with her alternately masticating the same hunk of spruce gum!

I sometimes chew gum nowadays to see if it will bring back the old pleasant sensations, but it don't. The teacher is not watching me now. There is too little restraint, and the companion too who then assisted in operating the gum business, and used to spit on her slate with such elegance and abandon, and wipe it thoughtfully off with her apron, she too is gone. One summer day when the little birds were pouring forth their lay, and the little lambs were frisking on the green sward, and yanking their tails athwart the ambient air, she lit out for the great untried West with a grasshopper sufferer. The fluff and bloom of existence for her too is gone. She bangs eternal punishment out of thirteen consecutive children near Ogallalla, Nebraska, and wears out her sweet girlish nature working up her husband's underclothes into a rag carpet. It seems tough, but such is life.

MY TOMBSTONE MINE.

Camp on Alder Gulch, June 18, 1880.

The general feeling of expectation and suspense which is the natural result of recent mineral discoveries near to any mining town, is still prevalent. If possible it is on the increase, and all the prevailing indications of profound mystery are visible everywhere. There is a general air of knowing something that other people do not. Almost every man is hugging to his bosom a ponderous secret which is slowly crushing him, while all his fellow men are trying to hold down the same secret.

Occasionally a man comes to me, takes my ear and wrapping it around his arm two or three times so that I can't get away, he tells me that he knows where there is the richest thing in America. Only he and his wife and another man and his wife know where this wonderful wealth is to be found.

He asks me to come into it so that capital will then be interested. I agree to it and on the way to the camp I overtake the able-bodied men of Wyoming, all of whom are trying in their poor, weak way to keep the same secret.

Such is life.

Sometimes I think that perhaps I had better give up mining. I do not seem to get the hang of the thing, somehow. All the claims I get hold of are rich in nothing but assessments, while less deserving men catch on to the bonanzas.

Once I located a vein which showed what I called good indications of a permanent vein, staked it out under the United States law and went to work on it. I paid out $11 for sharpening picks alone, in going down ten feet to hold it. It was mighty hard quartz, but the lead grew wider and better defined all the time till I got down ten feet and had an assay.

The assayer said that I had struck a marble quarry, but it was very inferior marble after all. Besides I found afterward that it was owned by Jay Gould and some other tender feet from New York.

Then I relocated the claim and called it The Marble-Top Cemetery Lode, and went away. Probably if I had gone down on it, the ore would have shown free milling tombstones and Power's Greek slaves and all that kind of business, but I felt kind of depressed all the time while I was at work on it. There was a kind of "Hark from the tombs a doleful sound," air about the whole mine.

Cummins City still booms. Building lots have gone up to $100 each. This for a place where a few weeks ago the song of the coyote was heard in the land, and where the valley of the river, and bald sides of the rugged mountains were unscarred, is a good showing.

The magical power of a mineral excitement to transform the bleak prairie and the rocky canyon into a thriving village at once, is something to command our admiration and wonder.

Two months ago, I might say, the little village of Cummins City was nothing but a little caucus of prairie dogs, and a ward meeting of woodticks.

Now look at it. Opera houses, orphan asylums, hurdy-gurdies, churches, barber shops, ice-cream saloons, dog-fights, musical *soirees*, spruce gum, bowling-allies, salvation, and three card monte. Everything in fact that the heart of man could yearn after.

As you drive up Euclid Avenue, you smell the tropical fragrance of frying bacon, and hear the recorder of the district murmuring with a profane murmur because his bread won't raise. Here and there along the river bank, like a lot of pic-nickers, the guileless miners are panning pounded quartz, or submitting their socks to the old process for freeing them from decomposed quartzite, and nonargentiferous clayite. Flying from the dome of the opera house is a red flannel shirt, while a pair of corpulent drawers of the same ruddy complexion, is gathering all the clear, bracing atmosphere of that locality.

As a picturesque tower on the roof of the Grand Central, the architect has erected a minaret or donjon keep, which is made to represent a salt barrel. So true to life is this new and unique design, that sometimes the cattle which roam up and down Euclid Avenue, climb up on the mansard roof of the Grand Central, and lick the salt off the donjon keep, and fall over the battlements into the moated culverin, or stick their feet through the roof and rattle the pay gravel into the custard pie and cottage pudding.

Bill Root, the stage driver, went out there during the early days of the camp, and with more or less red liquor stowed away among his vitals.

William is quite sociable and entertaining, even under ordinary circumstances, but when he has thawed out his digestion with fire-water, he talks a good deal. He is sociable to that extent that the bystander is steeped in profound silence while William proceeds to unfold his spring stock of information. On the following morning William awoke with a seal brown taste in his mouth, and wrapped in speechless misery. There was no cardinal liquor in the camp, (a condition of affairs which does not now exist,) so that William was silent. On the amputating table of the leading veterinary surgeon of Cummins City was found a tongue that had just been removed. It was really cut from the mouth of a horse that had nearly severed it himself, by drawing a lariat through it: but the story soon gained currency that an indignant camp had risen in its might, and visited its vengeance on William Root for turning loose his conversational powers on the previous day.

Great excitement was manifested throughout the camp, as William had not uttered a word as yet. Toward noon, however, a party of hardened miners, carrying a willow-covered lunch basket with a cork in the top, arrived in camp, and shortly after that it was ascertained that the conversational powers of Mr. Root still remained unimpaired.

The chaplain of the camp set a day for fasting and prayer, and the red flannel shirt on the dome of the opera house was hung at half-mast in token of the universal sorrow and distress.

This is a true story, which accounts for the awkward manner in which I have told it.

BANKRUPT SALE OF A CIRCUS.

As I write these lines my heart is filled with bitterness and woe. There is a feeling of deep disappointment this morning that has cast my soul down into the very depths of sadness. Some years ago the legislature of Wyoming conceived the stupendous idea that the circus instead of being man's best friend and assistant in his onward march through life, was after all a snare and a delusion.

This august body then passed a law that fixed the licenses of circuses showing in Wyoming Territory at $250, which was of course an embargo on the show business that, as I might say, laid it out colder than a wedge so far as Wyoming Territory was concerned.

The history of that law is a history of repeated injury and usurpation. Our people were bowed down to the earth with the iron heel of an unjust legislature and forced to drag out the weary years without the pleasures which come to other States and other Territories.

In the midst of this overhanging gloom, there were two men who were not afraid of the all powerful legislature, but boldly lifted up their voices and denounced with clarion tone and dauntless eye the great wrong that had been done to our people.

One of these men was a tall, fine-looking man, with piercing eye and noble mein. He stood out at the front in this unequal war and with his silvery hair streaming in the mountain zephyrs, he told the legislature that a justly indignant people would claim at the hands of her law-makers a full and ample retribution for the tyrannical act.

Judge Blair, Associate Justice of the Supreme Court of Wyoming, whether at the social gathering or the quarterly meeting, never lost an opportunity to condemn the unrighteous act or to labor for its abolishment. He fearlessly adjourned court time after time in order that the jury might go to Denver or Salt Lake to attend the circus, and embodied in one of his opinions on the bench the everlasting truth that "the usurpation of the people's prerogatives by the lawmakers of any State or Territory, in so far as to deprive them of a divine right inherent in their very natures, and compelling them to undergo a slavish isolation from the Mammoth Aggregation of Living Wonder? and Colossal Galaxy of Arenic Talent, was unjust in its conception and criminal in its enforcement." See Boggs vs. Boggs, 981. The other dauntless antagonist of the tyrannical law was a young man with pale seldom hair, and a broad open brow that bulged out into space like a sore thumb. He was slender in form like a parallel of longitude, with a nose on him that looked like a thing of life. This young man was myself.

Together we talked in season and out of season, laboring with the lawmakers with an energy worthy of a better cause.

We met with scorn and rebuffs on every hand, and the cold, hard world laughed at us, and unfeelingly jeered at our ceaseless attempts. But we labored on till last winter, the welcome telegram was flashed over the wires that the despotic measure was no more.

Then there was a general joy all over the Territory. Judge Blair sang in that impassioned way of his, which makes a confirmed invalid reconciled to death, and I danced.

When I dance there is a wild originality about the gyrations that startles those who are timid, and causes the average, unprotected ballroom-belle to climb up on the platform with the orchestra, where she will be safe.

Bye-and-bye the young man with the step-ladder and the large oil paintings, and the long-handled paste brush came to town, and put some magnificent decalcomania pictures on the bill-boards and fences; and Judge Blair and I patted each other on the back; and laughed seven or eight silvery laughs.

But in the midst of our unfettered glee a telegram came from Denver that the circus that had billed our town had been attached by the sheriffs. It seems that the elephant had broken into a warehouse in Denver and had eaten 160 bales of hay, worth $100 each in the Leadville market. The owner of the hay then attached the show in order to secure pay for the hay.

This necessitated a long delay and finally a sale of the circus. Everything went, the big elephant and the baby elephant, the band chariot with a cross-eyed hyena painted on it, the steam calliope that couldn't play anything but "Silver Threads Among the Gold," the sacred jackass from North Park, the red-nosed baboon from New Jersey, the sore-eyed prairie dog from Jack Creek, the sway-backed grizzly bear from York State, and the second-hand clown from Dubuque, all had to go.

Then they opened a package of petrified jokes and antique conundrums that had been exhumed from the ruins of Pompeii. It seemed almost like sacrilege, but the ruthless auctioneer tore these prehistoric jokes from the sarcophagus and knocked them down to the gaping throng for whatever they would bring.

The show was valued at $2,000,000 on the large illustrated catalogues and bright-hued posters, but after the costs of attachment and sale had been paid there was only $231 left.

Oh! what a sacrifice. How little there is in this brief transitory life of ours that is abiding. How few of our bright hopes are ever realized. How many glad promises are held out to us for the roseate future that never reach fruition.

GREELEY VERSUS VALLEY TAN.

I stopped over one day at Greeley on my return. Greeley is the town after which Horace Greeley was named. It is enclosed by a fence and embraces a large tract of very fine agricultural land.

The editor of the *Tribune* had just received a brand new power press. I asked him to come out and take something. He did not seem to grasp my meaning exactly.

Afterward I wandered about the town thinking how much dryer the air is in Greeley than in Denver. The throat rapidly becomes parched, and yet the inducements for the visitor to step in at various places and chew a clove or two are very rare indeed. I thought what a dull, melancholy day the Fourth of July must be in Greeley, and how tame and dull life must be to those who experience a uniform size of head from year to year. The blessed novelty of rising in the morning with a dark brown taste in the mouth and the cheerful feeling that your head is so large that you can't possibly get it out through your bed-room door, are sensations that do not enter here.

All the water not used at Greeley for irrigating purposes is worked up into a light, nutritious drink for the people.

THE ETERNAL FITNESS OF THINGS.

An exchange comes out with an article giving the former residence and occupation of those who are immediately connected with the Indian management. It will be seen that they are, almost without an exception, from the Atlantic coast, where they have had about the same opportunity to become acquainted with the duties pertaining to their appointment as Lucifer has had for the past two thousand years to form a warm personal acquaintance with the prophet Isaiah.

With all due respect to the worthy descendants of the Pilgrim Fathers, and not wishing to cast a slur upon the ability or the integrity of the dwellers along the rock-bound coast of New England, I will say in the mildest manner possible that these men are no more fit to manage hostile Indians than Perdition is naturally fitted for a powder house.

A man may successfully cope with the wild and fierce codfish in his native jungle, or beard the salt water clam in his den, and still signally fail as an Indian agent. The codfish is not treacherous. He may be bold, blood-thirsty and terrible, but he will never go back on a treaty. Who ever heard of a codfish going back on his word? Who ever heard of a codfish leaving the Reservation and spreading desolation over the land? No one. The expression on the face of a codfish shows that he is perfectly open and above board.

We might say the same of the clam. Of course if driven to the wall, as it were, he will fight; but we have yet to find a single instance in the annals of history where the clam—unless grossly insulted and openly put upon, ever made an open outbreak.

This is why we claim that clam culture and Indian management are not analogous. They are not simultaneous nor co-extensive. They are not identical nor homogeneous.

I feel that in treating this subject in my candid and truthful way, perhaps the Administration will feel hurt and grieved; but if so I can't help it. The great reading public seems to look to me, as much as to say: "What are your views on this great subject which is agitating the public mind?" I can't evade it, and even if President Hayes were an own brother, instead of being a warm, personal friend and admirer, I would certainly speak right out as I have spoken out, and tell the whole broad Republic of Columbia that to successfully steer a hostile tribe of nervous, refractory and irritable Indian bummers past the rocks and shoals of war is one thing, and to drive a salt water clam up a hickory tree and kill him with a club, is entirely another thing.

THEY UNANIMOUSLY AROSE AND HUNG HIM.

I was talking the other day with a Laramie City man about Leadville, he said:

"In addition to the fact of Laramie money being now invested there, we have sent many good citizens there to build up homes and swell the boom of the young city. We also sent several there of whom we are not proud. We still hold them in loving remembrance. Sometimes we go through the motions of getting judgments against these men, and making transcripts with big seals on them, and sending to Leadville to be placed on the execution docket of Lake county.

"We also sent Edward Frodsham to Leadville. We intimated to him that life was very brief and that if he wanted to gather a little stake to leave his family perhaps he could do so faster in Leadville than anywhere else. So he went. He is there now. He at once won the notice of the public there and soon became the recipient of the most flattering attentions. A little band of American citizens one evening took him out on the plaza, or something of that kind, and hung him last fall.

"The maple turned to crimson and the sassafras to gold, and when the morning woke the song of the bunko-steerer and the robin, Mr. Frodsham was on his branch all right, but he couldn't seem to get in his work as a songster. There seemed to be a stricture in the glottis, and the diaphragm wouldn't buzz. The gorgeous dyes of the autumn sunrise seemed strangely at variance with the gen d'arm blue of Mr. Frodsham's countenance.

"His death calls to mind one sunny day in the midsummer of '78. It was one of those days when there is a lull in the struggle for existence, and the dreamy silence and hush of nature seem to be concurred in by a committee of the whole.

"It was one of those days when, in the language of the average magazine poet—

> The flowers bloomed, the air was mild,
> The little birds poured forth their lay,
> And everything in nature smiled.

"But soon from out the silence, bursting upon the quiet air, came the sharp report of a pistol. Then another and another in rapid succession. People who were going to trade in that locality suddenly thought of other places of business where the same articles could be obtained cheaper. Men who were not afraid of danger in any form, went away because they didn't want to be called as witnesses on the inquest.

"The shooting went on for some time. It sounded like the battle'of the Wilderness. After a while it ceased. A large party of men went out to gather up the dead and arrange for a grand funeral. But the remains were not so dead as they ought to be. There were bullet holes to be sure, penetrating various parts of the combatants, but the funeral had to be postponed. The sidewalks were plowed up, signs were riddled and windows shattered, but Edward Frodsham got off with a bullet hole through the side. The doctor pronounced it a very close call, but not necessarily fatal. It was a terrible disappointment to every one. As a shooting match it was a depressing failure, and as a double funeral it was not deserving of mention.

"The city council told Frodsham that if he couldn't shoot better than that he might select some young growing town outside of Wyoming and grow up with it. He did so. He favored Colorado with his stirring, energetic presence.

"His grave grows green to-day on the sunny hill-side 'neath the bending willow, and the soft, sweet breath that is sighing through the pines and stirring the delicate ferns beside the glassy depth of the mountain stream, is singing his requiem. [Perhaps, however, I am rushing the season for Leadville a little; if so the last refrain after the word 'presence,' may be wrapped up in warm flannels and stored away till July.]"

RHETORIC VS. WOODTICK.

Camp on the New Jerusalem Mine, June 15.

It is impossible at present to say anything about what the future of this district may bring forth. Every lead shows up beautifully, and so much so, in fact, that claim owners are working first one and then another in order to hold them under the new law, which requires an amount of work to be done on the lead within sixty days which is generally only required within one year. This new regulation, which is the act of the district of course, may not stand any very severe test, but at present the miners are respecting it.

It is severe on me, however, and virtually leaves me out. What I need is a law that will not ride over and overthrow and freeze out the poor man. This law is passed in the interest of capital and in direct violation of the rights and privileges of the great surging mass of horny-handed workingmen like Brick Pomeroy and myself.

I havn't the time to particularize or describe the different mines visited, and if I were to do so the chances are that I wouldn't cover myself or the district with glory.

It is true that I know a foot wall from a windlass, with one hand tied behind me, but if I were buying a mine I would be about as apt to purchase a deposit of sulphurets of expectations, showing traces of free milling telluride of disappointment, as anything else.

The camp has about 300 miners and prospectors now within the city limits. All up and down the picturesque valley of the swift-flowing river the low cabin and white tent dot the green sward, and far above the everlasting hills rear their heads on high, torn by the Titanic power of giant heat in the days of the long ago.

I said this to Professor Paige, the scientific correspondent of the *Inter-Ocean*, who accompanied me. I thought that perhaps it would tickle him to know that I could reel off a sentence like that, but it didn't affect him in that way. On the contrary, he seemed to think that the heat must have affected me in some way.

We climbed Jehu mountain on the evening that we arrived in camp. We thought it would be the proper thing to do, so we dug our toe-nails into the prehistoric granite and the micacious what's-his-name and climbed to the top.

For a few minutes we didn't mind it much and got along first-rate, trying to make each believe that climbing mountains was our regular business.

I began to tell the Professor a little harmless lie about how I had travelled among the Alps, but I didn't finish it. Somehow I felt like breathing in what atmosphere was not in actual use, but I didn't have any place to put it.

The air at Jehu Mountain is good enough what there is of it, but it is too rare. If a man could let out the back straps of his vest and breathe in the unoccupied atmosphere lying between the Laramie river and the Zodiac it would be all right, but he can't do it. His intentions are good, but his skin isn't elastic enough to hold the diluted fluid.

We climbed up to where we could see the silvery moon rising like a pale schoolma'am and looking sadly across the dark valley asleep in night's embrace. I thought it was time to say something.

"Professor," said I, as my brow lighted up like a torchlight procession, and my voice broke upon the hush and solitude of evening like the tremulous notes of the buzz saw, "do you not think that far away amid the unknown worlds which drift through space and along whose track the drifting systems of planets wheel and circle through countless ages, while man, clothed in a little brief authority, cuts such fantastic tricks Before high heaven as makes the angels weep, regarding himself as the center of the solar system, planning to frustrate the immutable laws of nature, violating the prime and co-ordinate common law of universes, going behind the returns, as it were, trying to peer behind the veil, as I might say, prognosticating the unprognosticatable, evading the axioms and by-laws which not only regulate worlds and their creation, but link the phantasmagoria of diagonal animalculæ and cast broadcast the oleaginous incongruity of prehistoric usufruct?"

The Professor didn't say anything. He didn't seem to have followed me. Somewhere the thread had been broken, and the glowing truths couched in such language as would light up the pages of history and astronomy, were lost upon the silent air.

The Professor seemed sad and anxious and preoccupied. There was a look of apprehension and doubt and distrust in his eye, and he moved about uneasily. I asked him if there were any last words that I could carry to his friends, and ii there were any little acts of humanity and friendship which I could perform to render his last moments more pleasant.

He said there were.

Then he told me that a wood-tick was slowly but surely boring a hole into his spinal column, near where the off scapula forms a junction with the nigh one, and asked me to help bring him to justice.

We should learn from this that heaven-born genius, with the music of poetic language and aflame with an inspiration almost miraculous, sometimes makes less impression upon the listener than a little insect no larger than a grain of mustard seed.

THE MODEL WIFE.

Dr. Westwood lectured here on Wednesday evening on the Model Husband. He wanted me to sit upon the stage as the horrible example, but I declined. He was quite pointed in his remarks all the way through, and seemed to have me in his mind when he described the model husband, although of course he used a fictitious name. The lecture was a good one, and very well liked by the husbands who had to sit and take it for an hour and a half. Let the gentle male reader imagine himself sitting for that length of time with his own wife on one side of him and another man's wife on the other side of him, and when the speaker makes a point on the old man to get alternate jabs in the side from the delighted ladies.

I shall lecture here during the winter on the subject of the "Model Wife." I will then get even. I will tell how the young man with bright hopes, and thinking only of the great, consuming love he has for his new spouse, is torn away from the hallowed ties of home and the sunny influences of young companions, and buried in the poverty-stricken cottage of a woman who cannot begin to support him in the style in which he has been accustomed.

It is high time that this course of disgraceful misrepresentation on the part of young women should be exposed. I once knew a young man with the most gentle and trustful nature. He had never known care or sorrow. But an adventuress with winsome smile and loving voice crossed his path and allowed him to think that she could maintain a husband like other women, and in his blind adoration for her he bade good-bye to his home and its joys and madly walked out with her into the great, untried future. She told him that he should never know the cruel sting of poverty, and other romantic trash, and look at him to-day. He is a broken-hearted man. His wife does not take him into society; does not keep him clothed as other men are clothed, and grudgingly gives him the little pittance from week to week which she earns by washing.

Is it strange that his pillow is wet with tears, and in his agony he cries out upon the still air of night, "Oh, mother, why did I leave thy kindly protection and overshadowing love and marry a total stranger?"

Then the woman who has sworn to protect and love and cherish him kicks him in the pit of the stomach and harshly tells him to "dry up."

I sometimes think that if mothers knew to what sorrow and gross and shameless treatment their sons were to submit all through their lives, they would put them out of their misery with a base-ball club. Some mothers do try this but they postpone it too long and the sons get too large and more difficult to kill than when their skulls are young and tender.

I have always maintained that a kind word and a caress will do more for the great yearning nature of the husband than harshness and severity. The tuue wife may reprove her husband when he spills coal all over the Brussels carpet and then steps on it and grinds it in, but how much better even that is than to kick him under the bed and then sit down on him and gouge out his eyes with a pinking iron.

I know that men are too often misunderstood. They may be rough on the exterior but they can love Oh, so earnestly, so warmly, so truly, so deeply, so intensely, so yearningly, so fondly and so universally!

Always kiss your husband good-bye when you go down town to your work. It may be the last time. I once knew a wife who went down town to price a new dolman, and because she was vexed about something she did not kiss her husband but slammed the door and left him. When she returned he was a corpse!

While peeling the potatoes for dinner with the carving knife, he had stepped on a clothes pin, which threw him forward over the baby carriage, the knife entering at the northeast corner of the gizzard and sticking out beneath the shoulder blade about two feet into space. What a scene for the now repentant wife. There, in the full vigor of his manhood, lay all that was mortal of her companion—dead as a mackerel!!!

Let us take this home to ourselves, and ask ourselves today if we are doing the square thing by the only husband we have. Are we loving him as we should, or are we turning this task over to the hired girl?

Intemperance, too, is a fruitful cause of connubial unhappiness. Young man, beware of a wife who loves the flowing bowl. I once knew a beautiful young lady, talented and with good business ability. The entire circle of her acquaintance admired and respected her, but alas! one evening at a banquet her companion, with a heavenly smile, asked her to drink wine. Gradually the taste grew upon her, and although she married, she could not support her husband, and he gradually pined away and died brokenhearted. He used to sit up nights for her to come home, and he caught the inflammatory rheumatism and swelled up and died. It was a terrible thing. I tell you we cannot be too careful. You take a handsome young man like the author of these lines and his power for good or evil is untold. I sometimes wish that I had not been constructed with so much dazzling beauty to the square inch, and I am almost tempted to go and disfigure myself some way. If I were to ask a fair gazelle on New Year's day to come and join me in a social glass and then throw one of those melting 2 by 8 glances of mine on her, I know for a moral certainty that before night she would be in the calaboose. But I shall guard against that. Nothing of that kind shall ever be laid at my door. I promised my aged parents when I left the old homestead that I would never set 'em up for anyone.

SOME OVERLAND TOURISTS.

The varied classes of tourists passing over the Union Pacific Railroad, representing as they do all classes of humanity, seem to call for a brief notice from the nimble pen of a great man.

During my short but eventful life I have given a large portion of my time to studying human nature. Studying human nature and rustling for grub, as the Psalmist has it, have occupied my time ever since I arrived at man's estate.

There is one style of tourist which I am more particularly devoted to, perhaps, than any other. It is the young man who is in search of health for his invalid mustache. Only last week I saw one of these gentle youths who was going to try sea air and California fruit to see if he couldn't rescue his consumptive mustache from the jaws of death.

When he got off here and took the poor thing out to where it could look about and see the green plains and snow-capped mountains, I felt sorry for him. It is hard for one to be a successful tourist with a pale invalid along with him night and day, and I could imagine how that young man would have to get up nights when his mustache got restless and needed fresh air or wanted to take its tonic.

It was certainly the most gentle, retiring, modest mustache I ever saw. It didn't seem to care for anything only to be loved.

Every little while the youth would reach up to where it was and feel around nervously to see if it had climbed the golden stairs or was still on deck.

It was not a heavy mustache at all. It was about as voluptuous as a buffalo gnat's eye-brow.

I never saw a mustache before that brought the scalding tears to my eyes like that one. I thought how lonely the young man would be when it had glided up the flume and left him in this cold, uncharitable world with nothing to love and cling to but an earnest and unhappy boil on the back of his neck that wouldn't come to a focus.

Sometimes I go down to the train to see some fair young girl who is on the overland trip. But I am not always gratified.

A short time ago I went over, feeling as though I would like to see a fair young creature full of life and joy and with the light of a joyous future shining in her lustrous eyes.

It didn't seem to be her train. It was the day that a woman was on board with a Russia iron alapaca dress and white eyes. She was from Winnipewankiegingersuappetymagoggery, Maine.

She had a little sore-eyed boy with cream-colored hair and freckles on his face as large as a veal cutlet.

The boy would occasionally walk along the platform with his fore finger rammed into his mouth and hooked around his wisdom tooth. He would walk along looking up into the sky, and running into everybody and falling over the baggage truck till his mother got quite irritated, and I told the boy that the future looked dark for him unless he braced up and stopped pulverizing people's corns.

Bye and bye the boy ran into a blind man and knocked the wind out of him, so that all he could do for ten minutes was to stand there and gasp for breath as though he wanted to breathe in the vast realms of space.

Then his mother extended a long, bony hand with a large silver ferule on the biggest finger, and she laid hold of that lemon-colored kid of her's and gathered in as much of his ear as her hand would hold. She churned him up pretty good, and it didn't seem to be very much exertion for her either. Every little while he would make an aerial flight and back he would come, his boots banging against the car with a loud report. Finally the woman with the white eye, from Winnipewankiegingersuappetymagoggery, Me., consolidated her efforts for one grand flourish, but while in mid-air the boy's ear unscrewed and he lit out through the firmament, falling in a shapeless mass on the other side of the second-class car, where his gentle mother found him and gathered him up in her gingham apron.

There are lots of these little queer and amusing circumstances taking place here almost every day, and I have often thought that if some one with a taste for the ridiculous would turn his attention in that direction he would make an interesting sketch of them.

During the month of June we had a heavy snow storm, and it pleased the average tourist very much to be able to snow ball in mid-summer, so that he could tell his friends about it when he got home.

One intellectual Hercules, with a head about as large as a gum drop and a linen hat like the dome of the Mormon Temple, thought it would be a frisky little thing to throw some snow in the face of a sensible man engaged in conversation on the hotel pavement. The sensible man mopped the snow out of his face and went on with his conversation till the train was ready to start and the mental giant had forgotten all about it.

Then the large man walked up to the watery-eyed youth with a big lunch basket full of snow and proceeded to stow it away around the features of the youthful snide with the skim-milk optic. He used what he could get near by, trying to fill his ears full, but couldn't get snow enough. Then he took what he had left and worked it down inside the voluptuous shirt collar of the bilious young man from the Normal school.

I enjoyed it first-rate because I can not bear to see a feminine tourist like this young man, wearing men's clothes and trying to play himself for a man. When a man wants to be a merry laughing girl and can't, and he stands trembling on the dividing line between manhood and womanhood and hesitating which way to fall, I often wish that I had a foot like Brigham Young's tombstone with a swing to it like a pile driver and I would like to kick the young man with the old gold hat band and the polka dotted necktie so far into the realms of space that when he fell people would think he was a red-headed meteor looking for a soft place to fall into.

CATCHING MOUNTAIN TROUT AT AN ELEVATION OF 8000 FEET.

A few days ago, in company with Dr. Hayford, I went over to Dale Creek on a brief extempore trouting expedition. Dale Creek is a beautiful and romantic stream running through a rugged canon and crossed by the beautiful iron bridge of the Union Pacific Railroad.

We went up Dale Creek at this season of the year is not very much of a torrent, and on the day we went over there all the trout had gone down to the mouth of the stream to get a drink.

Every little while the Doctor would put on his glasses and hunt for the creek while I caught grasshoppers and looked at the scenery. I did not catch any trout myself, but the Doctor drove one into a prairie-dog hole and killed him. I am frantically fond of field sports although I am not always successful in securing game. I love to wander through the fragrant grass and wild flowers, listening to the song of the bobolink as he sways to and fro on some slender weed; but it delays me a good deal to stop every little while and cut on No. 4 and returned on No. 3.

TROUT FISHING.

My fly hooks out of my clothes. I throw a fly very grace, fully, but when it catches under my shoulder-blades, and I try to lift myself up in that manner, my companions laugh at me and make me mad.

Dr. Hayford, who had command of the expedition, told me that we would have an hour and three quarters to fish and then we would have to go back and catch the train. Therefore we hurried a good deal, and I had to leave a decrepit trout that I had found in a dead pine tree and was almost sure of. We gathered a bouquet of wild roses and ferns and cut worms and went back to the bridge to wait for No. 3. We sat there for an hour or two on a voluptuous triangular fragment of granite, telling large three-ply falsehoods about catching fish and shooting elephants in Michigan. Then we waited two or three more long weary hours, and still the train didn't come.

After a while it occurred to me that I had been made the victim of the man who had spent the most of his life telling the public about the pleasant weather of Wyoming. He enjoyed my misery and cheered me up by saying that perhaps our train had gone, and we would have to wait for the emigrant-train. We ate what lunch we had left, told a few more lies, and suffered on.

At last the thunder of the train in the distance was borne down to us, and we rose with a sigh of relief, gathered up our bouquets and decomposed trout, and prepared to board the car. But it was a work train and didn't stop.

Then I went away by myself and tried to control my fiendish temper. I thought of the doctor's interesting family at home, and how they would mourn if I were to throw him over Dale Creek bridge, and pulverize him on the rocks below. So my better nature conquered and I went back to wait a few more weeks.

The next train that came along was a freight train, and it made better time going past us than at any other point on the road.

Toward evening the regular passenger train came along. I found out which coach the doctor was going to ride in, and I got into another one. I look my poor withered little bouquet and looked at it. All the flowers were dead and so were the bugs that were in it. It was a ghostly ruin that had cost me $9.25. An idea struck me, and I gave the bouquet to the train boy to sell. I told him what the entire array of ghastliness had cost me, and asked him to get what he could out of it.

He took the collection and sold it out to the passengers, realizing, $21.35. Passengers bought them and sent them home as flowers collected at Dale Creek bridge in the Rocky mountains. Then a kind hearted gentleman on the train, who saw how sad I looked, and how ragged my clothes were, where I had cut fish-hooks out of them, took up a collection for me.

Hereafter when a man asks me to join a fishing excursion to the mountains, I hope that I shall have the moral courage and strength of character to refuse.

HOME-MADE INDIAN RELICS.

Sherman, on the Union Pacific Railroad, is the loftiest by a considerable majority of any point on the road. This fact has occasioned some little notoriety for Sherman, and on the strength of it a small reservoir of Western curiosities has been established there.

I went over to the curiosity ranche while the train was taking breath, to see what I could see and buy it if the price were not too high.

There were a great many Western curiosities from various parts of the country, and I got deeply interested in them.

I love to find some old relic of ancient times or some antique weapon of warfare peculiar to the noble Aztecs. I can ponder over them by the hour and enjoy it first-rate.

Among the living wonders I noticed a bale of Indian arrows. These arrows are beautiful to look upon, and are remarkably well preserved. They are as good as new. I asked, simply as a matter of form, if they were Indian arrows. The man said they were. Then I asked who made them, and he got mad and wouldn't speak to me.

I do not think I am unreasonable to want to know who makes my Indian arrows, am I?

I am willing to pay a fair price for the genuine Connecticut made arrow with cane shaft, and warranted cast steel point, but the Indian arrow made at Omaha is not durable.

This curiosity man would make more money and command a larger trade if he were not so quick-tempered.

He had also some Western cactus as a curiosity for the tenderfoot who had never fooled with a cactus much.

It was the clear thing, however. I sat down on one to test its genuineness. It stood the test better than I did. When you have doubts about a cactus and don't know whether it is a genuine cactus or a young watermelon with its hair banged, you can test it by sitting down on it. It may surprise you at first, but it tickles the cactus almost to death.

For a high-priced house plant and gentle meek-eyed exotic that don't care much for affection, the Rocky Mountain cactus takes the cake.

It is very easy to live, and don't require much fondling. It will enjoy life better if you will get mad at it about once a week and pull it up by the roots, and kick it around the yard. Water it carefully every four years; if you water it oftener than that, it will be surprised, and gradually pine away and die.

Another item I must not forget in giving directions for the cultivation of this rare tropical plant: get some one to sit down on it occasionally—if you don't feel equal to it yourself. There's nothing that makes a cactus thrive and flourish so much as to have a victim with linen pants on, sit down on it and then get up impulsively like. If a cactus can have these little attentions bestowed upon it, it will live to a good old age, and insinuate itself through the pantaloons of generations yet unborn. Plant in a gravelly, coarse soil, and kick it every time you think of it.

Returning to our subject, however, I think the Indian is a trifle uncertain and at times tricky by nature. Of course I do not wish to say anything that would have a tendency to injure the reputation of the Indian, for in all candor I will say that he means well.

I do not wish to have what I may say published as coming from me, because the Indian has always used me well, perhaps because I never allow myself to stray into his jurisdiction, but he has little, hateful, mean ways which I despise. Some think that if he were to have more chance to learn, more normal schools and base-ball clubs and upright pianos, he would have more ambition to do right and get ahead, but I almost doubt it.

I am very humane myself, but I am more apt to be harsh in my measures with the Indian than most Eastern people of culture are. Perhaps this is because I have seen people who had been shot full of large size bullet holes by the red man. This makes a difference, and I may be prejudiced.

When the average philanthropist has seen a family lying scattered around promiscuous and shot so full of holes that even the coarsest kind of food is of no use, he begins to ask in his mind whether a more severe method of treatment would not be beneficial to the Indian.

I want to look this matter calmly in the face, and ask whether night shirts and civilization and suspenders will make good citizens out of these unfettered children of the forest or not? Is it the opinion of the gentle reader that a nation of flea-bitten, smoke-tanned beggars will come forward and submit to the ennobling influences of Christianity and duck vests and horse-shoe scarf pins and quarterly meetings and gauze underwear? Methinks not.

Nature constructed the noble red man with certain little mental, moral and physical eccentricities, and these eccentricities can be better worn away and remodeled on the evergreen shore.

Poor, weak, fallible man cannot successfully grapple with the task of working over an entire nation of human beings and changing the whole trend, so to speak, of a nation's mental and moral nature.

Let us not, therefore, usurp the prerogative or attempt to perform the Herculean task which a wise Creator has laid out for Himself.

The policy of Divine administration, if I mistake not, is to improve the Indian and reform him in a future state in a large corral where the worm dieth not. This of course is only my private opinion, and I am offering it now in packages containing six each, securely boxed and sent free to any address on receipt of $1. I would sell it cheaper were it not for the excessive freight and the recent rise in white paper.

Supposing then the above to be the correct theory, what can poor erring man do to forward the good work? Evidently he can do nothing unless it be to change the state of the red man from a discouraging and annoying mortality to a bright and shining immortality.

I would suggest that this be done so far as possible by those who can spare the time and ammunition to do so. I will give to such all the encouragement and moral support I can. I would assist in the good work, but I am most too busy now planting my raspberry jam and setting out my early Swedish dried apple pie plant.

THE PREVIOUS REPORTER.

Fluke MaGilder, an old Washington reporter, who afterward was well known among Western newspaper men, was one of the most tireless and persistent news-gatherers I ever knew. He used to tell with considerable apparent pleasure how he didn't obtain the points on a prominent military court martial which was held at Cheyenne in 1876. It happened on this wise:

When it was known for a dead certainty that the court-martial had closed, and that the result was sealed up in an envelope in the possession of General Pope, who roomed at the Inter-Ocean, Fluke got up an infernal lie to tell the General, and thus got him away from his room. He induced a little negro boy, by promising him an old pair of pants, to go up and deliver a note to General Pope, saying that General Merritt was out at Fort Russell, and that he wanted to see him immediately. After the General had gone Fluke crawled into the transom of his room, and began to ransack things. It turned out, however, that the documents were safe in the General's overcoat pocket, and MaGilder was baffled. He searched all the drawers in the room, looked under the bed, rummaged the pockets of all the extra clothes in the room, and the more he searched the madder he got, and when at last it dawned upon him that he was foiled, his wrath knew no bounds. He filled his pockets with the General's cigars, drank the General's wine, and wiped his nose on the General's best clean handkerchiefs. He spit tobacco juice in the General's slippers, wiped his feet on the pillow shams, dressed the coal-stove up in the General's night shirt, and spread a few spare hairpins which he had in his pockets, under the General's pillow. He was pretty mad. He took the spittoon and stood it on the center-table, with a tooth brush sticking in the middle, and wound up by trying on the General's underclothes and tearing the ruffles off. It is so well established that Fluke had a great deal of *embonpoint*, that it is unnecessary to say he had a good deal of trouble to get into General Pope's apparel, as the General is a slim man. However, as MaGilder stood in the position of a boy who is just on the point of going in swimming, and had the last garment drawn over his head, so that he could not see very well, General Pope slipped in with a large snow-shovel, which he applied with great vigor. When they offered Fluke a chair at a party after that he would murmur, "No, thank you, I prefer to stand up. I've been sitting down all day and wish a change." But everybody knew that he hadn't sat down for over a week.

THE PEACE COMMISSION.

EVIDENCE OF JOHNSON BEFORE THE COURT.

Los Pinos, Col., Nov. 17.

Chief Johnson was again called on the stand this morning, and administered the following oath to himself in a solemn and awe-inspiring manner:

"By the Great Horn Spoons of the pale-face, and the Great Round Faced Moon, round as the shield of my fathers; by the Great High Muck-a-Muck of the Ute nation; by the Beard of the Prophet, and the Continental Congress, I dassent tell a lie!"

When Johnson had repeated this solemn oath—at the same time making the grand hailing sign of the secret order known as the Thousand and One—there was not a dry eye in the house.

Question by General Adams.—What is your name and occupation, and where do you reside?

Answer—My name is Johnson, just plain Johnson. The rest has been torn off. I am by occupation a farmer. I am a horny-handed son of toil, and don't you forget it. I reside in Greeley, Colorado.

Question—Did you, or did you not hear of a massacre at White River agency, during the fall, and if so, to what extent?

Objected to by defendant's counsel because it is irrelevant, immaterial, unconstitutional, imitation, and incongruous.

Most of the forenoon was spent in arguing the point before the court, when it was allowed to go in, whereupon the defendant's counsel asked to have the exception noted on the court's moments.

Answer—I did not hear of the massacre, until last evening, when I happened to pick up a copy of the Evanston *Age* and read it. It was a very sad affair, I should think.

Question—Were you, or were you not, present at the massacres?

Objected to by defendant's counsel on the ground that the witness is not bound to answer a question which would criminate himself.

Objection sustained, and question withdrawn by the prosecution.

Question—Where were you on the night that this massacre is said to have occurred?

Answer—What massacre?

Question—The one at White River?

Answer—I was attending a series of protracted meetings at Greeley, in this State.

Question—Were Douglass, Colorow and other Ute chiefs with you at that meeting in Greeley?

Answer—They were.

Court adjourned for dinner.

General Adams remarked to a reporter that he was getting down to business now, and that he had no doubt that in a few months he would convict all these Utes of falsehood in the first degree.

After dinner, court was called, with Johnson at the bat and Douglass on deck; General Adams, short stop; Ouray, center field.

Question—You say that you were not present at the White River massacre; were you ever engaged in any massacre?

Objected to, but objection afterward withdrawn.

Answer—No.

Question—Never?

Answer—Never.

Question—What! Never?

Answer—Well, dam seldom.

(Great applause and cries of "ugh!")

Question—Did you, or did you not, know a man named N. C. Meeker?

Answer—Yes.

Question—Go on and state if you know where you met him and at what time.

Answer—I met him in Greeley, Colorado, two or three years ago. After that I heard that he got an appointment as Indian Agent somewhere out west.

Question—Did you ever hear anything of him after that?

Answer—Nothing whatever.

Question—Did the account of the White River massacre that you read in the *Age* mention the death of Mr. Meeker?

Answer—No. Is he dead?

General Adams—Yes, he is dead.

At that the witness gave a wild whoop of pain and anguish, fell forward into the arms of General Adams, and is unconscious as we go to press.

We do not wish to censure General Adams. No doubt he is conducting this investigation to the best of his ability; but he ought to break such news as this as gently to the Indian as possible.

SOME ANSWERS TO CORRESPONDENTS.

Lock Malone, Beaver, Utah, writes as follows:

"I am now making some important scientific experiments with Limberger cheese as a motor, but have no data whereby to work. So new and unusual is the motor to science, that I am unable to get anything relative to its history.

"1. When was Limberger cheese first discovered, and by whom?

"2. What did he do it for anyway?

"3. To what do you attribute the bad odor in which Limberger cheese is held by scientists?

"4. Looking from what may be termed a purely utilitarian standpoint, and not allowing ourselves to be influenced by incongruous incandescence, should you say in all respects that virtually in view of the heterogeneous mobility of attended animalculate it might had or couldn't possibly was?"

ANSWER.

1. Limberger cheese was first discovered by Galileo, floating through space, during his studies relative to the heavenly bodies.

This was about 1609.

The body had, however, been floating through space for many millions of years previous to that, as Galileo remarks in his diary that he wasn't proud of it at all for it was evidently in a very poor state of preservation.

Galileo caught some of it and tamed it, but the scientific minds of that age had not yet made the attempt to utilize it as a motor.

The discovery was purely accidental. At about the time referred to, Galileo had constructed his powerful telescope which would bring the moon down so that the valleys and hills of that body were plainly visible. One day the telescope brought down a fragment of Limberger cheese that was floating through space. It magnified the cheese to such an extent that Galileo could smell it distinctly.

This was the true cause of Galileo's abandonment of the Copernican theory and eventually of astronomy.

3. The last answer really disposes of your third question.

4. Grappling with the abstruse and alarmingly previous usufruct embodied in the omnipresent, and constantly emanating and noticeably refractory

diagnosis, herein set forth, and still wandering on through the ever changing yet constantly invariable and fluctuating, yet undeviating perihelion of the heavenly bodies, with unprejudiced mind and unbiased judgment.

Arriving at the conclusion that perhaps in some cases it might not, or yet again it might or might not, and still it might.

Numerous Husband, writes from Jehosephat Valley as follows:

"I am twenty-seven and am going on twenty-eight years of age. A few years ago I joined on to the Mormon Church, and with my usual enthusiasm begun to get married.

"I have been getting married with more or less recklessness ever cents. When times was dull and I was out of employment, I Would go and get married.

"The ofishal count shows that I am an easy and graceful marryer.

"I now find that I am hopelessly involved financially. I had intended this summer to build a collosle villa for my multitoodinous wife; but it will cost me more than I can now command.

"Besides that the surkass is now on the weigh, and I am called upon to secure voluptuous woven wire mattress stuffed opera reserved seats, for my household aggregation of living wonders.

"I am willing to take all I can pay for if she will sit on a hard blue scat with me, and let her feet dangle down; but I cannot abide by the excessive tariff for preserved seats.

"I love the high moral tone of the sho, and dearly love the grand display of arenick tallent, but I cannot croll under the canvuss with my domestic carryvan, without attracting attention.

"When I was a boy and had not yet entered with my wild impetuous nacher in 2 the mattrymoniall biziness, I used to carry water to the elephant, and thus see the World's Congress of Rair and Beautyful Zoologickal Wonders, but I cood not do that now.

"By the time I got the Jordan carried up to the elephant, to pay my admittance, the sho would be over and gone, and I would be more or less left.

"I thereupon ask in all kandor for your valyable advise on these points?"

ANSWER.

The case before us is one which would evoke sympathy from the stoniest heart. It is also one which requires a close scrutiny and cool, deliberate investigation.

You probably at first married a wife whom you considered a treasure, and at once set yourself about amassing wealth of this kind until you find that you are carrying over on your inventory year after year, a large stock of undesirable wives which you are unable to dispose of.

You probably thought when you first married, that there were only two or three unmarried young ladies in the broad and beautiful universe who were worthy of you.

This was a fatal error, and one very common to the bran new bridegroom.

The census will show that there are several, if not more, desirable young ladies who are still on deck.

I am sorry that you have placed yourself in the position you have, and so far as possible will assist you; but these suggestions which I might offer, could only be partially successful.

Could you earlier in the season have given your wives say a dozen able-bodied hens apiece, with instructions that they were to be stimulated to the utmost by their respective owners, the egg-crop might have assisted very materially in purchasing circus tickets with the consequent concert tickets and vermilion lemonade.

There are other suggestions that might be made but it is too late now to make them. I can only offer one more balm to your deeply wounded and disappointed heart. You might by economy and frugality, secure an available point on the route with your mass meeting of household gods and goddesses, where you could sit on the fence and see the elephant meander by.

Yours, enveloped in a large wad of dense gloom.

THE CROW INDIAN AND HIS CAWS.

Early in the week five Crow chiefs passed through here on their way to Washington.

I went down to see them. They were as fine looking children of the forest as I ever saw. They wore buckskin pants with overskirt of same. The hair was worn Princesse, held in place with Frazer's axle grease and large mother of clamshell brooch. Down the back it was braided like a horse's tail on a muddy day, only the hair was coarser.

When an Indian wants to crimp his hair he has to run it through a rolling mill first, to make it malleable. Then the blacksmith of the tribe rolls it up over the ordinary freight car coupling pin, and on the following morning it hangs in graceful Saratoga waves down the back of the untutored savage.

I said to the interpreter who seemed to act as their trainer, "No doubt these Crows are going to Washington to try and interest Hayes in their Caws."

He gave a low, gurgling laugh.

"No," said he with a merry twinkle of the eye, as he laid his lip half way across a plug of government tobacco, "as spring approaches they have decided to go to Washington and ransack the Indian Bureau for their gauzy Schurz."

I caught hold of a car seat and rippled till the coach was filled with my merry, girlish laughter.

These Indians wear high expressive cheek-bones, and most of them have strabismus in their feet. They had their paint on. It makes them look like a chromo of Powhattan mashing the eternal soul out of John Smith with a Bologna sausage.

One of these chiefs, named Raw-Dog-with-a-Bunion-on the-Heel, I think, chief of the Wall-eyed Skunk Eaters, looked so guileless and kind that I approached him and said that no doubt the war-path in the land of the setting sun was overgrown with grass, and in his mountain home very likely the beams of peace! lit up the faces of his tribe.

He did not seem to catch my meaning.

I asked him if his delegation was going to Washington uninstructed.

In reply he made a short remark something like that which the shortstop of a match game makes when a hot ball takes him unexpectedly between the gastric and the liver pad.

Somehow live Indians do not look so picturesque as the steel engraving does. The smell is not the same, either. Steel engravings of Indians do not show the decalcomania outline of a frying-pan on the buckskin pants where the noble red man made a misstep one morning and sat down on his breakfast.

A dead Indian is a pleasing picture. The look of pain and anxiety is gone, and rest, sweet rest—more than he really needs—has come at last. His hands are folded peacefully and his mouth is open, like the end of a sawmill. His trials are o'er. His swift foot is making pigeon-toed tracks in the shifting sands of eternity.

The picture of a wild free Indian chasing the buffalo may suit some, but I like still life in art. I like the picture of a broad-shouldered, well-formed brave as he lies with his nerveless hand across a large hole in the pit of his stomach.

There is something so sweetly sad about it. There is such a nameless feeling of repose and security on the part of the spectator.

Some have such sensitive natures that they cannot look at the remains of an Indian who has been run over by two sections of freight, but I can. Somehow I do not feel that nervous distrust when I look at the red man with his osophagus wrapped around his head and tied in a double bow knot, that I do when he is full of the vigor of health.

When a train of cars has jammed his thigh-bone through his diaphragm and flattened his head out like a soup plate, I feel then that I can trust him. I feel that he may be relied upon. I consider him in the character of ghastly remains as a success. He seems at last so in earnest and as though he could be trusted.

When the Indian has been mixed up so that the closest scrutiny cannot determine where the head adjourns and the thorax begins, the scene is so suggestive of unruffled quiet and calm and gentle childlike faith that doubt and distrust and timidity and apprehension flee away.

THE NUPTIALS OP DANGEROUS DAVIS.

On the morning on which Adam Forepaugh entered the city of Laramie, and with a grand array of hump-backed dromedaries, club-footed elephants, and an uncalled-for amount of pride, and pomp, and circumstance, captured the town, Dangerous Davis, clad in buckskin and glass beads, and ornamented with one of Smith & Wesson's brass-mounted, self-cocking, Black Hills bustles, entered his honor's office, and walking up to the counter where the Judge deals out justice to the vagabond tenderfoot, and bankrupt non resident, as well as to the law-defying Laramite, called for $5.00 worth of matrimony.

On his arm leaned the fair form of the one who had ensnared the heart of the frontiersman, and who had evidently gobbled up the manly affections of Dangerous Davis. She was resplendent in new clothes, and a pair of Indian moccasins, and when she glided up to the centre of the room, the casual observer might have been deceived into the belief that she was moving through the radiant atmosphere like an $11.00 Peri, if it had not been for the gentle patter of her moccasin as it fell upon the floor with the sylph-like footfall of the prize elephant as he moves around the ring to the dreamy strains of "Old Zip Coon." A large "filled" ring gleamed and sparkled on her brown hand, and vied in splendor with a large seed-wart on her front finger. The ends of her nails were draped in the deepest mourning, and as she leaned her head against the off shoulder of Dangerous Davis, the ranche butter from her tawny locks made a deep and lasting impression on his buckskin bosom.

At this auspicious moment His Honor entered the room, with a green covered German almanac for 1852 and a copy of Robinson Crusoe under his arm, and as he saw the young thing who was about to unite herself to the bold, bad man from Bitter Creek, he burst into tears, while Judge Blair, who had adjourned the District Court in order to witness the ceremony, sat down behind the stove and sobbed like a child. At this moment William Crout, who has been married under all kinds of circumstances and in eleven different languages, entered the room and inspired confidence in the weeping throng.

Dangerous Davis changed his quid of tobacco from one side of his amber mouth to the other, spat on his hands, and asked to see the Judge's matrimonial price list. The Judge showed him some different styles, out of which Dangerous Davis selected the kind he wanted.

By this time about one hundred and thirteen men, who had been waiting around the court room during the past week in order to be drawn as jurymen, had crowded in to witness the ceremony.

After all the preliminaries had been gone through with, the Judge commenced reading the marriage service out of a copy of the Clown's Comic Song Book. When he asked if anyone present had any objections to the proceedings, Price, from force of habit, rose and said, "I object;" but Dangerous Davis caressed his brass-mounted Grecian bend, and Price withdrew the objection. Everybody admitted Price's good judgment, under the circumstances, in withdrawing the objection.

After the usual ceremony, the Judge put the bridegroom through some little initiations, instructed him in the grand hailing signs, grips, passwords and signals, swore him to support the Constitution of the United States, pronounced the benediction on the newly-wedded pair, and the ceremony closed with an extemporaneous speech by Judge Brown and profound silence and thoughtfulness on the part of Brockway, as he reflected upon the dangers which constantly surround us.

Dangerous Davis mounted his broncho, and tying his new wife on behind him on the saddle with an old shawl strap, plunged his spurs into the panting sides of his calico colored steed, and in a few moments was flying over the green plains, while the mountain breeze caught up the oleaginous saffron-hued tresses of the bride and in wild glee mingled them with the broncho's sorrel tail, and tossed them to the four winds of heaven.

THE HOLIDAY HOG.

Dear reader, did you ever go along past the market these cold December mornings and study the expression of the frozen holiday hog as he stands at the door with his mouth propped open by a chip, and the last hardened outlines of a diabolical smile lingering about the whole face? Did it ever occur to you that he has ways like Charles Francis Adams?

And yet he was not always thus—a cold, hard, immovable pork statue. Once he was the pride of some Nebraska home. He was petted and caressed no doubt, and had more demoralized melon rinds, and cold potatoes, and dish water than he actually needed. But think of it, gentle, kind-hearted reader; he has been torn from those he loved, and butchered to make a Caucasian holiday; snatched from the home of his youth, and frozen into a double and twisted post mortem examination. Perhaps, dear reader, you have never had to stand as a model for the picture of the man in the front of the almanac, who looks like the victim of a buzz saw, with the various members of the Zodiac family floating around him. If you have not, and we will take your word for it, you cannot fully realize the feelings of the Nebraska hog on a December day, without a stitch of clothes to his back.

SOME CENSUS CONUNDRUMS.

It was in the prime of summer time,
An evening calm and cool—

When the census enumerator came to the sanctity of my home, and opened a valise which contained a large duodecimo volume, and about nine gallons of brand new interrogation points.

He opened his note book, which was about the size of the White River Reservation, and proceeded to get acquainted. I thought at first that he had come from Chicago to interview me about the Presidential convention, and get my views. This was not the case, however.

I think he is going to write my biography and sell it at $2.00 each.

I gave him all the information I could, and telegraphed to my old Sabbath School Superintendent at home for more.

Among other little evidences of his morbid curiosity, I will give the following:

When were you born, and looking calmly back at this important epoch in your life, do you regret that you took the step?

If yes, state to what extent and under what circumstances?

Do you remember George Washington, and if so to what amount?

What is your fighting weight?

Who struck Billy Patterson?

Did you ever have membranous croup, and what did you do for it?

Do you keep hens, or do you lavish your profanity on those of your neighbors?

Have any of your ancestors ever been troubled with ingrowing nails, or blind staggers?

What is your opinion of rats?

Are you a victim to rum or other alcoholic stimulants, and if so, at what hour do you usually succumb to the potent enemy?

Would you have any scruples in asking the enumerator to join you in wrestling with man's destroyer at that hour?

Do you eat onions?

Which side do you lie on while sleeping?

Which side do you lie on during a political campaign?

What is the chief end of man?

Are you single, and if so what is your excuse? Who will care for mother now?

THE GENTLE POWER OF A WOMAN'S INFLUENCE.

Cummins City is still a crude metropolis. Society has not yet arrived at the white vest and lawn sociable period there. There is nothing to hamper any one or throw a tiresome restraint around him. You walk up and down the streets of the camp without feeling that the vigilant eye of the policeman is upon you, and when you register at the leading hotel the proprietor don't ask how much baggage you have, or insist upon it that your valise ought to be blown up with a quill to give it a robust appearance.

Speaking of this hotel, however, brings to my mind a little incident which really belongs in here. There are two ladies at this place, the only ones in the city limits, if my memory serves me. One of these ladies owns a lot of poles or house logs which were, at the time of which I speak, on the dump, as it were, ready to be used in the construction of a new cabin.

It seems that some of the prospectors of the corporation, without the fear of God or the Common Council of Cummins City, had been appropriating these logs from time to time until out of a good, fair assortment there remained only a dejected little pile of "culls." The owner had watched with great annoyance the gradual disappearance of her property from day to day, and it made her lose faith in the final redemption of all mankind. She became cynical and misanthropical, lost her interest in the future, and became low spirited and unhappy.

One day, however, after this thing had proceeded about far enough she went to her trunk, and taking out the large size of navy revolver, the kind that plows up the vitals so successfully and sends so many Western men to their long home. Then she went out to where a group of men had scattered themselves out around camp to smoke.

She wasn't a large woman at all, but these men respected her. Though they were only rough miners there in the wilderness they recognized that she was a woman, and they recognized it almost at a glance, too. There she was alone among a wild group of men in the mountains, far from the protecting arm of the law and the softening influences of metropolitan life, and yet the common feeling of gallantry implanted in the masculine breast was there.

She indicated with a motion of her revolver that she desired to call the meeting to order. There seemed to be a general anxiety on the part of every man present to come to order just as soon as circumstances would permit. Then she made a short speech relative to the matter of house logs, and suggested that unless a certain number of those articles, now invisible to the naked eye, were placed at a certain point, or a certain amount of kopecks placed on file with the chairman of the meeting within a specified time, that perdition would be popping on Main Street in about two and one-half ticks of the chronometer.

There didn't seem to be any desire on the part of the meeting to amend the motion or lay it on the table. Although it was arbitrary and imperative, and although an opportunity was given for a free expression of opinion, there didn't seem to be any desire to take advantage of it.

A committee of three was appointed to carry out the suggestions of the chair, and in about half an hour, the house logs and kopecks having been placed on deposit at the places designated, the meeting broke up, subject to the call of the chairman.

It was not a very long session, but it was very harmonious—very harmonious and very orderly. There was no calling for the previous question or rising to a point of order. The pale-faced men who composed the convention did not look to the casual observers as though they had come there to raise points for debate over parliamentary practice. They kept their eye on the speaker's desk and didn't interrupt each other or struggle to see who would get the floor.

It is wonderful this inherent strength of weakness, as I might say, which enables a woman amid a throng of reckless men to command their respect and obedience sometimes where main strength and awkwardness would not avail.

THE NATIVE INBORN SHIFTLESSNESS OF THE PRAIRIE DOGS.

I had read in my Fourth Reader about prairie dogs, and I thought, according to Washington Irving, that they knew more than a Congressman. He says a great deal about the sagacity and general mental acumen of the prairie dog, but I don't just exactly somehow seem to see where it comes in.

If it be an indication of shrewdness and forethought to establish a village nine hundred miles from a railroad, wood, water and grub, and live on alkali and moss agates and wander down the vista of time without a square meal, then the prairie dog is beyond the barest possibility of doubt, keen and shrewd to a wonderful degree. But if instinct or animal sagacity be reckoned according to the number and amount of creature comforts afforded within a given space, I have a cow in my mind that will double discount all the chuckle-headed, cactus eating prairie dogs west of the Missouri.

I do not wish to say anything relative to Mr. Irving's opinion of the prairie dog which would not be perfectly respectful, for I learn with great sorrow that Mr. Irving is dead, but I do think that there is hardly an animal in the entire arcana of nature that will not beat the prairie dog two to one as a provider for his family or himself.

I have an old hen at my home here who certainly approximates very closely to my ideal of an irreclaimable fool that has grown childish with old age, and outside of the Democratic party perhaps she is entitled to distinction. But even she has lucid intervals, and she hasn't yet fallen to where she would willingly take up a home under the desert land act like a prairie dog.

ANSWERS TO CORRESPONDENTS.

The following answers to correspondents contain a great deal of useful information, and I publish them in order to avoid the constant annoyance of writing the same in substance to so many inquiring friends.

"Sweet Sixteen" writes from "Hold-up Hollow."

I am betrothed to a noble youth from Rice Lake, Minnesota, but he seems too have soured on his betroth.

"At first he seemed to love me according to Gunter, but he has grown cold. About the first of the round-up he went away, and I soon afterward heard that he was affianced to another.

"I understand that he says I am not of noble lineage enough for him. It is true. I may not be a thorough-bred, but I have a pure, loving nature, which is now running to waste. The name of my beloved is De Courtney Van D'Edbeete. He comes from the first families, and O, I love him so!

"Can you tell me what to do?

"Sweet Sixteen."

Answer.—Yes, I can tell you what to do. I have been there some, too. If you will only do as I tell you, you are safe.

You must win him back. I think you can easily do so.

Select a base-ball club of about the weight you can handle easily, and then go to him and win him back.

You are too prone to give up easily. Do not be discouraged.

All will yet be well.

He may think now that you are not of noble blood but you can make him change his mind. Go to him with the love light in your eye and put a triangular head on him with your base-ball club, and tell him that he does not understand the cravings of your nature. Drive him into the ground and sit down on him, and then tell him that you are nothing but a poor, friendless girl, and need some one to cling to. Then you can cling to him. All depends upon how successful you are as a clinger.

I see at a glance that De Courtney needs to be flattened out a few times. Do not kill him, but bring him so near to the New Jerusalem that he can see the dome of the court house, and he will gradually come back to you and love you, and your life will be one long golden dream of never-fading joy, and De Courtney will wring out the colored clothes for you and help you do the washing, and he will stay at home evenings and take care of the children while you go to prayer meeting, and he will not murmur when you work off an inexpensive meal of cold rice and fricasseed codfish on him.

If he gets to feeling independent, and puts on the old air of defiance, you can diet him on cold mush and mackerel till he will not feel so robust, and then you can reason with him again, and while he is recovering you can take your baseball club and your noble self-sacrificing love, and win him back some more.

"Lalla Rookh" writes from Waukegan, Illinois, as follows to wit:

"My classmates and I have had quite a serious discussion recently, on several questions of table etiquette, and we have finally agreed to leave the matter with you.

"First—If one is asked to say grace at the table, and does not wish to do so, or is not familiar with the forms, what should he do?

"Second—If one has anything in his mouth, or gets any foreign substance like a piece of bone or a seed in his mouth, how should he remove it, and what is the proper thing to do with it?

"Third—Would you kindly add a few general rules of table etiquette, which would be useful to the many admirers of your classic style?"

Answer—It would be hazardous for a gentleman unaccustomed to asking grace at the table to attempt it, unless he be a naturally fluent extemporeaneous speaker.

It is more difficult for one unacquainted with it, than to address a Sabbath school, or write a letter accepting the nomination for President.

It is, therefore, preferable to say in a few terse remarks that you are profoundly grateful for the high compliment, but that your health will not admit of its acceptance.

Second—Care should be used while at table not to get large foreign substances like hair-pins, soup-bones, or clothespins into the mouth with food, as it naturally requires some little *sang froid* and tact to remove them. One accustomed to the mysteries of parlor-magic may slide the articles into his sleeve while coughing, and thence into the coat pocket of his host, thus easily getting himself out of an unpleasant situation, and at the same time producing roars of laughter at the expense of the host.

If, however, you are not familiar with sleight of hand, you may take in a full breath, and expel the object across the room under the whatnot, where it will not be discovered until you have gone away.

I will add a few general rules for table etiquette, which I have learned by actual experience to be of untold benefit to the active society man.

First—It is proper to take the last of anything on the plate if it comes to you, instead of declining it. It is supposed that there is more in the house, or if not, the host may go down town and get some. Do not, therefore, decline anything because it is the last on the dish, unless it looks as though it wouldn't suit you.

Second—If by mistake you get your spoon in the gravy so far that the handle is more or less sticky, do not get ill-tempered or show your displeasure, but draw it through your mouth two or three times, laughing a merry laugh all the time. Do not attempt to polish it off with your handkerchief. It might spoil your handkerchief.

Third—In drinking wine at table do not hang your eyes out on your cheek, or drink too fast and get it up your nose.

Do not drain your glass perfectly dry and then try to draw in what atmosphere there is in the room. This is not only vulgar, but it tends to cast large chunks of three-cornered gloom over the guests.

When you have drained your glass, do not bang it violently on the table and ask your host "how much he is out." This gives too much of the air of wild, unfettered freedom, and the unrestrained hilarity of the free-lunch.

Fourth—When you get anything in your mouth that is too hot, do not get mad and swear, because the other guests will only laugh at you, but remove the morsel calmly and tell the waiter to put it on ice a little while for you.

Fifth—When your coffee is out and you desire more, do not pound on your cup with your spoon, but be gentle and ladylike in your demeanor, telling some fresh little anecdote to please the guests, looking yearningly toward the coffee urn all the while.

Sixth—If you have to leave the table as soon as you are through, do not jump up suddenly and upset the table, but make an original and spicy remark about "having to eat and run like a beggar," and this will create such a hearty laugh over your sally of wit that you can slip out, select the best hat in the hall, and be half way home before the company can restrain its mirth.

There are some more good rules that I have on hand, not only relative to the table, but the ball-room, the parlor, the croquet lawn, the train, the church, and, in fact, almost everywhere that the society man might be placed. These I will give the public from time to time, as the growing demand seems to dictate.

THE SECRET OF GARFIELD'S ELECTION.

Headquarters in the Field,}

September 19, 1880.}

As I start for Chicago to-morrow I take this opportunity to write.

The trip so far has been one continuous ovation. I have been swinging round the circle, leaving the flag and the constitution with the people, and living out of a valise—and my friends—till I begin to yearn for home. It has been my fortune to run into several Garfield meetings during the time that I have been here, and to make short but telling speeches for the Republican candidates. As one of the local papers very truthfully said:

"Mr. Nye certainly reaches the very core of the subject matter in his admirable campaign speeches this fall. His commanding appearance and wild, peculiar beauty win the attention of the audience even before he says one word, and when speaking his air of candor and searching truth secures the earnest and prayerful consideration of those before him. He seems to supply a want long felt, and in case of Garfield's election we have no hesitation in saying that it will be due largely to the scorching truths and heaven-born genius of this remarkable man."

It is a novel sensation indeed, after five years of silent suffering in Wyoming, disfranchised and helpless, to mingle in the campaign and give free utterance to the blood-curdling truths that have for years been bottled up in these brain. Perhaps the people here do not deserve it, but they need purification through suffering.

I have one Garfield speech that I have used here a number of times with telling effect, and which I shall turn over to the State Central Committee when I go West.

By taking out the front breadths, turning the overskirt and revising the peroration, it will wear till November easily. I would insert it in this letter only for the fact that it seems rather tame in print, owing to the absence of gestures.

In my public speaking most everyone who is near me seems to be forcibly struck with my gestures. Hear what the press says. The Minneapolis *Tribune*, speaking of my wonderful effort, concludes as follows:

"Perhaps the most potent weapon of this campaign is the soothing, poetical style of gesture owned and operated by William Nye. In his speech last evening before the Young Men's Republican club, those who were on the fence were harassed with soul-destroying doubts as to which was most to be feared, the success of an unprincipled Democracy or the frolicsome gestures of the speaker. The general feeling at the close of the speech seemed to be that Minneapolis had never listened to a speech so rich with wild, impetuous and death-dealing gesticulations before."

The Stillwater *Lumberman* says:

"The speech last evening was noticeable for its grandeur of conception and the picturesque grace of its calisthentics. The speaker seemed to be largely made up of massive brow and limbs. When he rose and with easy grace unrolled his speech and untangled his legs, a general smile seemed to ripple the faces of the immense audience, but when he took a drink of water and began to make his new style of gesture, the mirthful manifestations gave place to a horrible apprehension of danger. Toward the close of the speech when Mr. Nye got warmed up to his work, and seemed to be lost in a wilderness of dissolving limbs, the police interfered and prevented the sacrifice of human life."

The Clear Lake *News* of the 17th says:

"One of the distinguishing features of the meeting held here on Wednesday evening, under the management of the Temple of Honor, was a short speech on temperance by Bill Nye, of Wyoming.

"His work in the line of temperance seems to have been mainly that of furnishing the horrible examples, so that young men might avoid the demon of rum.

"After the speaker got well under way and began to emphasize his language with some gestures that he has imported at great expense for his own use, the congregation seemed at a loss whether it would be best as a matter of safety to flee from intemperance or the death-dealing gestures of the speaker.

"Mr. Nye to-day gave bonds in the sum of $500 to keep the peace, shipped his gestures to Chicago, and will leave on the first south-bound train."

PERILS OF THE BUTTERNUT PICKER.

Speaking of trains reminds me that I have been scooting around the country lately on mixed and accommodation trains.

They are a good style of conveyance in some respects. For instance, if a man has a car-load of wheat that he wants to run into St. Paul with and sell, he can have it attached to the mixed train, and then he can get into the coach and go along with it, and attend to it personally. But where a man's time is worth $9 a moment, as mine is, it is annoying.

At first I couldn't get accustomed to it. I couldn't overcome my inertia when the car started or stopped, and it kept me worn out all the time apologizing to a corpulent old lady in the third seat from me. Had I been given a little time to select a lady whose lap I would prefer to sit down in, there were a dozen perhaps in the car more desirable than this old lady, but in the hurry and agitation I always seemed to select her.

Finally the conductor said that kind of business had gone far enough, and he tied me into my seat with a shawl-strap.

The train was very long, and when it got under full head-, way it was almost impossible to stop it at the various stations. We either stopped out in the country prematurely or passed the station at the rate of nine miles a minute, and then repented and came back. I was struck with the similarity of the first five or six towns on the line and spoke of it to a friend who accompanied me.

It seemed to me that Clarksville, Mapleton, Eldorado Junction, Pine Grove and Brookville had been planned by the same architect, but my friend only laughed and showed me that we had been switched and side-tracked for two or three hours at the first-named place.

We stopped in the woods once and I went out after butternuts.

It was a lovely autumn day, and after the thick nutritious air of the car, it was paradise to get out into the forest, where the fresh, sweet odor of the falling leaves was everywhere, and the hush of nature's annual funeral checked the thoughtless word and noisy laughter of the invader.

I wandered on, thinking of the brevity and comparative unimportance of our human life. How short the race we run, and how unsatisfactory our achievements at last. How like the leaves of the forest we spring forth in the early summer of our existence, nod pleasantly to our fellows a few brief mornings, and then die.

Thoughtlessly and aimlessly I had wandered on until I came to a large butternut, which I climbed with the old and almost forgotten enthusiasm of boyhood. At the top I tried some of my old and difficult tricks, and just as the train moved silently away I was going through the difficult and dangerous act of hanging to the upper limb of a butternut tree by the seat of the pants, and waiting patiently for the bough or the cassimere to yield and let the artist down into the arena by force of gravitation.

Dear reader, did you ever go through this thrilling experience? Did you ever feel the utter insecurity and maddening uncertainty which it yields? If not, then these lines are not to you?

Gently the tree swayed to and fro with the motion of the autumn breeze. Sadly the pines were sighing like lost souls, and the dead leaves fell softly to the ground, like the footfalls of departed spirits. I began to wish that I could fall softly to the ground like the footfalls of departed spirits, too.

I began to get bored and unhappy after awhile. My feet and hands hung in a cluster, and the position seemed strained and unnatural. I began to yearn for society, and the comforts of a home. I mentally calculated the distance I would have to fall, and wondered which of my bones I would shatter the most, and what the doctor's bill would be.

All at once I heard what seemed like a sound of smothered laughter. It was no doubt nothing but a sound which my fevered imagination had conjured up, aided by the torrent of blood that rushed to my head and thumped so loudly in my ears, but it maddened me, and I summoned all my strength in the mighty struggle to free myself. Finally, there was a short, sharp crash, and I felt myself rapidly descending through space. I fancied that I was an acrobat, and had fallen from the center pole that holds up the sky. I thought I lay in the dust and sawdust of the ring in a shapeless mass; and over all, and above all, there was the maddening sensation that my wardrobe was not complete. In my tortured imagination I could hear demoniac laughter, and occasional words of derision. They became more pronounced and distinct at last, and I fancied I heard one of these grinning imps saying:

"How peaceful he looks, and how young and fair. See how carelessly he has inserted his nose in the moist earth. He must have suffered a good deal through life, and yet his face is calm and happy in its expression. His general appearance is that of perfect rest, and the glad fruition of every hope.

"Let us go up into the tree and get the rest of his remains, and send them all home together."

This last speaker reminded me of the conductor, and the similarity struck me even in my trance. Slowly I opened my eyes. It was he. I almost wished that the fall had killed me. I did not fall from the tree to be humorous, but if I had I should have considered it the crowning triumph of an eventful career.

Most everyone from the train was there, and several from the nearest towns along the line. I bowed my thanks in silence, and backed over to the car. I got aboard and sat down. I found that I attracted less attention when I was sitting down, and I never cared so little for public notice in my life as I did that day.

It seems that the train had gone away some distance, but when it got by itself it remembered that I was not on board, and the peanut boy remembered seeing me get off at this point. So, as the train was already two weeks and four days behind, the conductor decided to go back. He says now that he does not regret it. He says that the life of a conductor at the best has but few bright spots in it, and the oases along the desert which he treads are widely separated, but he told me with tears in his eyes that Providence had made me the humble instrument for great good, and he felt grateful to me.

When he breaks out into a glad ripple of childish laughter now without any apparent cause, he takes a piece of checked cassimere out of his pocket and explains how he got it, and tells the whole story to his friends, so there are a great many people along that line of travel who know me by reputation although they have never seen me.

A WORD OR TWO ABOUT THE SWALLOW.

Lately I have made some valuable discoveries relative to ornithology, and I will give some of them to the public, for I love to shed information right and left, like a Normal school.

When the soft south wind began to kiss our cheeks, and the horse-radish and North Park prospector began to start, the swift-winged swallows drew near to my picturesque home on East Fifth street, and I hoped with a great, anxious, throbbing hope, that they would build beneath the Gothic eaves of my $200 ranche.

I would take my guitar at the sunset hour, and sit at my door in a camp-chair, with the fading glory of the dying day bathing me in a flood of golden light, and touching up my chubby form, and I would warble, "When Sparrows Build," an old solo in J, which seems to fit my voice, and the swallows would flit around me on tireless wing, and squeak, and sling mud over me till the cows came home.

This thing had gone on for several days, and the little mud houses under the eaves were pretty near ready, and in the meantime the spring bed bug had come with his fragrant breath, and turpentine, and quicksilver, and lime, and aquafortis, and giant-powder, and a feather, has made my home a howling wilderness, that smelled like a city drug store.

But it didn't kill the bugs. It pleased them. They called a meeting and tendered me a vote of thanks for the kind attentions with which they had been received. They ate all these diabolical drugs, not only on regular days, but right along through Lent.

I got mad and resolved to insure the house and burn it down. One evening I felt sad and worn, and was trying to solace myself by trilling a few snatches from Mendelssohn's "Wail," written in the key of G for a baritone voice. A neighbor came along and stopped to lean over the gate, and drink in the flood of melody which I was spilling out on the evening air. When I got through and stopped to tune my guitar anew, and scratch a warm place on my arm, he asked if I were not afraid that those swallows would bring bed bugs to the house.

I had heard that before, but I thought it was a campaign lie. I acted on the suggestion, however, and taking a long pole from behind the door, where I keep it for pictorial Bible men, I knocked down a 'dobe cottage, and proceeded to examine it.

It was level full of imported Merino and Cotswold and Southdown and Early Rose and Duchess of Oldenburg and twenty-ounce Pippins and Seek-no-further bed bugs. There were bed bugs in modest gray ulsters and bed bugs in dregs of wine and old gold, bed bugs in ashes of roses and beg bugs in elephants' breath, bed bugs with their night clothes on and in morning wrappers, bed bugs that were just going on the night shift, and bed bugs that had been at work all day and were just going to bed.

I killed all I could and then drove the rest into a pan of coal oil. When one undertook to get out of the pan I shot him. This conflict lasted several days. I neglected my other business and omitted morning prayers until there was a great calm and the swift-winged swallows homeward flew. When these feathered songsters come around my humble cot another spring they will meet with a cold, unwelcome reception. I shall not even ask them to take off their things.

I have formed the idea somehow from watching the eccentric nervous flight of the swallow, that when he makes one of those swift flank movements with the speed of chain lightning he must be acting from the impulse of a large, earnest, triangular bed bug of the boarding house variety. I may be wrong, but I have given this matter a good deal of attention, and whether this theory be correct or not I do not care. It is good enough for me.

LAUGHING SAM.

During the past week I have experienced the pleasure of an acquaintance with Laughing Sam, a character well known throughout the West. Samuel Thompson was introduced to me on Tuesday last, and, although he has a look of subdued pain and half concealed anguish, I soon found that he was capable of exhibiting the most wild and ungovernable mirth.

LAUGHING SAM.

Laughing Sam is employed by Surveyor Downey, and the latter has often told me how he wished that I could employ Sam by the month to laugh at what I might write, so that I could be encouraged.

After the formalities of an introduction were over, we began to tell anecdotes in order to get Sam into a cheerful frame of mind. When one would get tired and lay off for a rest, some other one would come forward to the bat and tell some more humorous tales. But Sam had evidently heard all these anecdotes, and looked disgusted and fatigued and bored.

Downey whispered to me that it wouldn't do; we must have something entirely different, and that I had better fix up one of those custom-made lies of mine, such as we used to tell at the boarding house in '75.

I did so with some hesitation, but Sam kindly gave me his attention and cheered me with an occasional pleased grunt. Then I threw my whole soul into it. I put in all the pathos of which I am capable at certain parts, and then where it was grand and terrific I got up and sawed the air, and where it was ludicrous I enlarged upon it till Sam's eye began to glisten.

By-and-by the fountains of the great deep opened, and Sam lay on the floor a quivering mass. Sometimes we thought he was dead, but then one leg would fly through the air and he would give a wild whoop of pain. Then, in a lucid moment, he would try to get up, but he would fall back again, and his lips would spasmodically relax and contract, and the air would be filled with a wild mixture of yells and whoops and gurgles and contortions.

It was not what was said that made him laugh, but it was because his time had come to indulge in a little mirth. I tried the same story afterward on an ordinary laughter, and when I got through he was bathed in tears. So it wasn't the story.

When Laughing Sam looks at his watch and sees that a large amount of mirthfulness is due he calmly puts away anything that may be near him of a fragile nature and proceeds to laugh in a way that shakes the stars loose in the firmament and disarranges the entire planetary world.

This fall he has an engagement to laugh for Eli Perkins during the lecture season. Eli is to give him half the proceeds of the lectures and Sam has got to laugh whether he feels like it or not.

THE CALAMITY JANE CONSOLIDATED.

I have one claim—at least myself and two or three other capitalists have—which has shown itself to be very rich, but it is not for sale. We are sinking on it now. We set a force of men at work on it two weeks ago consisting of genial cuss from Bitter Creek. He dug a few hours in a vertical direction, when overworked nature yielded and he went to sleep.

I discharged the entire gang. Shortly after that at a great expense we secured a day shift by the name of O'Toole. He is Greek I think.

He is still at work, though he found it very difficult to use the long handle shovel at first. He insisted on pouring the dirt down the back of his neck and then climbing out of the shaft with it and undressing himself with a gentle repose of manner which indicated that he had perfect command of himself and knew that his time was going right on all the same.

Still there are drawbacks about this style of mining. The work does not progress as rapidly as the present rush and hurry and turmoil of the American people seem to demand.

Two weeks ago the perilous undertaking of sinking this shaft to a depth of ten feet in a perpendicular direction was begun, and although we have shipped several mule loads of the choicest grub, consisting of bacon in large packages done up in corn-colored overshirts and XXX Nebraska flour, yet the top of Mr. O'Tool's head is visible to the naked eye from a considerable distance as he stands in the shaft.

Occasionally the Count De O'Toole fancies that he has been bitten by a tarantula, and the stockholders of the Calamity Jane Consolidated have to ship a large lunch basket with a willow cover to it and a cork in the top in order to counteract the poison that is rankling in his system.

THE NOCTURNAL COW.

With the opening up of my spring movements in the agricultural line comes the cow.

Laramie has about seven cows that annoy me a good deal. They work me up so that I lose my equanimity. I have mentioned this matter before, but this spring the trouble seems to have assumed some new features. The prevailing cow for this season seems to be a seal-brown cow with a stub tail, which is arranged as a night-key. She wears it banged.

THE NOCTURNAL COW.

The other day I had just planted my celluloid radishes and irrigated my turnips and sown my hunting-case summer squashes, and this cow went by trying to convey the impression that she was out for a walk.

That night the blow fell. The queen of night was high in the blue vault of heaven amid the twinkling stars. All nature was hushed to repose. The people of Laramie were in their beds. So were my hunting-case summer squashes. I heard a stealthy step near the conservatory where my celluloid radishes and pickled beets are growing, and I arose.

It was a lovely sight. At the head of the procession there was a seal-brown cow with a tail like the handle on a pump, and standing at an angle of forty-five degrees.

That was the cow.

Following at a rapid gait was a bewitching picture of alabaster limbs and Gothic joints and Wamsutta muslin night robe.

That was me.

The queen of night withdrew behind a cloud.

The vision seemed to break her all up.

Bye-and-bye there was a crash, and the seal-brown cow went home carrying the garden gate with her as a kind of keepsake. She had a plenty of garden gates at home in her collection, but she had none of that particular pattern. So she wore it home around her neck.

The writer of these lines then carefully brushed the sand off his feet with a pillow sham and retired to rest.

When the bright May morn was ushered in upon the busy world the radish and squash bed had melted into chaos and there only remained some sticks of stove wood and the tracks of a cow, interspersed with the dainty little footprints of some Peri or other who evidently stepped about four yards at a lick, and could wear a number nine shoe if necessary.

Yesterday morning it was very cold, and when I went out to feed my royal self-acting hen, I found this same cow wedged into the hen coop. O, blessed opportunity! O, thrice blessed and long-sought revenge!

Now I had her where she could not back out, and I secured a large picket from the fence, and took my coat off, and breathed in a full breath. I did not want to kill her, I simply wanted to make her wish that she had died of membranous croup when she was young.

While I was spitting on my hands she seemed to catch my idea, but she saw how hopeless was her position. I brought down the picket with the condensed strength and eagerness and wrath of two long, suffering years. It struck the corner of the hen-house. There was a deafening crash and then all was still, save the low, rippling laugh of the cow, as she stood in the alley and encouraged me while I nailed up the hen-house again.

Looking back over my whole life, it seems to me that it is strewn with nothing but the rugged ruins of my busted anticipations.

THE RELENTLESS GARDEN HOSE.

It is now the proper time for the cross-eyed woman to fool with the garden hose. I have faced death in almost every form and I do not know what fear is, but when a woman with one eye gazing into the zodiac and the other peering into the middle of next week and wearing one of those large floppy sun bonnets, picks up the nozzle of the garden hose and turns on the full force of the institution, I fly wildly to the Mountains of Hepsidam.

Water won't hurt anyone of course if care is used not to forget and drink any of it, but it is this horrible suspense and uncertainty about facing the nozzle of a garden hose in the hands of a cross eyed woman that unnerves me and paralyzes me.

Instantaneous death is nothing to me. I am as cool and collected where leaden rain and iron hail are thickest, as I would be in my own office writing the obituary of the man who steals my jokes. But I hate to be drowned slowly in my good clothes and on dry land and have my dying gaze rest on a woman whose ravishing beauty would drive a narrow-gauge mule into convulsions and make him hate himself to death.

A WAIL.

To the Editor of the Bass Drum:

I appeal to the charity of more favored sisters of the east, who live in an atmosphere of music to throw a crumb of comfort to one who lives in the wilderness and has, in the past ten years, heard positively no music.

I want a list of contralto songs for the voice, compass two octaves G, in bass clef to G, above the line, treble. I should also like a list of piano solos, third or fourth grade, the Trauemerei order of music preferred. I will make any compensation desired, and forever bless my friends in need. No Name.

It is pretty sad to suffer along for ten years and not hear any music. It must seem dull and quiet, especially to one who has lived in an atmosphere of music. Ten years with no one at hand to churn up the atmosphere occasionally with something extending "from G in bass clef to G above the line treble" is a long while. But here in the "wilderness" we have to squeeze along the best way we can. We can't go and hear Ole Bull every two weeks here. Sitting Bull is about as near as we can approximate to the Bull family. It is pretty tough, and there is no denying it.

Speaking about crumbs of comfort, however, if "No Name" will drop around to the *Bass Drum* office, say about 12:30 to-morrow, we will attend to the crumb business. We do not, as a general rule, warble much, but if she will come around at that hour we will trill two or three little olios for "one who lives in the wilderness, and has in the past ten years heard positively no music." If we had known that she was starving along that way without five cents' worth of music to lay her jaw to, we would have hunted her up and given her a blast or two. There's nothing mean about us. We may be rough and perhaps impulsive at times, but we will never hush our merry lay so long as anybody is suffering. Always come right to us when hungry for music.

THE GREAT, HORRID MAN RECEIVETH NEW YEAR CALLS.

In my Boudoir, Dec. 20, 1879.

New Year's Day will be Leap Year, and the ladies want to make calls.

The masculine man will, therefore, have to receive. Some of us will club together at private houses and receive, while others will "hire a hall" and sling a great deal of agony, no doubt. I shall be at home to some extent. I shall wear my organdy, looped up with demi-overskirt of the same, and three-ply lambrequins of Swiss, with corded edges and button-holes of elephant's breath cut plain. My panier is down at the machine shop now and will be done in a few days. I shall be assisted by Superintendent Dickinson and First Assistant Postmaster General Spalding of the Laramie post-office department, and the grand difficulty will no doubt occur at the residence of the latter.

Mr. Dickinson will wear a lavender *moire antique* with all wool underclothes. The costume will be draped on the side with bevel pinions, and looped back with English button-holes, and cut low in the neck.

Mr. Spalding will wear a cream-colored walking suit with train No. 4. He will also wear buttons with buttonholes to match. Sleeves cut Princesse, with polished elbows of same. Boots plain with cranberry sauce. Brocaded silk overskirt, with lemon sauce. Fifty-three button kids, fastening to the suspenders, open back, with Italian dressing.

I give these notes to the reporter in advance, because women are so apt to get these things all mixed up. After we have spent so much time constructing an elaborate wardrobe, we do not wish the journals of the Territory to come out the next day, and make each one of us appear like "a perfect dud." Our table will also look the nicest of any in town. We have designed it ourselves. We have arranged the hose so that we can play it on the dishes after we have used them, and save splashing around in hot water between meals. We intend to feed the first three or four delegations without doing any work on the dishes. After that we will of course have to turn on the hose. Visitors will be made to feel perfectly at home. Callers will be required not to spit on the floor. Parties making calls will not be allowed to throw peanut shells in the card-receiver, or leave their muddy articles on the piano. Callers will please remain seated while the frigid sustenance is circulated. No standing callers allowed. Standing collars are going out of style anyhow.

JUST THE THING.

Office of The Twilight Bumble Bee.

We have just received a copy of the Nebraska *Staats Zeitung-Tribune* a nice little eight page German paper, published at Grand Island, Nebraska. We have not read it all through yet, but it is a mighty good paper. We do not understand much German. We are a little rusty. "Zwei glass lager" is about all the German we know, and that isn't very pure.

But this paper we like. There is a tone about it that seems to indicate a lofty conception of true journalism. A noble ambition to cope with vice and the prevailing errors of the day, and to conquer ignorance and wrong. As we said before, there are a great many things in the paper which we fail to quite "catch on" to, owing to our ignorance of the German language, but there is a picture of a cook stove on the eighth page that is first-rate. It is in the English language. There is also a picture of a wind mill, in fractured English, on the same page. It is very correct in its sentiment, and we endorse it.

In conclusion we will say that from what we have seen of this paper, we are prepared to say that it meets a want long felt. It is pure in tone, noble in politics, fearless in its attack upon the popular shortcomings of the day, and well deserving of the hearty approval of the public.

THANKS.

M. E. Post, M. C., of Cheyenne, will please accept our thanks for an indestructible pumpkin pie, presented on the 9th inst. It is the most durable pie that we ever wrestled with. Probably it was not picked early enough and got too ripe. It is the first genuine cane-bottomed pie, with patent dust damper and nickle-plated movement that we have tasted since we came west. He says it was raised on the Laramie plains. If this be true, we have opened up before us another resource of which we may be justly proud. We have valuable marble quarries, but marble may be cracked and broken. We also have mountains of iron and leads of valuable quartz, but all these must yield to the superior strength of man. This style of pie, however, will defy the power of mortal ingenuity, and withstand the effacing finger of time. Men may come and men may go but this pie will last forever. We make bold to say that when Gabriel sounds the proclamation that time is no more, this blasted pie will stand up without a blush and say: "Here, Gabriel, is where you get your nice, fresh pie, and don't you forget it, either."

AN ANTI-MORMON TOWN.

A Mormon missionary turned himself loose in Rawlins the other night and attempted to proselyte the good people into getting another invoice of wives to assist in taking off the chill of the approaching winter; but there was a feeling in the audience that the man who represented the church of the Latter Day Saints was a little off in addressing them, so they went to a dealer in old and rare antiquities and purchased some eggs that had a smell which is peculiar to eggs that have yielded to the infirmities of age.

The Rawlins people raised the windows on the sides of the building and broke eleven and one-half dozen out of a possible twelve dozen of these eggs, which had been coined in the year of the great crash. It was the year when so many hens were not feeling well; they broke them against the brass collar button of the orator, and they ran down in graceful little brooklets and rivulets and squiblets and driblets overleven and one-half dozen out of a possible twelve dozen of these eggs, which had been coined in the year of the great crash. It was the year when so many hens were not feeling well; they broke them against the brass collar button of the orator, and they ran down in graceful little brooklets and rivulets and squiblets and driblets over his white lawn tie and boiled shirt.

Rawlins is not strictly a Mormon town, and the lecturer who took some clothes through in a valise the other day bound for Evanston, where he could get them washed, was arrested by a New York detective who was sure he had at last caught the man who had Stewart's body.

A CHRISTMAS RIDE IN JULY.

I've just returned from a long ride to the Soda Lakes.

The ride reminded me of a tour I took in July from Laramie over to Cheyenne, two years, ago. We had experienced the pleasure of riding over the mountain, on the Union Pacific train, and had held our breath while crossing Dale Creek bridge, and viewed with wonder the broken billows of granite, lying here and there at the tip-top of the mighty divide. But some one had said that it was nothing compared with the mirth-provoking trip by carriage across the mountains, over a fine wagon road to Cheyenne.

In the morning I nearly melted riding up the sandy canyon, and took off my coat and gliding pleasantly along-alternately sang one or two low throbs of melody, and alternately swore about the extreme heat.

When we got nearly to the top, I thought it didn't look well for a man to whom the American people look for so much in the future, to be riding along the public highway without his coat, so I put it on. At the top of the mountain I put on a linen duster and gloves. Shortly after that I put on my overshoes and a sealskin cap. Later, I put on my buffalo overcoat, and got out and ran behind the carriage to keep warm.

When I got to Cheyenne, the Doctor looked me over and said that he could save my feet because they had so much vitality, and were in such a good state of preservation; but my ears—my pride and glory—the ears that I had defended through the newspapers for years, and had stood up for when all about was dark—they had to go.

That is, part of them had to go, and there was enough left to hear with; but the ornamental scallops and box plaiting, and frills, the wainscoating, and royal Corinthian entablatures had to go.

EXAMINING THE BRAND ON A FROZEN STEER.

A stock owner went out the other day over the divide to see how his cattle were standing the rigorous weather, and found a large, fine steer in his last long sleep. The stockman had to roll him over to see the brand, and he has regretted his curiosity ever since. He told me that the brand looked to him like a Roman candle making about 2,000 revolutions per moment, and with 187 more prismatic colors than he thought were in existence. Sometimes a steer is not dead but in a cold, sleepy stupor which precedes death, and when stirred up a little and irritated because he cannot die without turning over and showing his brand, he musters his remaining strength and kicks the inquisitive-stockman so high that he can see and recognize the features of departed friends. That was the way it happened on this occasion. The stockman fell in the branches of a pine tree on Jack Creek, not dead but very thoughtful. He said he was near enough to hear the rush of wings, and was just going to register and engage a room in the New Jerusalem when he returned to consciousness.

ONION PEELIN'S.

The Chinese agriculturalist does his hair up in a French twist because he don't want to have his cue cumber the ground.

Almost every day there is a new liver pad or lung pad or kidney pad, but in its way nothing has succeeded in giving instant relief like the Leadville foot pad.

A man can scratch his back against a hat rack or a whatnot for a year or two, and attribute it to buckwheat cakes, but after he has gone on this way for about seven years, the public and his friends begin to lose faith in him.

A handsome competence is in store for the man who will invent a neat, durable and portable pie opener that will successfully reach the true inwardness of the average box-toed, Bessemer steel, gooseberry pie which the hired girl casts in her kitchen foundry.

Along the dreary pathway of this cloud-environed life of ours there is no joy so pure, no triumph so complete, no success so fraught with rapture, as that of the female artiste who hangs on the flying trapeze by her chilblain and kisses her hand to the perspiring throng.

It is not the disheartening sense of failure alone which makes a man swear in the stilly night, nor yet the fact that he has slapped his alabaster limb harder than he needed to, but it is the trifling and heartless way in which the mosquito kisses his hand to the audience, and soars away humming a Tyrolean lay.

Putting up stovepipe is easy enough, if you only go at it right. In the morning, breakfast on some light, nutritious diet, and drink too cups of hot coffee. After which put on a suit of old clothes—or new ones if you can get them on time—put on an old pair of buckskin gloves, and when every thing is ripe for the fatal blow, go and get a good hardware man who understands his business. If this rule be strictly adhered to, the gorgeous eighteen-karat-stem-winding profanity of the present day may be very largely diminished, and the world made better.

It is strange that the human heart is so easily influenced by the change of seasons, and although spring succeeds winter, and summer follows upon the heels of spring, just as it did centuries ago, yet the transition from one to the other is ever new and pleasing, and the bosom is gladdened with the cheering assurance of spring, or the promise of the coming summer time, with its wealth of golden days, its cucumbers and vinegar, its green corn, its string beans, its baseball, its mammoth circus, its fragrant flowers, and its soda water flavored with syrup from a long-necked, wicker-covered bottle, just as it was in the days of Pharoah, and Hannibal, and Andrew Jackson.

Milton Keynes UK
Ingram Content Group UK Ltd.
UKHW051019250324
439991UK00008B/924